EXAM PRO

Torts

What is **Exam Pro–Torts**?

Exam Pro–Torts is a study aid that helps law students prepare to answer multiple choice questions on their exams.

How should you use **Exam Pro–Torts** most productively?

First, **Exam Pro–Torts** is divided into chapters that approximates the usual organization of Torts casebooks and classes that are used in Law Schools. After studying a particular topic during a semester, you should read, analyze and try to answer the questions in the chapter that covers the material that was just covered in the class. Work through a substantial block of questions before checking your answers against those given in the book.

As you compare your answers to those given in the book, do not be content merely to check to see if you selected the correct letter. The answers given in the book provide a good discussion of why the correct answer should be chosen and why the other answers are incorrect. It is important for a student to be able to make those distinctions. Many of the question and answer sets in this book will allow you to make fine, subtle distinctions in the law. A careful use of the questions and answers will assist you in understanding those distinctions. In addition, that close study will allow you to be better prepared for a final exam.

Second, when it gets close to time to study for an exam, review the questions and answers in **Exam Pro–Torts** for the material that will be covered on the exam. This use of the book will allow you to review quickly and test yourself on the material.

What **Exam Pro–Torts** offers you:

•   **Exam Pro–Torts** contains specific subject matter multiple choice questions and answers that allow a detailed study of the material found in most law school torts classes.

•   **Exam Pro–Torts** contains fact based hypothetical questions and answers that are of the type typically found on law school torts multiple choice exams.

D1127481

Why **Exam Pro–Torts** will work for you:

- **Exam Pro-Torts** questions and answers help you to understand the fine/subtle distinctions found in the complex area of the law known as torts.

- **Exam Pro–Torts** will help you prepare confidently for a torts examination.

Exam Pro–Torts
from Thomson Reuters

TORTS

By

John H. Bauman

Professor of Law
South Texas College of Law

Ronald W. Eades

Professor of Law, Emeritus
Louis D. Brandeis School of Law at the
University of Louisville

Exam Pro

WEST.

A Thomson Reuters business

Mat #40371005

© 2010 Thomson Reuters
  610 Opperman Drive
  St. Paul, MN 55123
  1–800–313–9378

Printed in the United States of America

ISBN: 978–0–314–16147–5

To Kathee

JHB

To Lillian

RWE

Table of Contents

Chapter   **Page**

1. Intentional Torts 1

  Questions: 1

  Answers: 18

2. Privileges: Defenses To Intentional Torts 29

  Questions: 29

  Answers: 37

3. Negligence 41

  Questions: 41

    A. Duty 41

      1. Adults 41

      2. Children 48

      3. Professionals 49

      4. Negligent emotional distress 55

      5. Negligence per se 57

    B. Breach 58

      1. Burden of proof 58

      2. Res ipsa loquitur 60

    C. Injury 62

    D. Causation 63

      1. Cause in fact 63

      2. Proximate cause 68

    E. Defenses 70

      1. Contributory/Comparative Fault 70

      2. Assumption of Risk 72

      3. Statutes of limitations 73

      4. Immunities 74

Chapter   **Page**

    Answers: 77

       A. Duty 77

          1. Adults 77

          2. Children 78

          3. Professionals 79

          4. Negligent emotional distress 81

          5. Negligence per se 82

       B. Breach 82

          1. Burden of proof 82

          2. Res ipsa loquitur 84

       C. Injury 84

       D. Causation 85

          1. Cause in fact 85

          2. Proximate cause 87

       E. Defenses 88

          1. Contributory/Comparative Fault 88

          2. Assumption of Risk 89

          3. Statutes of limitations 89

          4. Immunities 90

4. **Vicarious Liability** 91

    Questions: 91

    Answers: 110

5. **Strict Liability** 117

    Questions: 117

       A. Animals 117

       B. Ultrahazardous and abnormally dangerous
          activities 126

    Answers: 134

       A. Animals 134

       B. Ultrahazardous and abnormally dangerous
          activities 137

Chapter		**Page**
6.	**Nuisance**	141
	Questions:	141
	A. Public	141
	B. Private	145
	C. Substantial harm	146
	D. Bases of liability	147
	E. Remedy	149
	F. Defenses	151
	Answers:	153
	A. Public	153
	B. Private	154
	C. Substantial harm	154
	D. Bases of liability	155
	E. Remedy	155
	F. Defenses	156
7.	**Wrongful Death And Survival**	159
	Questions:	159
	Answers:	167
8.	**Products Liability**	171
	Questions:	171
	Answers:	183
9.	**Defamation**	191
	Questions:	191
	Answers:	198
10.	**Privacy**	201
	Questions:	201
	Answers:	206

Chapter   **Page**
11. Misrepresentation Torts 209

        Questions: 209

        Answers: 216

12. Damages 221

        Questions: 221

        Answers: 227

CHAPTER 1
INTENTIONAL TORTS

QUESTIONS:

Use the following facts for Questions 1 through 3. Jess, who walked with the aid of a cane, was standing on a street corner one day, waiting for the traffic light to change. Pranks quietly walked up behind Jess and, thinking it would be a good gag, kicked the base of Jess's cane. Although the bottom of the cane came off the ground, Jess had not been leaning on it heavily. Jess lost his balance slightly, but did not fall, and was not injured. Jess turned around to see Pranks laughing at him. Jess got mad and whacked Pranks over the head with the cane.

1. If Jess sues Pranks for battery, who will prevail?

    A. Jess will prevail because losing his balance counts as "harm."

    B. Jess will prevail because the contact with his cane, while he was holding it, is the equivalent of an offensive contact with his person.

    C. Pranks will prevail because he intended only to play a joke, not to cause any physical harm.

    D. Pranks will prevail because Jess suffered no actual injury.

2. If Jess sues Pranks for assault, who will prevail?

    A. Jess will prevail because the intent sufficient for battery will also support a claim of assault.

    B. Jess will prevail because every battery includes an assault.

    C. Pranks will prevail because he intended only contact with the cane, and not to cause apprehension.

D. Pranks will prevail because Jess never saw the contact coming and therefore experienced no apprehension of harmful or offensive contact.

3. If Pranks sues Jess for battery, who will prevail?

A. Jess will prevail because Pranks was the original aggressor.

B. Jess will prevail because most jurisdictions do not require the victim of an assault or battery to retreat before engaging in self-defense.

C. Pranks will prevail because he actually suffered an intended harmful contact.

D. Pranks will prevail because Jess used a weapon.

4. A mentally disturbed individual went into a crowded gym, pulled out a gun, and began firing into the crowd, wounding several people. Later, after being arrested, the individual insists that he did not intend to hit anyone in particular, and in fact did not care if he hit anyone or not. If those who were wounded in the incident sue the shooter for battery, who will prevail?

A. The plaintiffs will prevail if the shooter knew that, by firing into the crowd, it was substantially certain that someone would be struck by a bullet.

B. The plaintiffs will prevail because the shooter created an unreasonable risk of harmful contact.

C. The shooter will prevail because it was not his purpose to cause a harmful contact with anyone, and he therefore lacked the intent necessary for battery.

D. The shooter will prevail because the mentally ill cannot commit an intentional tort.

5. A landowner decided to do some target practice on her rural land. She went to an open field and began firing at large, dead tree about 400 yards away. The landowner was aware that the tree was near her property line and that hikers used a trail in the state forest on the other side of the line. One of her shots missed the dead tree and carried onto public property, where it wounded a hiker whom the landowner had not seen.

If the hiker sues the landowner for battery, who will prevail?

A. The hiker will prevail, because the landowner knew that members of the public visited the state forest on the other side of the property line.

B. The hiker will prevail, because harmful contact in fact resulted.

C. The landowner will prevail because she did not have the intent necessary for liability for battery.

D. The landowner will prevail because she was on her own property when she fired.

6. Alex saw Barber, whom he disliked intensely, walking about fifty yards away. Alex picked up a large rock, took aim at Barber, and threw. In a one in a million chance, Alex hit Barber in the head with the rock. If Barber sues Alex for battery, who will prevail?

A. Barber will prevail because she suffered an intended harmful contact.

B. Barber will prevail only if Alex was skilled enough at rock-throwing that harmful contact was substantially certain to occur.

C. Alex will prevail because, at that distance, he only created a remote risk of harmful contact.

D. Alex will prevail because he must have known that it was unlikely that he could hit Barber with the rock.

7. Art, Phil and Susan were walking along the street engaged in a heated argument. Art became angry at something Phil said and violently shoved him against Susan. Susan was knocked to the ground and hurt her leg. Phil landed on top of her, but was not physically injured. Which of the following statements is true?

A. Susan can successfully sue both Art and Phil for battery.

B. Susan and Phil can both successfully sue Art for battery.

C. Phil can successfully sue Art for battery, and Susan can successfully sue Phil for battery.

D. Phil has the only valid battery action since he is the only one whom Art intended to contact.

Use the following facts for Questions 8 and 9. Matty, ten years old, was riding her bicycle along the street when she saw Tom standing on the sidewalk. A big puddle of muddy water lay in the street near where Tom stood. As a joke, Matty steered her bike into the puddle for the purpose of splashing Tom. Matty did not see Hannah, a pedestrian walking across the street from the other direction. Matty rode through the puddle, throwing muddy water on Tom and running into Hannah, knocking her down.

8. If Tom sues Matty for battery, who will prevail?

    A. Matty will prevail because muddy water does not cause bodily harm.

    B. Matty will prevail because she was too young to be capable of an intentional tort.

    C. Tom will prevail if he saw her coming and suffered apprehension.

    D. Tom will prevail because being splashed with muddy water in this way constitutes an intended offensive contact.

9. If Hannah sues Matty for battery, who will prevail?

    A. Hannah will prevail because Matty intended an offensive contact with Tom.

    B. Hannah can only recover for offense, and not for physical harm, because Matty only intended offense.

    C. Matty will prevail because she did not see Hannah, so that the contact with her was unintended.

    D. Matty will prevail in a battery claim because her conduct toward Hannah constituted negligence.

10. Ashley downloaded a ring-tone to her cell phone that sounds exactly like the buzzing of an angry bee. Ashley then snuck up behind Bart, whom she knew to be severely allergic to bee stings and therefore deathly afraid of bees. Ashley activated the ring-tone while holding the cell phone inches away from the back of Bart's head. Bart was startled and jumped away, waving his hands frantically to ward off the supposed bee.

    A. Bart has no claim so long as Ashley did not actually touch him with the cell phone.

    B. Bart has no claim because no bee was actually present, so Ashley could not have in fact inflicted a harmful contact.

    C. Bart has an assault claim because Ashley knew of his fear of bee stings.

    D. Bart has a battery claim because the cell phone was so close to his head.

11.   Zach and Al were engaged in a heated argument. Zach became enraged and said to Al, "I am going to go get my baseball bat and beat you to a pulp." Zach walks away in the direction of his car, where Al has reason to believe that Zach does, in fact, keep a baseball bat. If Al sues Zach for assault, who will prevail?

  A.   Al will prevail because Zach threatened him with a harmful bodily contact.

  B.   Al will prevail only if he actually feared that Zach not only had a baseball bat in his car, but also would actually hit him with it.

  C.   Zach will prevail if he did not intend to actually hit Al with the bat.

  D.   Zach will prevail because the threat of harmful bodily contact was not imminent.

12.   Use the following facts for Questions 12–14: Dale insulted Mark in front of a number of people. Mark told Dale, "I can't deal with you here, in front of all these people, but if I ever run across you when you are alone, I will beat you up with my bare hands." The next day, Dale was jogging in the park. No one was around. Suddenly, Mark stepped out onto the jogging trail about twenty feet in front of him. "Prepare to meet your doom," said Mark, smiling evilly. Dale turned around and ran (not jogged) in the opposite direction. If Dale sues Mark for assault under these facts, which of the following is correct?

  A.   Dale will prevail because the facts show he apprehended a harmful contact with his person.

  B.   Dale will only prevail if Mark was stronger than he was.

  C.   Mark will prevail because he had not actually started to attack before Dale ran away.

  D.   Mark will prevail because he was too far away for the threat to be "imminent."

13.   Use the same facts as Question 12. In addition, assume that Dale was known to Mark to be a timid person who always tried to avoid any physical confrontation. Mark himself was rather small and puny, so that a normal person would not have feared him at all. If Dale sues Mark for assault under these facts, which of the following is correct?

  A.   Dale will prevail because the threat is enough, and Dale does not in fact have to believe that Mark will actually attack.

B.   Dale will prevail because Mark in fact intended to cause him apprehension of a harmful contact.

C.   Mark will prevail because Dale's fear was unreasonable.

D.   Mark will prevail because he knew Dale would run away, so that he would not have to actually carry out his attack.

14.   Use the same facts as Question 12. For this question, however, assume that Dale was a champion martial artist who had no doubts that he could defend himself from attack by Mark. However, he turned and ran away because he was on parole from a prison sentence for a criminal battery on another person. Dale knew that his parole could be revoked and he could be sent back to prison if he became involved in another fight. Under these circumstances, which of the following statements is true?

A.   Mark will prevail because Dale did not fear him.

B.   Mark will prevail because Dale could have defended himself from Mark's attack.

C.   Dale will prevail because public policy encourages people to avoid physical confrontations.

D.   Dale will prevail because he need only experience apprehension of harmful contact.

15.   Pam was searching for a parking place in a crowded mall parking lot on a holiday weekend. Seeing another motorist backing out of a spot two rows over, Pam sped up, drove the wrong way down that row of parking spaces, and backed up into the now empty spot. In doing so she cut off Rob, who had been approaching the space from the proper direction. Rob, angered, shook his fist at Pam and shouted obscenities at her through the closed windows of his car, before driving off to look elsewhere for a place. Pam was upset and unnerved by the violence of Rob's reaction. If Pam sues Rob for assault, who will prevail?

A.   Pam will prevail because Rob's gesture was a threat of harmful contact, and put Pam in apprehension.

B.   Pam will prevail because she in fact felt threatened by Rob's actions.

C.   Rob will prevail because, sitting in his car, he did not have the present ability to inflict a harmful contact on Pam.

D.   Rob will prevail because Pam's fears were unreasonable.

16.   Bet, the owner of Bet's Bookstore, a small establishment in a modest strip mall, was standing at the door to her establishment one morning when she saw a particularly annoying political canvasser emerge from one of the other stores in the mall and then enter the next store closer to Bet's. Not wanting to deal with the canvasser, Bet watched him come down the line of stores until he exited the store next to hers. Bet quickly locked the door of her store, switched the "Open" sign to "Closed", and hid behind the counter. While she was doing this the only other person in her store was Bill, who was browsing the magazines in the rear. Bill began to walk towards the front of the store as the canvasser left, and he saw Bet quickly unlock the door, switch the sign back, and return to her sales counter. Bill asked what had happened and was incensed that Bet had locked him in the store. If Bill sues Bet for false imprisonment who will prevail?

   A.   Bet will prevail because Bill voluntarily entered the store.

   B.   Bet will prevail because Bill was not aware of the confinement until it was over.

   C.   Bill will prevail providing that Bet knew he was in the store.

   D.   Bill will prevail because confinement itself counts as "injury" in a false imprisonment claim.

17.   This question is set in the same bookshop as Question 16. Bet, the owner, was in the habit of locking up each day at 1:00 p.m. so that she could eat her lunch in peace. One day she locked the front door of the shop and heated some soup in her microwave oven. She was just sitting down to enjoy her nice, hot soup when Mary, a customer whom she did not know was still in the store, tried the front door and found it locked. Mary asked Bet to open the door so she could leave, but Bet told her she would have to wait until she finished her lunch. This took about 15 minutes, after which Bet opened the door and let a very angry Mary depart. If Mary sues Bet for false imprisonment, who will prevail? (Assume in this question that no rear entrance is available.)

   A.   Mary will prevail because she was confined without her consent.

   B.   Mary will prevail because Bet was negligent in locking the store without checking to see if customers were present.

   C.   Bet will prevail because she did not know Mary was there when she locked the door.

D. Bet will prevail because the confinement was brief.

18.   Use the same facts as Question 17, except that when Mary asks to leave, Bet tells her to use the rear entrance to the store, which was locked but could easily be opened from the inside. The rear entrance opens on a service alley which was clean, free of obstructions and normally empty of people. Mary insisted that Bet open the front door, and sued Bet for false imprisonment when she refused. Who will prevail?

   A. Mary will prevail because she was confined without her consent.

   B. Mary will prevail because Bet had a duty to let her leave the way she had entered.

   C. Bet will prevail because Mary was never completely confined.

   D. Bet will prevail because Mary's demand that she open the front door was unreasonable.

19.   Use the same facts as Question 17, except that when Bet told Mary to use the rear entrance, Mary went to the back of store and opened the rear door. She looked out and saw that the alley today was filled with a crowd of tough looking teenagers who were smoking, throwing knives at a telephone pole, and fighting. Mary returned to the main part of the shop, but Bet still would not let her out the front door until she had finished her soup. If Mary sues Bet for false imprisonment, who will prevail?

   A. Mary will prevail only if the persons in the alley were presently involved in violations of the law.

   B. Mary will prevail because the alternative exit involved a risk of harm to her person.

   C. Bet will prevail because Mary was never completely confined.

   D. Bet will prevail because she is not responsible for the actions of third parties in a public right of way.

20.   This question is also set in Bet's Bookstore. One day Arnie was in the back of the store looking at magazines. Bet was in the front of the store and was unaware that Arnie was still on the premises. At this point Marla entered the store to browse. Marla was the proprietor of a nearby sandwich shop, and Bet was annoyed with her about the condition of her establishment, which was run-down and

detracted from the attractiveness of the shopping area. Bet locked the door to her store and told Marla that she would not let her leave until she had agreed to clean her place up. Voices were raised, as Marla demanded that Bet allow her to leave, and Bet continued her demands that Marla clean up her store. Arnie tried to leave the store at this point, but discovered the doors were locked. Arnie rattled the front door and yelled for Bet, who did not hear him because she was arguing with Marla. If Arnie sues Bet for false imprisonment who will prevail?

    A.   Arnie will prevail because Bet intended to confine Marla.

    B.   Arnie will prevail because Bet should have exercised greater care to make sure the store was empty before locking the door.

    C.   Bet will prevail because she never knew that Arnie was in the store.

    D.   Bet will prevail because she was protecting her own interests when she confined Marla.

21.   Polly was called into the human resources office at the store where she worked as an accountant and payroll officer. The head of human resources, the chief financial officer of the store, and the store's chief of security were there, and the head of human resources told her that she was suspected of embezzlement and that an accounting team from headquarters was investigating her work. Polly protested her innocence, but the head of security told her that she would have to stay in the office if she wanted any hope of keeping her job. "We are leaving now," the head of human resources said, "and if you leave this office before we return you will lose your job no matter what the audit shows." They left Polly in the room with the door open. Polly sat in the office for an hour before the chief of security returned and told her she was free to go: "It turns out that the mistakes occurred at headquarters, not here, so you are free to return to work." If Polly sues her employer and the other employees for false imprisonment, who will prevail?

    A.   Polly will prevail because the threat to fire her means her consent to remain in the room was invalid.

    B.   Polly will prevail because the presence of three people in the office constitutes a threat of force sufficient to confine her.

    C.   The defendants will prevail because employers have a privilege to confine their employees.

D. The defendants will prevail because Polly was not completely confined.

22.   The chief financial officer of the store in Question 20 had hoped that the accusation of embezzlement would justify firing Polly, whom she disliked for purely personal reasons. After Polly was cleared in the investigation, the chief financial officer called Polly into her office and told her that he would call the police and have her charged with larceny if she did not immediately resign. "I will ruin your career," she told Polly. "I will see to it personally that you never get another job, that your bank forecloses on your mortgage, and that your children are taken away from you and put in foster homes. I will leave you nothing but your eyes to weep with." Polly was infuriated by the threat, told the chief financial officer to go ahead and try, and promised to sue the company if she did. Polly stormed out of the meeting and called a lawyer friend who specialized in employment cases. She later reflected that if the chief financial officer was out to get her like that, she should probably start looking for another job. If Polly sues the chief financial officer for intentional infliction of emotional distress, who will prevail?

A. Polly will prevail because threats of false criminal charges amount to outrageous conduct.

B. Polly will prevail because she in fact was upset.

C. The defendant will prevail because Polly's emotional distress was not severe.

D. The defendant will prevail because the proper remedy for a false criminal charge is a suit for malicious prosecution.

23.   The chief financial officer in the previous question was disappointed in the failure of her threats to get rid of Polly. She decided to try a different approach. She knew that Polly's son, who was about fourteen years old, suffered from a severe anxiety disorder. The chief financial officer went to Polly's house one day when she knew that Polly would be at work and her son would be home alone from school. The chief financial officer knocked on the door and announced that she was from the police, and that whoever was there better open up. When the chief financial officer saw the nervous boy open the door, she knew her plan would work. She told Polly's son that she knew his mother was embezzling money from work and that he was helping her. She told him that if he did not confess it would go hard on his mother: she would be sent to prison, he would never see her again, and it would be all his fault. Polly's son began to cry, ran away, and locked himself in his room. When Polly came home it took her an hour to get the story from her son. The boy was

so traumatized that he had to be admitted to an inpatient care facility and he has fallen behind in school as a result. If Polly's son sues the chief financial officer for intentional infliction of emotional distress, who will prevail?

    A.   Polly's son will prevail because he is a minor.

    B.   Polly's son will prevail because the outrageous conduct caused him severe emotional distress.

    C.   The defendant will prevail because obviously empty threats do not constitute outrageous conduct.

    D.   The defendant will prevail because the reaction of Polly's son was unforeseeably severe.

24.   This question is based on the same facts as Question 22. The chief financial officer's conduct towards Polly's son has caused Polly herself great distress. She now cannot sleep, has periods of blinding rage in which she breaks furniture, and has become unable to work. Polly has had to seek treatment herself for her emotional condition, and now has lingering problems of distrust of other people which makes it hard for her to function at work. If Polly sues the chief financial officer for intentional infliction of emotional distress arising out of the conduct towards her son, who will prevail?

    A.   Polly will prevail because the conduct was outrageous.

    B.   Polly will prevail based on the doctrine of transferred intent.

    C.   The defendant will prevail because Polly's emotional distress was not severe.

    D.   The defendant will prevail because Polly was not present when the outrageous conduct occurred.

25.   Bingo was driving his car during a torrential rainstorm. As he drove past a low spot on the highway, a stream of rainwater swept across the road, causing Bingo to lose control of his car. Bingo's car swerved off the road and onto land belonging to Duke. Bingo got out of his car as water began to rise up above the level of the wheels. Bingo could have walked back onto the road, but he chose instead to climb up to higher ground on Duke's land, to a spot where some trees provided some shelter from the rain. Duke later discovered Bingo and his car, and ordered Bingo to get himself and his car off Duke's property. Bingo tried, but his car would not start because of water damage. If Duke sues Bingo for trespass based on the initial entry of Bingo's car onto Duke's property, who will prevail?

A. Duke will prevail because trespass to land is a strict liability tort, and Bingo's car in fact ended up on his property.

B. Duke will prevail because Bingo's entry violated Duke's right of exclusive possession.

C. Bingo will prevail because he did not intend for his car to end up where it did.

D. Bingo will prevail because his trespass caused no harm to Duke or his land.

26. This question is based on the same facts as Question 25. If Duke sues Bingo for trespass based on Bingo's taking shelter from the storm under Duke's trees, which of the following statements is true?

A. Duke cannot recover because the initial entry was not tortious.

B. Duke can state a prima facie case of trespass to land against Bingo

C. Since Bingo entered Duke's land unwillingly, Bingo still lacks the intent needed to commit trespass

D. Duke cannot recover because his order to Bingo to leave the land was unjustified under the circumstances

27. This question is based on the same facts as Question 25. If Duke sues Bingo for trespass based on the failure of Bingo to remove his car from Duke's property, which of the following statements is true?

A. Duke cannot recover because the initial entry was not tortious.

B. Duke can state a prima facie case of trespass to land against Bingo for the failure to remove the car.

C. Bingo has no duty to attempt to move the car.

D. Bingo has acquired a license to leave the car there indefinitely.

28. Connie bought an eighteenth century cottage in a seaside community. Connie's cottage is separated from the ocean by a road and an estate belonging to Baron. Baron's estate stands on a towering cliff, high above the ocean below. So steep is the cliff that

Baron has no practical access to the water, even though there is a small sand beach below the cliff at low tide. According to the laws of the jurisdiction, that beach is public land since it is below the high tide mark. One day Connie discovered a secret trap door in her basement. The door led to an ancient tunnel, probably dug by smugglers, which runs below Baron's land and exits below the cliff at the water's edge. During the summer, Connie regularly uses the tunnel to visit the beach at low tide. Baron has discovered this and sues Connie for trespass to land. Who will prevail?

A. Baron will prevail provided he owns the subsurface rights on his property.

B. Connie will prevail because Baron has no access to the beach from his own property.

C. Connie will prevail because her trespass was not visible to Baron.

D. Connie will prevail because the beach she uses is public land.

29. Which of the following is most likely to be found to constitute trespass to land?

A. A homeowner grills food on a backyard grill, and the smoke drifts over to a neighbor's backyard.

B. A private plane from a nearby airport flies over a house at an altitude of one thousand feet.

C. A rural landowner hunts ducks on her own property, and the noise of the shotgun disturbs her neighbor's sleep.

D. A rural landowner hunts ducks on her own property. The shotgun pellets pass over but do not land on the neighbor's property.

30. Which of the following is most likely NOT to be found to constitute trespass to land?

A. A person constructs a building close to the lot line, and the eave of the building extends over the neighboring lot.

B. Rainwater runs off a person's land in a natural flow onto the property of a neighbor.

C. A person piles dirt from an excavation in a tall heap close to the lot line, so that the dirt runs onto the neighboring land by the action of rain and gravity.

D. A person constructs a dam across a stream on the person's property, with the result that the stream backs up and floods part of the neighboring land.

31. Porter owned an antique porcelain dish. One day his friend Danzig visited and expressed interest in seeing the dish. Porter showed him the dish, but told him explicitly not to touch it. In violation of this request, Danzig picked up the dish in order to see whether it had a maker's mark on the bottom. Danzig then put the dish down without damaging it. Porter brings suit against Danzig for trespass to chattels.

A. Porter will prevail because Danzig's conduct amounts to dispossessing Porter of the dish.

B. Porter will prevail because Danzig intermeddled with the dish.

C. Danzig will prevail because the dish was not damaged.

D. Danzig will prevail because Porter was unreasonable in forbidding him from touching the dish.

32. After dinner at Porter's house, Danzig goes into Porter's bathroom and brushes his teeth using Porter's toothbrush. Danzig then rinses the brush and replaces it. The brush is not noticeably impaired by this use. Porter sees Danzig do this, however, and he now cannot bring himself to use that toothbrush any more.

A. This is a trespass to chattel because Danzig has intentionally dispossessed Porter of the toothbrush.

B. This is a trespass to chattel because the toothbrush was rendered unusable as a result of Danzig's conduct.

C. This is not an actionable trespass to chattel because the toothbrush was not physically damaged.

D. This is not an actionable trespass to chattel because Potter did not forbid Danzig from using the toothbrush.

33. Tami picks up what she believes to be a school workbook and begins filling out the questions in it with a ballpoint pen. Only after she completes several pages of the book does she discover that the book is not hers, but belongs to her classmate, Biff.

A. This is a trespass to chattel because Tami has intermeddled with the chattel and impaired its condition.

B. This is a trespass to chattel because Tami was negligent in not making sure the book belonged to her before she began writing in it.

C. This is not a trespass to chattel because Tami lacked intent to interfere with the possessions of another.

D. This is not a trespass to chattel because Tami's harm to the book was minor.

34. Parma owns an antique wooden writing desk made in Providence, Rhode Island, in 1750. While visiting Parma's house one day, Derby sat down at the desk and wrote a letter, even though Parma wanted no one to touch it. While writing the letter, Derby left a scratch in the finish of the desk.

A. This is trespass to chattels for which Parma could recover the full value of the desk.

B. This is trespass to chattels for which Parma could recover any loss in value of the desk.

C. This is a conversion for which Parma could recover the full value of the desk.

D. This is a conversion for which Parma could recover the rental value of the desk for the time it took to write the letter.

35. Parma was leaving for an indefinite vacation, so he sent his antique writing desk to Lyon's Antique Store for safekeeping, because Lyon's has an excellent security system. When Parma finally returned and went to reclaim the desk, Lyon was out of town on a buying trip and the store was closed. Parma had to wait several days before Lyon returned and Parma could reclaim the desk.

A. This is conversion because Parma's right of possession was seriously interfered with.

B. This is trespass to chattels because Parma's right of possession was interfered with, but not seriously enough to constitute conversion.

C. This is trespass to chattels because Lyon should have exercised more care not to interfere with Parma's right to the desk.

D. No tort was committed.

36. Parma was again leaving for vacation, and this time he hired Buck's Delivery to transport the antique desk to Lyon's Antiques for

safekeeping. Buck's Delivery deliberately sent the desk to Milan's Antiques instead. Milan's Antiques then sold the desk to Cormac, who paid value for the desk in ignorance of the fact that it really belonged to Parma and was not for sale. Under these facts, which of the following are converters of the desk?

    A.   Only Buck's Delivery is a converter of the desk.

    B.   Buck's Delivery and Milan's Antiques converted the desk.

    C.   Buck's, Milan's and Cormac all converted the desk.

    D.   Buck's, Milan's, Cormac, and Lyon's all converted the desk.

37.   Kluck, while a guest in Parma's home, noticed that the finish on the antique writing desk was extremely dirty. Although Parma had told Kluck not to touch the desk, Kluck decided to do Parma a favor and clean up the desk. In doing so, Kluck removed the original finish on the desk, which had not been disturbed since 1750. By so doing, Kluck destroyed the value of the desk as an antique. With the original dirty finish the desk had been worth $50,000; cleaned up the desk was only worth about $10,000. In an action for conversion by Parma against Kluck, which of the following is correct?

    A.   Kluck would prevail because Kluck did not intend to damage the desk.

    B.   Parma would prevail, but could only recover at most $40,000, the difference in value of the desk before and after the refinishing.

    C.   Parma would prevail and could recover the full market value of the desk, $50,000; Kluck would now own the desk.

    D.   Parma would prevail and could recover the full market value of the desk, $50,000; Parma would retain ownership of the desk.

38.   Without permission, Bolton placed an old car in the abandoned barn on the farm belonging to his neighbor, Fisk. Without knowing that the car was in the barn, Fisk sold the farm to Wedge. While inspecting the property, Wedge discovered the car in the old barn. Wedge moved some of his own farm equipment into the barn, put a padlock on the barn door, and asked Fisk who owned the car. Fisk said he didn't know, but suggested it might belong to Bolton. Bolton meanwhile had discovered that the door to the barn was locked, which prevented him from removing his car. The next day, Wedge contacted Bolton and told him he could remove the car from the barn. Bolton then sued Fisk and Wedge for conversion.

A. Bolton will not prevail because he was a trespasser.

B. Bolton will not prevail because no conversion occurred.

C. Bolton will prevail against Fisk, but not against Wedge.

D. Bolton will prevail against Wedge, but not against Fisk.

39. This question uses the same facts as Question 38, except that Wedge refused to allow Bolton to remove the car. Wedge claimed ownership of the car, since it was in the barn when the farm was sold. Bolton then sued Fisk and Wedge for conversion.

A. Bolton will not prevail because he was a trespasser.

B. Bolton will not prevail because no conversion occurred.

C. Bolton will prevail against Fisk, but not against Wedge.

D. Bolton will prevail against Wedge, but not against Fisk.

40. This question uses the same fact as Question 38, except that Wedge started the car and drove it out of the barn. Wedge then drove the car around the farm for a while before parking it in his driveway under an oak tree and notifying Bolton to come get it. When Bolton arrived he found that droppings from a flock of starlings in the oak tree had soiled (but not damaged) the finish on the car. Bolton then sued Wedge for conversion.

A. Wedge will prevail because the he did not exercise sufficient dominion over the car.

B. Wedge will prevail because he has an absolute right to use chattels left on his property without permission.

C. Bolton will prevail because Wedge exercised dominion and control of the car by driving it around the farm.

D. Bolton will prevail because the condition of the car was impaired.

ANSWERS:

1: The answer is B. Battery requires an intended harmful or offensive contact with the person of another, but such a contact with something closely connected to the person's body, such as clothing or something the person is holding, will be considered contact with the other's body and so sufficient to support a battery claim. Furthermore, kicking someone's support in this manner, even as a joke, is at least offensive. Answers involving "harm" may be incorrect because what the plaintiff must show is a harmful or offensive *contact*. Also, it is not necessary that the defendant intend to cause "harm" in the sense of physical injury. If the joke that was intended involved intentionally inflicting an offensive contact, then the defendant had the intent necessary for a battery. Here the injury was the affront to Jess's personhood and dignity.

2: The answer is D. Assault requires that the victim actually experience apprehension of an imminent harmful or offensive contact. In this scenario, Pranks snuck up behind Jess and kicked the cane away without warning. Jess thus experienced the offensive contact, but not any apprehension of the contact. Note that in this question, Pranks's intent is not really the issue. The problem is that a different element of the cause of action, the required apprehension, is missing. It should also be noted that some courts actually say that every battery includes an assault, and further that this statement is true whenever the victim saw the blow coming. But under the general rules of the Restatement, this is not accurate. Finally, when a defendant acts with an intent to cause a harmful or offensive contact, but only succeeds in causing apprehension, an assault is established. A familiar example of this is the situation where the defendant aims a blow at the plaintiff, who sees it coming and ducks out of the way. The intent was to inflict contact, but the result was apprehension, and therefore an assault.

3: The answer is C. All the elements of a battery are present, and no privilege is established on these facts. Jess is not under threat of attack, so the blow amounts to an unprivileged retaliation. All the other answers suggesting the existence of a privilege are incorrect. Thus, Answer A is incorrect because it is based on the assumption that Jess would have a privilege of self-defense here because Pranks was the original aggressor. The problem is that the threat of harmful or offensive contact from Pranks seems to be over; he is just standing there laughing at Jess and is no longer attempting to inflict harmful or offensive contact. Jess has no privilege at this point to hit Pranks. For the same reason, Jess has no privilege of self-defense. Therefore, the issue of whether Jess must retreat from some threat from Pranks, or on the other hand may stand his ground and defend himself, does not arise. There is no threat, and therefore no privilege. Therefore, any suggestion that Jess had a privilege to inflict a harmful contact, which was lost by reason of the use of excessive force, in the form of a weapon, is similarly misguided. Jess had no privilege to strike Pranks at all, whether with his cane, his fist, or the back of his hand.

4: The answer is A. The requirement of intent for battery is satisfied if the defendant acts, knowing that a harmful or offensive contact is substantially certain to result from the action. Firing into a crowd of people illustrates this rule. The shooter may not know or care who is hit, but if the crowd is sufficiently dense it is a substantial certainty that the bullet will strike someone. In this type of intent, the shooter's purpose is not determinative, but rather the knowledge of the substantial certainty of the result. On the other hand, if the actor is aware that his or her actions will create only an unreasonable risk of harm, that is not sufficient for liability for battery. Unreasonable risk is the test for negligence. It is also necessary to distinguish knowledge that a result was substantially certain from the issue of motive. In this problem, the purpose of the shooter is not the issue. If the shooter knew that harmful contact was substantially certain, it does not matter that he was indifferent to who was actually struck by the bullet, or even if he did not care whether or not he hit anyone. So long as the shooter knew that contact was substantially certain, that is sufficient for intent.

Finally, note that mental illness does not necessarily immunize the actor from liability for intentional torts. The key issue is whether the mental condition still allows the actor to form the necessary intent. For example, if the mental condition caused the actor to develop an unreasoning hostility to persons who visit gyms, that delusion might lead him to commit an act of violence such as this. But if the condition allowed the actor to understand that a harmful contact was substantially certain to result from his actions, liability for battery would still follow. On the other hand, if the mental illness was so severe that it prevented the actor from understanding the nature of his act, or that it would impact other persons, then the actor would have neither purpose to inflict a harmful contact nor knowledge that such contact was certain to occur. In this case, it appears that the individual understood what he was doing and what the result would be, but was indifferent. That state of mind does not rule out liability for battery, because he could still know that harmful contact was certainly going to occur.

5: The answer is C. The landowner here neither has the purpose to shoot the hiker nor knows that this result is substantially certain to occur. The knowledge that the landowner has regarding the presence of hikers in the state forest is not knowledge that, if she misses the tree, the hikers are substantially certain to suffer harmful contact. Rather, the landowner knows that hitting a hiker is a possibility—a risk. In this situation, even if the shooter misses the tree and the bullet continues into the state forest, it is probable that it will not strike a person at all. It may hit a tree or simply fall to the ground, spent. In this situation, therefore, the landowner might well be negligent in creating an unreasonable risk to hikers, but lacks the intent necessary to commit battery. Note, therefore, that knowledge of the existence of a risk is not the equivalent of knowledge that a result is substantially certain. As noted, the landowner here creates a risk, and could be liable for negligence, but not for battery. Also note that simply being on one's own property does not create any privilege to injure those outside the premises.

6: The answer is A. These facts satisfy all the elements of the tort of battery. It is important to distinguish this situation from that in the previous question. In Question 5, the actor had neither purpose to inflict a harmful contact, nor knowledge that it was substantially certain. In this question, although it is no certainty that the rock will hit Barber, the actor does have the purpose of inflicting a harmful contact: Alex "took aim at Barber, and threw." The purpose of inflicting the harmful contact of course satisfies the intent element of battery. Thus, while knowledge that the result is substantially certain is an alternative basis for finding the intent needed to commit battery, the statement that such knowledge is necessary and required is incorrect. Even without knowledge of substantial certainty, having the purpose of inflicting the contact will satisfy the intent element. So long as it was Alex's purpose to hit Barber, it does not matter for purposes of intent that the success of the attack was questionable.

7.   The answer is B. Art inflicted a harmful or offensive contact on both Phil and Susan. He directly contacted Phil by pushing him, and indirectly contacted Susan by pushing Phil into her. Since they were walking together and Art shoved Phil against Susan, the facts support the inference that Art must have at least been substantially certain that Phil would contact Susan. On the other hand, Susan cannot successfully sue Phil for battery, even though he was the one who actually came into contact with her. For battery, it is necessary that the potential defendant "act" in some way to bring about the contact. Here, Phil did not engage in any volitional act, but rather was pushed into Susan. As far as Phil was concerned, the contact was wholly unintentional.

8.   The answer is D. This is a typical offensive contact situation. It does not matter that muddy water would not cause bodily harm,

since intended offensive contact also establishes liability for battery. In addition, Matty at ten years of age is old enough to understand that this would be offensive; the offense is no doubt what would make it a joke. Tom is not required to experience apprehension in order to recover, since that is an element only of assault.

9. The answer is A. This is a transferred intent situation. The intended tort towards Tom also results in a harmful and offensive contact with Hannah, and the intent to contact Tom then transfers into an intent to contact Hannah. In these situations, it may appear as if the contact with the third party is accidental and negligent, and indeed it would probably be possible to sue for negligence in many of these situations. That possibility, however, does not rule out battery, as several of the incorrect answers suggest. All the elements of battery are present thanks to the doctrine of transferred intent.

10. The answer is C. A buzzing ring-tone might cause apprehension in someone allergic to bees without it constituting an assault, so long as the possessor of the phone did not realize it would cause such a reaction. Here, Ashley knew of Bart's fears, and the activation of the cell phone therefore was intended to cause him to apprehend a sting. To most people, but especially to one allergic to bees, a sting would be considered a harmful contact. It is not necessary that the actor in fact be capable of inflicting the contact; apparent present ability is sufficient. Therefore, no actual bee needed to be present so long as it appeared that a sting might be imminent. On these facts, however, no actual contact with Bart occurred, so this could not constitute a battery.

11. The answer is D. Assault requires that the threat of harmful or offensive contact be imminent, and that the defendant have the apparent present ability to in fact inflict the contact. Here, Zach has to depart the immediate area and go to his car, supposedly to get the bat. Thus the threat to hit Al with the bat is not imminent, and Zach does not at that moment have the ability to carry out the threat. For these reasons, even if Al believes that Zach has a bat and will return with it, at this point there is no assault. Finally, Zach's intent to hit Al or not is not the issue here; the problem is the threat. Note that if Zach later returns with the baseball bat, any threatening actions at that point might constitute an assault, since he would appear at that point to be intending to and capable of inflicting the harmful contact.

12. The answer is A. Given the earlier threats and the present situation, all the elements of assault are present, and Dale's actions show he did in fact have apprehension of a harmful or offensive contact. Dale is not required to fear actually being beaten up, or

losing the fight, in order to prevail in a claim for assault. He need only suffer apprehension, meaning anticipation, of the required contact. Here the threat of attack was clear in light of earlier events and Mark's statements when he met Dale. Contrary to the last answer, Mark was certainly close enough to make the threat imminent.

13.   The answer is B. According to the Restatement Second, section 27, it does not matter that the plaintiff's apprehension is unreasonable. If the defendant intended to cause apprehension of harmful or offensive contact, and the victim in fact experiences such apprehension, that is sufficient to state a claim for assault. In other words, it does not matter that a reasonable person in Dale's position would not have experienced apprehension. It is sufficient that Mark intended it, and Dale in fact experienced it. It also does not matter that the defendant expected the plaintiff to flee so that he would not have to actually carry out the attack. So long as the defendant intended to cause apprehension, the intent requirement is met. Once the defendant takes action to put that intention into motion, and the required result occurs, the elements of assault are satisfied.

14.   The answer is D. The "apprehension" referred to in the elements of assault is not the same as "fear." Instead, it indicates that the plaintiff is put in the position of anticipating an unpleasant and unwanted contact of some sort, either harmful or offensive. Therefore, it does not negate the required showing of apprehension if the defendant proves that the plaintiff did not experience fear because the plaintiff believed that he or she could defend herself from the attack. The action of assault exists on the theory that people should not be put in this position with impunity, because it can lead to injury and breaches of the peace. On the other hand, it is not entirely accurate to say that public policy encourages people to avoid confrontations, because the common law recognizes a privilege to stand one's ground and defend oneself.

15.   The answer is C. Threatening gestures from one motorist to another, without more, are not assaults because there is no threat of imminent harmful contact. These encounters can be unpleasant, but unless some more serious attempt is made to inflict contact or create apprehension of imminent contact, it does not amount to assault.

16.   The answer is B. According to the Restatement Second of Torts, the plaintiff in a claim of false imprisonment must either be aware of the confinement or be harmed by it. Apparently the basis of the claim is that confinement of a person against their will and without consent is an actionable affront to their personhood. However, the affront is not present if the plaintiff was not aware of the confine-

ment, or was not harmed by it. In this case, Bill was not aware of the momentary confinement, and his movements were in no way hindered by it. This is true even though Bet knew he was in the store when she locked the door to keep the canvasser out. And while confinement is indeed the injury in these cases, it must be combined with knowledge on the part of the plaintiff. Finally, voluntarily entering the store does not include some sort of consent to be confined there.

17.   The answer is A. Although Bet did not know about Mary when she first locked up the shop, once she became aware of her presence and her demand to leave, she had no privilege to confine her in the store. At that point she had a duty to unlock the door so Mary could depart. Bet has intent at this point because now she is aware of Mary's presence. Since false imprisonment is an intentional tort, Bet would not have been liable for negligently locking Mary in. It is only after she becomes aware of Mary that her failure to unlock the door becomes a problem. Although the confinement was brief, it was sufficiently long to affront Mary and invade her interest in freedom of movement.

18.   The answer is C. If a viable exit from confinement is available, the plaintiff is not completely confined, as required by the elements of false imprisonment. The rear exit is slightly inconvenient, but on these facts presents no hazards or barriers that would make its use difficult for Mary. Accordingly, the existence of the rear exit means that Mary was not confined. Therefore, Bet had no duty to open the front door to avoid confining Mary.

19.   The answer is B. Mary is not required to run any risk of harm to her person in order to escape the confinement to which Bet has subjected her. Here, a person in Mary's position might reasonably fear harm from the actions of the people in the alley should she try to walk past them. Once Bet was informed of the problem with the rear exit she once again had a duty to allow Mary to exit. This is not a problem with the actions of third parties, but rather with Bet's own refusal to unlock the door of the store. Therefore, Mary was in fact completely confined. Also, so long as Mary in fact perceives a risk of harm, it is not required that the persons in the alley be presently engaged in illegal activity.

20.   The answer is A. This is a transferred intent type of situation in which an actor's wrongful conduct directed against one party ends up invading the rights of a third party. In these cases, the actor is liable to the injured third party for the intentional tort even if the actor was not aware of the third party's presence. In this case, Bet acted to confine Marla against her wishes, thus supplying the

necessary action and intent for false imprisonment. This conduct also confined Arnie against his wishes, with the result that Bet also is liable to him for false imprisonment.

21.   The answer is D. Consent obtained by improper duress is invalid, but this usually requires threats of physical harm to the victim or to others. In such a case the lack of actual physical barriers would not prevent a finding that the victim was completely confined by submitting to the threat and remaining. In this case, however, the store is investigating a possible embezzlement, and has requested that Polly remain on threat of being fired. This sort of moral duress is usually not considered to be enough, by itself, to constitute confinement for purposes of false imprisonment. Short of actual threats of physical force, moral duress sufficient to constitute confinement would require some more wrongful act on the part of the defendant, such as the seizure of the plaintiff's property. In this scenario there is not sufficient threat of physical force by the managers, and no physical barrier because the door remained open. On the other hand, employers do not have any general right to confine employees, beyond the normal requirement that employees stay at their posts and do their work.

22.   The answer is C. While intentional infliction of emotional distress requires outrageous conduct, that requirement is probably met in this scenario by the threat of what the defendant knows to be false criminal charges, together with the other threats of ruin. However, an important limitation on this tort is the requirement that the emotional distress suffered by the plaintiff be severe. This requirement is apparently one of those measures taken by courts to prevent the proverbial flood of litigation. Therefore, more than momentary upset is required. Here the facts show that Polly was angry but not overwhelmed or intimidated. She had the presence of mind to contact an attorney and to take other measures to protect herself. There is no indication on these facts that Polly was so overcome with emotion distress that it has affected her significantly. On this basis, she would probably not be able to show sufficient injury to allow her suit to succeed.

23.   The answer is B. Here, the conduct is particularly outrageous because the defendant knew that Polly's son was vulnerable and easily upset, and tried to exploit that vulnerability by threats and accusations against him. In contrast to the previous question, the facts here indicate severe emotional distress, shown by tangible symptoms that required professional treatment and that have affected the boy's daily living. The defendant will not be able to prevail by claiming that the threats were obviously empty or that the boy had an unusually severe reaction, since the defendant

targeted the boy precisely because she knew he was vulnerable, and therefore likely to believe in threats and react to them strongly.

24.   The answer is D. At least under the scheme laid out in the Restatement, the doctrine of transferred intent is not effective for the tort of intentional infliction of emotional distress. Instead, the Restatement limits liability when the outrageous conduct is directed at a person other than the plaintiff. In these situations, the plaintiff must actually be present when the outrageous conduct occurs, and the defendant must be at least reckless with respect to causing emotional distress to the third party. Thus, the defendant could be liable in this case if Polly had been present when the defendant falsely accused her son of helping her to embezzle funds from the company. It must be admitted, however, that Polly would have a strong argument for extending the reach of the tort in these circumstances, because the conduct of the defendant was aimed at affecting her and she was so closely related to the victim. However, under standard doctrine Polly could not prevail even though the facts suggest that her emotional distress in this case was in fact severe.

25.   The answer is C. For purposes of trespass to land, it is not necessary that the actor be aware that he or she is in fact entering onto land belonging to another, so long as it appears that the actor in fact intends to be on the particular piece of land in question. For example, a person who mistakenly enters land belonging to another is liable for the trespass. This actor would be liable for at least nominal damages even though the entry caused no damage to the owner or the land. In this case, however, Bingo did not intentionally enter Duke's property. Instead, Bingo's car was washed off the road and he involuntarily ended up on Duke's land. At that point, it appears he was not able to depart because of the depth of the water. Because Bingo did not intend to be on Duke's property at all, but was propelled there by forces beyond his control, Bingo is not liable for trespass.

26.   The answer is B. In this case, Bingo has a choice of where to go once his car is swept off the road. He chose to stay on Duke's land, and indeed walked further onto the property. Since he now has freedom of action and has deliberately remained on the property, he is committing trespass to land. He now intends to be on Duke's land.

27.   The answer is A. If the initial entry were wrongful, then Bingo would be liable for trespass for failing to remove his car even though it was now not possible to do so. For example, if Bingo had deliberately driven onto Duke's property, parked his car, and failed to move it when asked, Bingo would be liable for a continuing

trespass. Both the entry and the failure to leave would be wrongful. Also, if the car were moveable and Bingo simply refused to move it, that would also constitute a trespass, because Duke has a right to exclude Bingo from his property. In this case, however, Bingo entered unwillingly and now is unable to comply immediately with the order to remove the car. However, Bingo must make a reasonable effort to remove the car as soon as possible.

28.   The answer is A. Ownership of the surface at common law included ownership of the airspace above the land as well as everything below the surface as well. In some cases jurisdictions may have special rules that separate the subsurface rights from the ownership of the surface itself, but if Baron owns the subsurface interests then Connie is trespassing when she uses the tunnel to gain access to the beach below the cliffs. It does not matter that Baron has no access to the beach, or that the beach itself is public land. The trespass occurs when Connie enters the space below Baron's land.

29.   The answer is D. Smoke and noise might be nuisances, but are not trespasses because there is no tangible invasion. (The only exception would be in jurisdictions that allow a trespass claim where particulate pollution from smokestacks and other sources accumulate and cause damage to the property. A backyard grill is not going to achieve that level of harm.) Airplane over-flights are certainly a tangible invasion, but as a matter of policy are not trespasses. Modern rules suggest that such over-flights are only actionable if they invade the immediate airspace above the land and substantially interfere with the landowners use and enjoyment of the land.

30.   The answer is B. In all the other situations, the actor has intervened to cause a tangible invasion of the neighboring property.

31.   The answer is C. Danzig's conduct amounts to an intentional intermeddling with the dish, but not to dispossession. Dispossession requires intent to take control of a chattel in order to deprive the possessor of its use. A minor interference such as this will not lead to liability unless the chattel is damaged or impaired in some way.

32.   The answer is B. This short intermeddling with the toothbrush is not a dispossession. On the other hand, in this case the toothbrush is impaired in its condition. Danzig's rather disgusting conduct has left Porter with the reasonable feeling that the toothbrush is now unusable. Many people, with good reason, would not use something like a toothbrush that has been used by others. Although Danzig's use has not much altered the physical condition of the toothbrush, it

would be reasonable to state that the condition of the toothbrush has been substantially impaired. Revulsion at using someone else's toothbrush is common enough that Porter should not be required to specifically forbid it.

33.   The answer is A. Trespass to chattel requires intent, so negligence is not sufficient. However, the intent required is simply an intent to intermeddle with the chattel. It is not necessary that the defendant be aware that the chattel belongs to another, or that the intermeddling will interfere with another's rights of possession. Here, Tami intended to mark up the book, under the mistaken impression that it was her own. In the process she impaired its condition, making her liable for the harm done to Biff's book.

34.   The answer is B. The interference with Parma's rights of possession is not significant enough to count as conversion. Derby did, however, interfere with the desk and caused some minor impairment. While this might normally be too insignificant to count as harm, in the case of an antique it could possibly impair the value of the desk. If so, the remedy under trespass to chattel would be the loss in value of the desk. An alternative measure of recovery would be the cost of repair.

35.   The answer is D. Lyon's interference was at worst inadvertent. Lyon had no intent to interfere with Parma's rights or to intermeddle with the desk at all, and since Parma's vacation was indefinite, Lyon had no reason to know when Parma might return and want the desk back. Therefore this is neither conversion nor trespass to chattel.

36.   The answer is C. All three exercised dominion and control over the desk in a manner inconsistent with Parma's rights as owner: Buck's deliberately delivered it to wrong store, Milan's sold it, and Cormac bought it. Lyon's, however, had nothing to do with any of these transactions. Note that although Cormac was ignorant of the true state of affairs, he did not get good title to the desk because neither Buck's nor Milan's had title. One cannot obtain good title from a thief. Thus Cormac is an innocent converter, but a converter nonetheless. In situations of this sort, Cormac would probably be allowed to satisfy Parma's claim by returning the desk. Cormac would then have to pursue a claim against Milan's for return of the purchase price.

37.   The answer is C. Altering the desk in this manner is an act of dominion and control that would constitute a conversion. The remedy for conversion is in effect a forced sale. Parma can recover the full market value of the desk, but the ownership of the desk then

transfers to Kluck. If Parma wants to sue for the loss in value and keep ownership of the desk, Parma could do so in a trespass to chattels count. In conversion, however, it would be inaccurate to state that Parma could only recover the loss in value.

38.   The answer is B. The interference with Bolton's right to possession of the car was minimal, and neither Fisk nor Wedge acted with intent to interfere with Bolton's rights. Fisk did not even know the car was there, and Wedge acted promptly to locate the owner of the car. Neither made any claim to the car. It is true that Bolton was a trespasser in this situation, but that conduct does not cause a loss of the title to the car.

39.   The answer is D. By laying claim to the car, Wedge has exercised dominion and control of it in a manner that violates Bolton's rights. Fisk, on the other hand, never knew the car was in the barn, and so had no intent to deal with it or interfere with Bolton's ownership simply by selling the farm.

40.   The answer is A. Incidental usages of this sort, if not done under some claim of ownership, are not sufficient dominion and control to constitute conversion. If the car had been significantly damaged, the result might be different, but in this case the facts indicate that the droppings from the birds caused no harm. Thus there was only some superficial soiling which could be fixed simply by washing the car.

CHAPTER 2
PRIVILEGES: DEFENSES TO INTENTIONAL TORTS

QUESTIONS:

1. Marcus was standing in line at the local recreation center with many others, waiting to get a swine flu vaccination. Tolbert, a friend of Marcus, arrived at the center to play basketball. Tolbert saw Marcus and strolled over to say hello. As Marcus and Tolbert talked, they gradually approached the front of the line. Pimmy, a registered nurse who was administering the injections as fast as possible because of the number of people seeking the vaccinations, did not bother to look at Marcus's consent form or ask permission, but instead said, "Hold out your arm." Marcus held out his arm, but Tolbert did not. Nevertheless, Pimmy injected Tolbert, thinking he was also in line. Tolbert was allergic to the vaccination and suffered severe injury as a result. If Tolbert sues Pimmy for battery, who will prevail?

    A. Tolbert will prevail because the contact was in fact harmful.

    B. Tolbert will prevail because he did not consent to the contact.

    C. Pimmy will prevail because Tolbert impliedly consented by standing in line.

    D. Pimmy will prevail because he asked for consent.

2. At the recreational league softball tournament, Team Blue was losing by two runs in the last inning, but had two runners on base. When the batter for Team Blue hit a single to left field, Taylor decided to knock down the opposing Team Green's catcher so that the other runner could score as well, thus tying the score. Taylor ran into the catcher, whose name was Barnwell, grabbing him around the waist and slamming him into the backstop, breaking his arm. To

Taylor's surprise, the other runner was not allowed to score and Taylor was ejected from the game and banned from the league for a year. Barnwell sues Taylor for battery.

    A.   Taylor will prevail because professional baseball players take out the catcher all the time.

    B.   Taylor will prevail because Barnwell consented to this type of contact by agreeing to play in the softball league.

    C.   Barnwell will prevail because he did not consent to receive such a severe injury.

    D.   Barnwell will prevail because this type of contact is far outside the scope of any consent he may have given.

3.   Book consented to an exploratory spleen operation, which would take a small sample of spleen tissue for testing. While Book was heavily sedated before the operation, Dr. Fell induced her to sign a further consent form allowing the use of the spleen tissue in the development of gene therapies for spleen disorders. Dr. Fell then performed the operation in a competent fashion and completed the normal testing on Book's tissue. The tissue was then sent to Dr. Fell's laboratory for gene therapy development, as noted. Book later learned of the consent form she signed while sedated, and sued Dr. Fell for battery. Who will prevail?

    A.   Dr. Fell will prevail because Book consented to the operation.

    B.   Dr. Fell will prevail because Book consented to the use of her spleen tissue for experimentation.

    C.   Book will prevail because Dr. Fell exceeded the scope of her consent to the operation.

    D.   Book will prevail because her consent to the operation was obtained fraudulently while she was sedated, and is therefore invalid.

4.   Use the same facts as Question 3, except that the consent form obtained while Book was sedated authorized Dr. Fell to take additional spleen tissue beyond what would be required for medical testing for Book, and then further authorized the use of that tissue for gene therapy. After the operation Book learns of the additional consent form and the extension of the operation, and Book then sues Dr. Fell for battery. Who will prevail?

    A.   Dr. Fell will prevail because Book consented to the operation.

B. Dr. Fell will prevail because Book consented to the use of her spleen tissue for experimentation.

C. Book will prevail because Dr. Fell exceeded the scope of her consent to the operation.

D. Book will prevail because her consent to the operation was obtained fraudulently while she was sedated, and is therefore invalid.

5. Dr. Mills obtained consent to perform a serious surgical operation on Tip. In order to obtain consent from Tip, Dr. Mills withheld from Tip information about a serious risk of the operation. If Tip had known of the risk he probably would have refused the operation. Dr. Mills then performed the operation.

A. Because the consent was obtained without full disclosure, it is invalid, and Tip can sue for battery and recover for all the effects of the operation.

B. Because this involves mere non-disclosure, the consent is valid and Tip has no claim.

C. Tip can recover in negligence for any injury received in the course of the operation.

D. Tip can recover in negligence only if the undisclosed risk in fact materialized, resulting in injury to Tip.

6. Pat was walking down the sidewalk one day, sucking on a peppermint. He tripped on the uneven surface and, in his effort to catch his balance, inhaled the candy and began to choke. Darby, who saw what had happened, rushed over to help. Observing that Pat was turning blue, Darby tried to administer the Heimlich maneuver to dislodge the object that was blocking Pat's breathing. Although Darby had received some lifesaving training, he was not an expert, and he administered the procedure with too much force. He succeeded in dislodging the candy, but he cracked four ribs in the process. If Pat sues Darby for battery, Darby's best defense would be:

A. Pat was contributorily negligent for inhaling the candy.

B. The City was the sole proximate cause of the injuries for failing to maintain the sidewalks properly.

C. Pat is deemed to have consented to the life-saving treatment.

D. Darby did not intend to cause harm.

7.   Vandal was digging a hole in Ohner's front lawn one day, when he heard someone yelling at him to stop. Vandal kept digging until he felt a hand placed gently but firmly on his shoulder. The hand belonged to Ohner, who said, "That is my lawn, and you had better stop. You get off my land; I have called the police." Upon hearing those words, Vandal slapped Ohner's hand away and tried to hit Ohner with his shovel. Ohner grabbed his arm and told him again to get off his land. Vandal and Ohner were pushing and shoving one another when Meddler came walking down the sidewalk. Observing the altercation, Meddler rushed forward and knocked Ohner down by hitting him in the head with his briefcase. Vandal started to run away, but as he rounded the corner he ran headlong into Sarge, a uniformed police officer answering Ohner's earlier call. The impact nearly knocked Sarge down, but he grabbed Vandal and told him to stand still. Vandal punched Sarge to try to get free, so Sarge hit Vandal with his nightstick, thereby subduing him. If Vandal sues Ohner for battery, will Vandal prevail?

A.   No, because Ohner is privileged to use reasonable force to protect property.

B.   No, because Ohner had the privilege of private necessity.

C.   Yes, because Ohner is not privileged to use force to protect property.

D.   Yes, because Ohner did not need to use force, since he had already called the police.

8.   Use the same facts as Question 7. If Ohner sues Vandal for battery, who will prevail?

A.   Vandal will prevail if he did not know the lawn belonged to Ohner.

B.   Vandal will prevail because he was privileged to use force to defend himself against Ohner's touching.

C.   Ohner will prevail because his original contact with Vandal was privileged.

D.   Ohner will prevail on a theory of transferred intent (from the lawn to Ohner).

9.   Use the same facts as Question 7. If Ohner sues Meddler for battery, who will prevail?

A.   Ohner will prevail, because Meddler had no way of knowing which of the participants in the struggle was the aggressor.

    B.   Ohner will prevail, because Meddler had no duty to inter-
fere in the struggle.

    C.   Meddler will prevail, because Meddler had the privilege of
defense of third parties.

    D.   Meddler will prevail, because Ohner was the original
aggressor

10.   Moe and Jane were visiting a horse ranch one day. Moe, who
had a gross sense of humor, picked up a piece of fresh horse manure
and threatened to rub it in Jane's hair. Jane, repulsed at the notion,
drew her authentic Colt revolver and shot Moe in the arm. If Moe
sues Jane for battery, who will prevail?

    A.   Moe will prevail because he did not actually touch Jane
with the horse manure.

    B.   Moe will prevail because Jane used excessive force.

    C.   Jane will prevail because she had the privilege of self
defense.

    D.   Jane will prevail because the force was reasonable, since
she only shot Moe in the arm.

11.   Dave sincerely believed that people who claimed to have
allergies were faking or exaggerating. When Dave heard Marta talk
about her peanut allergy, he naturally insisted that it was all
nonsense and not a real health threat. In fact, Marta did have a
severe peanut allergy that could quickly bring about anaphylactic
shock and cause her to stop breathing unless she received an
immediate shot of medicine. Dave tried to force Marta to eat a
peanut to prove it was all a fake, and Marta kept backing away.
Finally Dave, who was getting angry, said he would shove the
peanut up Marta's nose to prove there was no problem. Dave
grabbed Marta, and Marta pulled a gun from her purse and shot
Dave. If Dave sues Marta for battery who will prevail?

    A.   Dave will prevail if he honestly thought the peanut was
harmless to Marta.

    B.   Dave will prevail because Marta used excessive force.

    C.   Marta will prevail only if Dave did not sincerely believe
that her allergy was fake.

    D.   Marta will prevail because she had the privilege of self
defense.

12.   While at work one, day, Brown notices that her gold ring is missing from her finger. Remembering that she removed it in the washroom, Brown returns there but cannot find the ring. A week later she notices that Jones is wearing a ring very similar to the one she lost. After thinking the situation over for another week, Brown comes to you to ask whether she can use force to recover the ring from Jones. You would advise her that:

  A.   She cannot use force to recover the ring.

  B.   She may use reasonable force to recover the ring and will be liable only if it turns out that the ring Jones is wearing is not in fact Brown's lost ring.

  C.   She may use reasonable force to recover the ring provided she is reasonable in her belief that the ring Jones is wearing is the lost ring.

  D.   She must first make a demand on Jones for the ring. If Jones refuses to surrender the ring then Brown may use reasonable force to recover it provided she is reasonable in her belief that the ring Jones is wearing is the lost ring.

13.   Bet, the owner of Bet's Bookstore, became concerned about shoplifting from her establishment. She purchased a security system that included a magnetic detector at the doors and an automatic locking system for the front door which could lock the front door remotely from Bet's position at the register. The system was also supposed to be integrated so that if the detector registered unpaid for merchandise it would automatically lock the door. This feature did not operate reliably, however, and Bet began to lock the front door herself whenever she saw a customer heading for the door without paying for anything. Bet would then make a quick check to make sure no shoplifting was occurring, and would then unlock the door. One day she triggered the door lock as Parton was heading for the door. Parton became angry at this affront, and refused to allow Bet to look in the briefcase he was carrying. Bet refused to unlock the door. After a tense five minute standoff, Parton relented and opened his briefcase, showing that he had none of Bet's merchandise. Bet then released the lock on the door. If Parton sues Bet for false imprisonment, who will prevail?

  A.   Bet will prevail because she has a shopkeeper's privilege to detain a departing customer to check for stolen merchandise.

  B.   Bet will prevail because Parton's refusal to open his briefcase provided Bet with a reasonable basis for suspicion.

    C.   Parton will prevail because Bet had no reasonable basis for a suspicion that he had taken any merchandise.

    D.   Parton will prevail because Bet's use of mechanical means to confine him amounted to unreasonable force.

14.   A large crowd celebrating the victory of the home team in the World Championships began to get out of control. Several stores were looted, and a large segment of the crowd started to head towards the Potstill Liquor warehouse. The warehouse contained thousands of cases of bottles of liquor. Police officer Finch saw what was happening and feared the effects if the crowd broke into the warehouse and got hold of the liquor. Finch rushed to the side entrance of the warehouse, broke in, and began smashing the cases of liquor, so that the bottles broke and the liquor poured out onto the floor and ran into the floor drains. By the time the crowd broke into the warehouse all the liquor was gone, and the rioters soon lost interest and went home. The owner of the liquor has sued Finch for trespass to chattels and conversion for the destruction of the liquor. Which of the following statements is correct?

    A.   Finch will be liable because he had no privilege to trespass on the premises or to destroy the liquor.

    B.   Finch was privileged to trespass on the premises of the warehouse, but will be liable for the harm actually caused.

    C.   Finch will be liable because he required a warrant to enter the premises.

    D.   Finch was privileged to destroy the liquor and will not be liable.

15.   Wilber was hiking in the woods near a lake where several summer cabins were located. As he rounded a large rock near the trail he surprised a bear, which approached him aggressively. Wilber ran back up the trail towards an unoccupied cabin belonging to Townes. The bear ambled after Wilber, who banged on the door of the cabin and then, as the bear approached, kicked in the door. The bear followed Wilber in and discovered the pantry, after which the bear lost interest in Wilber and began eating the food stored there. Wilber exited through a back door and ran back to his car. He called the local rangers, who were able to capture the bear. Before they did so, however, the bear had destroyed most of the interior of the cabin. Townes sues Wilber in trespass for the damage to the cabin.

    A.   Townes will recover for all damage to the cabin because Wilber had no privilege to trespass.

B. Townes will recover for all damage to the cabin because Wilber was using Townes's property to save himself.

C. Townes will recover only for the damage to the door, not for the damage caused by the bear.

D. Wilber will prevail because he had a privilege to use Townes's property to save himself from harm.

ANSWERS:

1.   The answer is B. Under these facts, there was no actual or implied consent. Consent can be manifested by conduct, but here all Tolbert did was stand in line with Marcus. When Pimmy asked for a show of consent, Tolbert did not provide it. Asking for consent is good, but Pimmy should have paid attention to the response.

2.   The answer is D. When one consents to participate in an athletic contest, one consents to the contacts that are a normal part of the game. If a more severe injury than normal results from such a contact, that would not be sufficient to invalidate the consent. However, it is always necessary to construe the scope of any consent. If the contact that occurred was outside the scope of the consent then the victim would have a valid claim for battery. In this case, the contact that occurred was well outside what would be covered by Barnwell's consent. That consent would cover contacts occurring as the result of a hard slide or even a collision on the base paths. In this case, however, Taylor picked Barnwell up and slammed him into an obstruction, which is outside the rules of the game–so far outside the rules that Taylor has been banned from playing for a year.

3.   The answer is A. Book gave two consents in this scenario, only one of which was suspect. The consent to the operation itself appears to be valid and knowing, and would cover the technically harmful contact of the operation. Nothing in the facts suggests that the operation was unnecessary or that Dr. Fell fraudulently induced Book to consent to it. This consent would therefore block any claim based on battery from the operation itself. The second consent form covered the use of the tissue obtained from the operation once testing was completed. It was not the consent to the operation itself. While this consent may be invalid, it would not invalidate the original consent to the operation. The invalidity of this second consent may give Book some claims for misuse of her tissue, but it would not likely include a claim for battery.

4.   The answer is C. The second consent form is invalid because Book was too sedated to understand it. Unlike Question 3, in this scenario the second consent not only allowed use of the tissue after the operation, but also purported to allow Dr. Fell to extend the scope of the operation and harvest more tissue than would be medically necessary simply to treat Book and test for her problems. Therefore, Book did not consent to the additional harmful contact of the operation in harvesting additional tissue. Since this contact was unconsented, Book would have a valid battery claim.

5.   The answer is D. Modern cases treat non-disclosure in these situations as negligence, and recovery is allowed under the doctrine of informed consent. Under that doctrine, Tip can only recover if the non-disclosed risk in fact occurred with resulting injury. Modern cases do not treat the consent as totally invalid, so that any harmful contact by the doctor (such as making the incision) would constitute battery. Battery would be reserved for situations in which the patient gave no consent whatever.

6.   The answer is C. In emergency situations courts imply consent to treatment, on the theory that the victim would probably give consent to it if he or she could. This is particularly true in situations like this in which failure to successfully give aid would likely result in the death of the victim. The statement that Darby did not intend harm is true but not the point. Darby intended what would other-wise be a harmful or offensive contact; what prevents it from being a battery in spite of the injury inflicted is the presence of implied consent.

7.   The answer is A. Ohner does have a privilege to protect property, although this privilege does not allow the use of deadly force. Generally the owner of the property must ask the other to leave unless it appears that would be futile or would result in significant harm. In this case, Ohner apparently yelled at Vandal to stop, but Vandal ignored the request and continued to damage Ohner's lawn. Ohner then used only gentle force in an attempt to get Vandal off his property. Ohner is not required to wait for the police to arrive before trying to stop Vandal from damaging his property.

8.   The answer is C. In situations such as this, Ohner is privileged to use reasonable force to remove the trespasser, and so long as Ohner does not exceed the scope of this privilege, the contact is not a battery. Because Ohner's force is privileged, Vandal does not have a privilege to resist. When Vandal does resist, that intentional harmful contact with Ohner is unprivileged and therefore a battery. Ohner is also privileged to increase the amount of force used if Vandal resists, because now Ohner is also acting in self-defense against Vandal's unprivileged use of force.

9.   The answer is A. Meddler will invoke the privilege of defense of others, claiming that it appeared that Ohner was attacking Vandal. However, both self defense and defense of others are based on the reasonable appearance of the need for defense. Meddler would therefore be privileged if he mistakenly, but reasonably, believed that Ohner was unjustifiably attacking Vandal. Meddler must therefore have a reasonable basis for thinking that Vandal is the victim and Ohner the aggressor. In this scenario, the facts do not

supply such a reasonable basis. Meddler comes upon the altercation after it has already begun, and the facts show that the two were pushing and shoving one another when Meddler intervened. There is nothing to suggest that Vandal was in greater need of protection than Ohner. Meddler would not be able to invoke the privilege of defense of others.

10. The answer is B. On these facts the force used was excessive, resulting in the loss of the privilege of self defense. Moe's threat is disgusting and highly offensive, but not obviously harmful. Jane does have the right to defend herself from Moe's threatened contact. However, because Jane is not threatened by death or serious bodily injury, she does not have a right to defend herself using such force. The use of a gun is calculated to inflict serious bodily harm, harm out of proportion to the threat represented by Moe. This is true even though she shot Moe in the arm rather than some more vital area. It should be noted that the facts do not suggest that this attack would be anything but a gross joke. If the facts indicated a likelihood of escalation into some more serious threat to Jane's person then the use of greater force would be justified.

11. The answer is D. Because Marta reasonably feared death or serious injury from contact with the peanut, she was entitled to use deadly force to protect herself. Because of the seriousness of the threat, this would not be excessive force. It is also worth noting that Marta backed away from Dave to try to avoid the threatened contact, so that even if the jurisdiction required that a person retreat if possible before using deadly force, Marta would have satisfied that requirement. She did not use the gun until Dave had actually grabbed her, so that the threat was imminent and escape was no longer an option. Note also that self defense is judged from the point of view of the person threatened with harmful or offensive contact. The question is whether it appears necessary from that person's perspective to use force in defense. For this reason, Dave's beliefs and motivations are not relevant; Marta does not have to risk serious injury to prove to Dave that his beliefs about allergies are mistaken.

12. The answer is A. A person has a privilege to use reasonable force to recapture chattels, but that privilege requires what used to be called fresh pursuit. Although that term has fallen out of favor, it is still required that the possessor of property act promptly to effectuate recovery of the chattel. In this case, a week elapsed after loss of the ring, during which time it is not stated that Brown did anything to recover it. Brown waited another week after possibly discovering it before seeking advice about recapture. At this point, any privilege to use force to retake the ring is gone, and Brown will

have to use other means, such as a request for return followed by legal proceedings of some sort. Further arguing against the use of force to recapture the ring is the uncertainty of ownership (is it really Brown's ring?) and of the circumstances under which Jones acquired the ring. The privilege to recapture is based on the tortious nature of the taking or acquisition of the chattel. If the ring was properly acquired Brown has no right to use force to take it. Under these circumstances, the advice here should certainly be that Brown not use force.

13. The answer is C. The shopkeeper's privilege is a privilege to detain for a reasonable time for investigation. It is not a privilege to arrest. Even this limited privilege, however, must be based on a reasonable suspicion. The privilege does not permit a general detention of every shopper for purposes of investigation. In this scenario, Bet has begun to lock the front door automatically every time a customer heads for the door without first stopping at the register to buy. Her detention of these customers is therefore not based on any individualized suspicion of shoplifting, and is therefore unprivileged. Since it is unprivileged, Bet cannot use Parton's objections to bootstrap herself into reasonable suspicion. In this scenario the confinement of Parton was brief but not negligible, and was accomplished without privilege.

14. The answer is D. This case involves a threat of harm to the public at large if a group of rioters should get hold of the liquor, become intoxicated, and possibly get even further out of control. One is privileged to take and destroy property in such situations in order to avoid the threat of public disaster. Since Finch is acting to avert harm to the public, the privilege is absolute, and Finch would not be liable for the loss of the property.

15. The answer is B. This case involves the privilege of private necessity, which is an incomplete or qualified privilege. Under this privilege an individual threatened with serious injury may use the real or personal property of another for protection. If in the course of doing so, however, the property is damaged, the user must compensate the owner. Therefore, Townes would have a right to compensation for the damage to the cabin. There is no real basis for trying to distinguish the harm done by Wilber from the harm done by the bear. The bear was able to cause the damage because Wilbur's trespass made the bear's entry possible. So Wilber did have a privilege, in the sense that if Towne had been present he could not have forced Wilber off the property and into the jaws of the bear. But Wilber must pay for the damage done by his trespass.

CHAPTER 3
NEGLIGENCE

QUESTIONS:

A. Duty

1. Adults

1.   Use the following facts for Questions 1 through 5. Farmer Sue was building a new barn for her farm. She did the design work herself, and then hired people to come on and help her construct the barn. After she had set the main poles for the barn and had begun to add the structure for the loft, several of her neighbors came to visit. Farmer Joe, one of the neighbors, looked at the structure for a long time. Joe finally said, "I don't think you are doing that right. We do get some high winds here on the plains, and I don't think you have enough support for that loft." Farmer Fred who had accompanied Joe agreed with Joe. Fred said, "You better get someone knowledgeable about barn building to take a look at that." That thing will probably come down in a high wind. Sue ignored their comments. She figured she had been a farmer for 30 years and knew enough about barns. In addition, she figured that she would just do her best and hope it worked out. Finally, she also knew she was very short of money. Farming just wasn't as profitable as it use to be. She needed the barn, but didn't have the money to pay for outside help. After the barn was built, it only managed to stand for about three months. When some high winds came up one night, the barn blew down. Some of the framing from the barn blew across the field onto the farm closest to Sue and owned by Farmer Mike. The framing blew through his chicken coop, destroyed the coop and killed 15 chickens. Mike wants to bring an action against Sue. Sue claims that she did her best and that should be sufficient. As Sue asked, "If someone does their best, what else can the law expect?" If confronted with this issue in a negligence case, the court should rule:

A.   A person's best is all that the law will require.

41

    B.   A person must act as a reasonable person even if that requires more than the individual's best effort.

    C.   A person must act in light of the best information and experience available.

    D.   A person is liable for injuries due to his or her own conduct even if the best available conduct was used.

2.   Use the facts from Question 1. Sue will also claim that she built the barn based upon her understanding of barn building. She had been in the farming business for 30 years and figured she knew enough about barns. She claims that her knowledge and understanding of barn building should be enough. How should the court rule on this claim?

    A.   A person's own best knowledge may not be enough. They are expected to have the ordinary knowledge of the community in which they live.

    B.   A person who acts must be held to the highest level of knowledge that is available.

    C.   A person who acts on their own property is not held to a standard of care of knowledge.

    D.   A person is held to a standard of care of their own level of knowledge.

3.   Use the facts from Question 1. Sue will claim that money was tight. She just did not have the money to pay someone to assist with the barn design and building. She will also claim that she absolutely had to have a new barn. It was necessary to keep her equipment in working order and to store some hay. Sue wants to claim that this condition of tight money will excuse her failure to build a reasonably safe barn. How should the court rule on that claim?

    A.   A person's personal financial situation will excuse a failure to act reasonably.

    B.   A person must only act reasonably in light of all the circumstances that exist including his or her own ability to finance conduct properly.

    C.   Circumstances are not to be considered with deciding whether a person's conduct was reasonable.

    D.   Although circumstances may be considered when deciding whether conduct was reasonable, lack of finances would not excuse the unreasonable behavior in this case.

4.   Use the facts from Question 1. When the case of Mike v. Sue goes to trial, how will the issues be decided?

   A.   The court will determine that the duty is one of a reasonable person of ordinary prudence under similar circumstances and the jury will decide if that duty has been breached.

   B.   The court will determine that the duty is one of a reasonable person of ordinary prudence under similar circumstances and then determine whether it has been breached.

   C.   The jury will determine that the duty is one of a reasonable person of ordinary prudence under similar circumstances and then the court will determine whether it has been breached.

   D.   The jury will determine that the duty is one of a reasonable person of ordinary prudence under similar circumstances and then decide whether it has been breached.

5.   Use the facts from Question 1. Sue will want to claim that the barn fell because of the wind. The wind, she will say, was an act of God. She wants to argue that she should not be liable for acts of God. How should the court rule on that claim?

   A.   Acts of God relieve defendants of liability.

   B.   Defendants must behave in light of reasonable care and ordinary prudence. If the act of God was one that reasonable people of ordinary prudence would have planned for, then the act of God does not relieve liability.

   C.   Due to the First Amendment to the U.S. Constitution, evidence of "Acts of God" is irrelevant to tort cases.

   D.   Defendants who place articles in the way of "Acts of God" are liable for the damage those articles cause.

6.   Use the following facts for Questions 6 through 9. Boater Bill was out on his boat on a warm summer afternoon. He was enjoying himself with a great day at the lake. Bill enjoyed seeing just how fast his boat would go and was pushing it to full throttle. Since it was such a beautiful day, Bill was going as fast as he could while looking around at the lovely scenery. Bill failed to notice that another boater was pulling a water skier in the water. Bill ran right at the water skier and hit her. The water skier, Jane, suffered serious personal injury. Jane sued Bill in negligence for those

injuries. Bill claimed that he was doing the best he could in light of the warm day and beautiful scenery. Will that argument relieve Bill of liability?

    A.   No. Bill will be held to the standard of a reasonable person of ordinary prudence under similar circumstances.

    B.   Yes. Negligence requires that Bill use his own best judgment and skills. The facts indicate that Bill was "doing the best he could."

    C.   No. Bill will be held liable for intentionally driving the boat.

    D.   Yes. Boating is a hazardous activity and all people upon the water are responsible for their own safety. The skier cannot sue someone else for injury.

7.   Use the facts from Question 6. Bill wants to claim that he was not aware of how long it would take the boat to stop. He alleges that he had only had the boat for one season and did not realize that it would coast after he shut the engine off. He says he saw the skier, shut off the engine, turned the rudder, but the boat just slid right into Jane. Will Bill's lack of experience with the boat be a defense?

    A.   Yes. A person cannot be held to have more knowledge then they actually have. That would be strict liability.

    B.   No. A person is held to the ordinary prudence of the community in which they live and act.

    C.   Yes. The law allows for those in the community who are less well able to mentally function.

    D.   No. Boating is a hazardous activity and strict liability ought to apply.

8.   Use the facts from Question 6. Bill claims that he was being careful during the whole boating event. He claims, however, that his wife was sitting in the back of the boat while they were going across the lake. Just a few moments before Bill hit the skier, his wife fell off the back of the boat into the water. Since Bill's wife cannot swim and was not wearing a life jacket, Bill was in a panic. He quickly turned the boat around and was searching the water for his wife. It was during this maneuver that Bill hit the skier. It appears that these facts are true and Bill's wife was pulled from the water after the accident. She suffered harm also from being in the water. Does the fact that Bill's wife fell in the water have any bearing on the case by the skier?

A. Yes. The existence of the emergency relieves Bill of liability in the accident.

B. No. Bill is still held to act as a reasonable person since another individual was injured.

C. Yes. The existence of an emergency will be a circumstance for the jury to consider. Bill's conduct must still be reasonable in light of this emergency.

D. No. Boating is a hazardous activity and Bill is liable for all injuries he causes.

9. Use the facts from Question 6. Evidence will show that Bill was out in the boat by himself. He liked to go boating alone, drive the boat very fast and spend the day drinking beer. At the time of the accident with the skier, Bill had already had 3 cans of beer within the hour. Bill would like to convince the judge that he should be able to use the intoxication as a circumstance to consider. Bill claims that he actually controls the boat better than most people who have consumed three beers. Bill wants to argue to the jury that he actually behaved as well as a reasonable person of ordinary prudence that happened to have consumed three cans of beer. In fact, Bill wants to allege that reasonable people of ordinary prudence always drink beer while boating on the lake. How will the consumption of three beers be treated in the case?

A. The three beers will be a circumstance that Bill can use to reduce his responsibility for the accident.

B. The three beers be evidence of what reasonable people do when boating on the lake.

C. Boating is a hazardous activity and Bill will be liable regardless of the evidence concerning the beer.

D. Intoxication is not a circumstance that can be used to reduce the duty. Bill will be held to the standard of a reasonable person of ordinary prudence. In fact, his consumption of three beers while driving a boat is probably, in itself, unreasonable.

10. Ms. Smith was driving her car along the interstate one day when she suddenly lost consciousness. The car swerved into another lane and hit a car being driven by Mr. Jones. Mr. Jones wants to sue Ms. Smith for the accident. Ms. Smith claims that she had never lost consciousness before and had no indication that anything was wrong on this day. What impact will Ms. Smith's claim have on the litigation?

A. The sudden, unexpected loss of consciousness will be considered under the reasonable person standard as an issue of how a reasonable person would respond to such an event.

B. The sudden, unexpected loss of consciousness will relieve Ms. Smith of any liability.

C. The sudden, unexpected loss of consciousness is irrelevant to the litigation. Ms. Smith is liable for auto accidents that she causes.

D. Ms. Smith will be liable since reasonable people do not lose consciousness.

11. Mr. Baker went to the doctor with symptoms of the flu. The doctor gave Mr. Baker a prescription to have filled at the pharmacy. When Mr. Baker got the prescription filled, the pharmacist said, "Be careful when you take this. It makes some people sleepy." The packaging for the medication also said, "Do not operate automobiles or heavy machinery for the first hour after taking this medication. It may cause drowsiness." Mr. Baker was feeling poorly, so he took the medication before he left the pharmacy. His drive home was about 30 minutes. After driving about 20 minutes Mr. Baker got very sleepy, drifted off to sleep and ran into another car. The driver of the other car sued Mr. Baker.

A. Mr. Baker will not be liable since it was the medication and not Mr. Baker that caused the accident.

B. Mr. Baker will be liable since a reasonable person of ordinary prudence under similar circumstances would have followed the directions given by the pharmacist and the package instructions.

C. Mr. Baker will not be liable since he was sick and sick people cannot be responsible for their actions.

D. Mr. Baker will be liable since the driver of an automobile is liable for accidents.

12. Mr. Davis had a very difficult day. When he awoke, everything seemed just fine and he went to work. Before he went to work, he stopped to get some coffee at the local coffee chop. While in the coffee shop, he suddenly felt that he had to do something to save the other people in the shop from suffocating. He grabbed one of the chairs and threw it through a window. He was trying to get some air into the room. It was later discovered that Mr. Davis had a sudden occurrence of mental illness. He had to be hospitalized. There was

nothing wrong in the coffee shop. The coffee shop would like to sue Mr. Davis for the damage to the window.

    A.   Mr. Davis will avoid liability by using an insanity defense to the claim.

    B.   Mr. Davis will avoid liability by proving that a reasonable person would not be able to plan for a sudden mental illness.

    C.   Mr. Davis will be liable since mental illness, even sudden mental illness, is not a defense to a negligence claim.

    D.   Mr. Davis' mental illness will shift the burden of proof to the coffee shop.

13.   Ms. Glena was driving home from work and decided to have a drink before going all the way home. She stopped at a local night spot and had two gin and tonics. She then got in her car and started driving home. She had not gotten more than about 2 blocks before she ran into another car. The police arrived quickly and smelled the gin on her breath. The driver of the other car wants to sue Ms. Glena for the accident.

    A.   Ms. Glena will not be liable since reasonable people find it necessary to have a couple of drinks after work.

    B.   Ms. Glena will not be liable since two gin and tonics is a reasonable number of drinks to have before dinner.

    C.   Ms. Glena will be liable since she failed to drive as a reasonably, ordinarily prudent drunk.

    D.   Ms. Glena will be liable since reasonable people do not get drunk and drive.

14.   Mr. Hawk got a new shotgun and wanted to go out shooting. He went into the woods but was careful to look around before starting to shoot. After making sure that there was no one around, he set a couple of cans up on a log in order to practice shooting. After firing the first shot, he heard a scream just beyond where he was. Mr. Hawk ran towards the sound and found that Mr. Klim had been hit by several pellets. If Mr. Klim sues Mr. Hawk for the injury, what is the best basis of the claim?

    A.   Intent, since Mr. Hawk intended to shoot the gun.

    B.   Negligence, since Mr. Klim will claim that Mr. Hawk failed to use reasonable care.

C. Strict liability, since guns are an abnormally dangerous instrumentality.

D. Under the Second Amendment to the U.S. Constitution, there is no liability for gunshot wounds.

2. Children

15. Suzie (age 8) and Billy (age 7) were playing jacks. The game involves bouncing a small ball, picking up little metal stars and then catching the ball. As the game progresses, it is necessary to pick up more of the stars at once. Suzie was clearly winning the game and Billy was getting frustrated. It was Billy's turn and he tried to bounce the ball a little too hard. It hit one of the metal stars and caused it to fly up and hit Suzie in the eye. Suzie suffered a personal injury from this event. If Suzie tries to sue Billy for the injury, the standard of care that would be applied to Billy would be:

A. Reasonable person of ordinary prudence under similar circumstances.

B. A reasonably prudent child.

C. A child of like age, intelligence, and experience.

D. A child of similar age.

16. Use the following facts for Questions 16 through 17. Suzie (age 16) has just gotten her automobile driver's license. She went to pick up her friend Billy (age 15) to go for a ride. While Suzie was driving around, they had an accident. Billy would like to sue Suzie for the personal injuries that he suffered. What standard of care will apply to Suzie?

A. Reasonable person of ordinary prudence under similar circumstances.

B. A reasonably prudent child.

C. A child of like age, intelligence, and experience.

D. A child of similar age.

17. Use the facts from Question 16. Driving an automobile seems like a different type of activity than one of playing children's games. What factors would courts use to apply an adult standard rather than a child standard? To state it differently, under what circumstances would the court apply an adult standard to a child?

A. When the child is over 14 years of age.

B.   When the child is engaged in an adult activity.

C.   When the child is engaged in a dangerous activity.

D.   When the child is engaged in an activity normally only engaged in by adults that is also a dangerous activity.

3.   Professionals

18.   Use the following facts for Questions 18 through 19. Carol was an architect. She designed a 5 story building that would house retail shops on the first floor and office space above that. The building was beautiful and finished on time. While movers were moving some office furniture onto the fifth floor, the building collapsed. It was discovered that the load, stress calculations in the original design by Carol were not correct. She did not allow for enough weight in the upper floors. The movers have sued Carol for their personal injuries. What standard will be used to measure Carol's duty of care?

A.   Reasonable person standard.

B.   An architect in good standing.

C.   To use her own best judgment.

D.   To use the highest duty of care.

19.   Use the facts from Question 18. Since the jury will be required to determine whether an architect used the appropriate skills and training, which of the following best describes how the jury will reach those conclusions?

A.   The jurors will rely on their own best judgments.

B.   The judge will tell the jury how an architect should have performed.

C.   Expert witnesses will give evidence on how an architect should have performed.

D.   Jurors will receive text books to read in the deliberation room about how architects should have performed.

20.   Use the following facts for Questions 20 through 23. Dr. Watson was a general surgeon. He was doing a gall bladder surgery on Mr. Smith. After the surgery was over, Mr. Smith had a couple of problems. The first problem was that there seemed to be some internal bleeding after the surgery. Dr. Watson had to take Mr. Smith back to the operating room, reopen the surgery, and repair

the bleeding. If Mr. Smith sues for having to undergo this second surgery, what is the standard of care to which Dr. Watson will be held?

    A.   The reasonable person standard.

    B.   The reasonable doctor standard.

    C.   The care and skill of a qualified surgeon.

    D.   The highest degree of care.

21.   Use the facts from Question 20. Dr. Watson will claim that internal bleeding is a common side effect from surgery. Although it happens, it is not the sign of something going wrong with the surgery. Dr. Watson will bring other doctors who will testify to the same facts. What impact will this evidence have on the case?

    A.   Dr. Watson is still liable since the surgery was not completed without a problem.

    B.   Dr. Watson is still liable since doctors guarantee that such routine surgery will go well.

    C.   Dr. Watson will not be liable since surgery is an ultrahazardous activity.

    D.   Dr. Watson will probably not be liable since even using the care and skill of other doctors this type of circumstance may arise.

22.   Use the facts from Question 20. After doing the second surgery to stop the internal bleeding, the surgery site would not heal. After several weeks, Dr. Watson had to reopen the site again. This time it was discovered that Dr. Watson had left a small sponge in the surgery site when he went in to stop the internal bleeding. If Mr. Smith wants to sue Dr. Watson for leaving the sponge in the surgery site, he must:

    A.   Prove the fact that the sponge was left in the site. That fact should make negligence so obvious that no other proof would be necessary.

    B.   Offer expert testimony to prove that the care and skill of surgeons requires that sponges be removed from the patient.

    C.   Offer evidence by other surgeons that they would not leave sponges in the patient.

D. Prove that sponges should never be used in surgery.

23. Use the facts from Question 20. Dr. Watson has been sued for leaving a sponge in Mr. Smith. Dr. Watson wants to offer evidence that although most doctors nationally view that as inappropriate, his local community of surgeons takes a different view. They feel like surgery is such a difficult skill, that surgeons just can't take the time to be responsible for counting sponges. The local community of surgeons feels that it is not that big of an issue. If a sponge is left in a patient, it can be easily removed with additional surgery. What impact will this argument have on the case?

A. The evidence of community standard will be excluded and the jury will be instructed to use the national standard.

B. The evidence of the national standard will be excluded and the jury will be instructed to use the community standard.

C. The jury will hear all of the evidence and decide which standard seems best.

D. The judge will hear all of the evidence, decide which standard seems best and then so instruct the jury.

24. Will Walker was out for his morning walk. Without watching, he crossed a major highway. A car hit him and knocked him into a ditch. Will was seriously injured by the accident. His left leg, for example, was completely crushed. An ambulance came and took Will to the hospital. The emergency room doctor decided that Will's life could only be saved if the left leg was amputated. A well known surgeon, Dr. Cutter, came in and examined Will. Dr. Cutter told Will, "We will have to amputate your left leg. There is no other way to save your life." Will said, "You may operate on me, but do not amputate my leg. I would rather die than lose the leg." Dr. Cutter took Will to the operating room, administered a general anesthesia and when Will was unconscious, Dr. Cutter amputated the leg. When Will regained consciousness, he was furious. He again claimed that he would have rather died then lose the leg. Will recovered from the accident and surgery although he had lost his left leg. Several well known experts have stated that there was no way that Will could have lived without the amputation. If Will sues Dr. Cutter, which of the following answers is most accurate?

A. Will has no claim since Dr. Cutter saved Will's life.

B. Will can sue for the tort of Battery.

C. Will can sue for negligence since his consent to the surgery was not fully informed.

D.   Will has no claim since the emergency situation allows the doctor to do what is best for the patient.

25.   Use the following facts for Questions 25 through 28. Sandy, age 40, was feeling poorly and went to the doctor. Her doctor, Dr. Pam, did a complete physical. Dr. Pam then informed Sandy that she had a rare disease that would require one of two treatments. Sandy could take medication "A" that was very strong, but would only require taking it for 10 days. In the alternative, Sandy could take medication "B" which was not as strong and had to be taken for 30 days. Sandy asked if there were any other differences. Dr. Pam that the prices were about the same and health insurance would pay for both. The stronger medication could cause some upset stomach, but there were no other differences. Sandy took the stronger medication for 10 days, had a little upset stomach, but was completely healed by the medication. A year later, Sandy returned to Dr. Pam with another issue. Sandy informed Dr. Pam that Sandy was trying to get pregnant and it didn't seem to be happening. It seems that Sandy didn't have any children, had gotten married at age 38, and now she and her husband wanted children. Dr. Pam said, "Oh. I know why you can't get pregnant. That medication "A" you took last year causes women to be sterile. Medication "B" would not have caused that problem, but I didn't think that was important. I just assumed that since you were 40 years old that you wouldn't want to get pregnant." Sandy wants to sue Dr. Pam for not being able to have children. Which of the following seems most accurate?

A.   Sandy can recover from Dr. Pam for battery since the consent to take medication "A" was not fully informed.

B.   Sandy cannot recover from Dr. Pam since the medication "A" cured Sandy's illness.

C.   Sandy can recover from Dr. Pam for negligence since the consent to take medication "A" was not fully informed.

D.   Sandy cannot recover from Dr. Pam since pregnancy or sterility is too remote of a cause.

26.   Use the facts from Question 25. Assume that Sandy went to Dr. Pam with the same illness. In this set of facts, however, Dr. Pam does not mention medication "B." Dr. Pam is aware that medication "A" causes sterility, but feels that Sandy should not have children. At age 40, Sandy would have additional risks in child bearing that a younger woman would not have. Although Dr. Pam realizes that Sandy might try to have children some day, Dr. Pam just believes it is in Sandy's best interest to take the stronger medication, get over the illness as quickly as possible, and forget about having children.

If Sandy later tries to have children, and sue Dr. Pam for the sterility, which of the following is correct?

   A. Sandy cannot recover from Dr. Pam, since Dr. Pam used the judgment of a physician in good standing in treating Sandy.

   B. Sandy cannot recover from Dr. Pam, since Dr. Pam acted in Sandy's best interest.

   C. Sandy can recover from Dr. Pam for the negligence in failing to provide informed consent.

   D. Sandy can recover from Dr. Pam for battery since Sandy did not consent to sterility.

27. Use the facts from Question 25. When Sandy comes to Dr. Pam with the illness, Dr. Pam tells Sandy the following. "The illness you have can be treated in one of two ways. Medication "A" is the strongest. You only have to take it for 10 days. It is a highly successful medication and will cure this disease in 90% of the cases. Its one major side effect is that it can cause sterility in women who take it. There is a 20% chance it can cause that sterility. Medication "B" is not as strong. You must take it for 30 days. It is only 50% effective. If it does not cure the disease, you would have to take another round of the medication. In fact, you might ultimately have to take the stronger medication. There is no risk of sterility with medication "B." " Sandy decided to take medication "A." One year later, when Sandy discovered she was now sterile, she wants to sue Dr. Pam. Which of the following is most accurate?

   A. Sandy can recover from Dr. Pam for causing harm with the treatment.

   B. Sandy can recover from Dr. Pam for battery for injuring her ability to have children.

   C. Sandy can recover from Dr. Pam for negligence in failing to fully inform Sandy.

   D. Sandy cannot recover from Dr. Pam.

28. Use the facts from Question 25. Assume that Dr. Pam gave the explanation for the treatments that also appears in Question 27. When Sandy sues Dr. Pam, however, Sandy makes one additional claim. Sandy claims that Dr. Pam had a duty to protect Sandy from mistakes. Although Sandy may have thought that curing the disease quickly was more important then having children in the future, once Sandy decided to have children, it was Dr. Pam's fault that Sandy was sterile. Sandy claims that because of their superior knowledge,

skill and experience, physicians have a duty to protect patients from making decisions that may later turn out to have not been correct. Which of the following is most accurate?

A. Sandy cannot recover from Dr. Pam since Dr. Pam acted as a physician in good standing in the community can gave full information before getting consent.

B. Sandy can recover from Dr Pam for a batter for causing the harm to child bearing.

C. Sandy can recover from Dr. Pam for Dr. Pam's failure to fully protect the patient from injury.

D. Sandy can recover from Dr. Pam for Dr. Pam's failure to make decision for Sandy that was in Sandy's best interest.

29. Use the following facts for Questions 29 through 30. Sally was injured in a car accident. She went to see Jane Adams to seek legal representation. Jane Adams is a well known plaintiff's personal injury lawyer in the city. Jane represented Sally in the case and brought an action again Mary who was the driver of the other car. After two years of trial preparation and three weeks of trial, Sally lost her case. The jury returned a verdict for Mary. Mary had not sued Sally, so Sally did not have to pay a judgment. Sally was just upset that she did not win a big judgment. During the case, Sally had told her lawyer, Jane, about cases she had read about all over the country. Jane kept reminding Sally that Jane would have to apply local law and every case was different. In Sally's action against Jane, which of the following is the most accurate statement?

A. Jane should have used principles from other states since national standards apply for professionals.

B. Jane would be held to a national standard of care, but had to use local state law since lawyers must use local state law for tort cases.

C. Jane would be held to a community standard in deciding the duty of care.

D. Jane would have to use national tort principles to litigate the case, but would be held to a community standard of care.

30. Use the facts from Question 29. Sally wants to sue Jane for losing the car wreck case. Sally feels that Jane should not have taken the case unless it was a sure winner. When lawyers take a case, which of the following applies?

A. Lawyers can only take a case if it is a sure winner.

B. Lawyers imply a guarantee of the results of a case when they file the lawsuit.

C. Failure to win a case is prima facie evidence of legal malpractice.

D. The lawyer's duty is to use care and skill of a qualified lawyer and there is not a guarantee of success.

4. Negligent emotional distress

31. Bill was watching television one evening. The evening news was on and Bill was catching up on the day's events. The newscaster noted that they had some news films of a terrible tornado that they were getting ready to show. The newscaster suggested that it might be too harsh for some people. Bill watched the news films. One of the films showed a tornado approaching a farm house. The tornado hit the farm house, a nearby barn and destroyed everything. In the picture, a cow could be seen flying through the air. The newscaster reported that the family and all of the farm animals were killed. Bill became very upset over what he had seen and could not sleep that night. Bill wants to sue the newscaster for causing so much stress. What is the likelihood of success?

A. Bill will win the lawsuit by suing for the tort of assault.

B. Bill will win the lawsuit by suing for negligent infliction of emotional distress.

C. Bill will win the lawsuit by suing for the tort of battery.

D. Bill will lose the lawsuit.

32. Use the following facts for Questions 32 through 35. John was walking along a sidewalk. He observed two cars run into each other in the middle of road about 100 yards from where he was walking. It was obvious that the accident was caused by the "red" car since the "red" car had been speeding and veering over the center line. The other car in the accident was merely an innocent car caught in an accident due to the negligence of the "red" car's driver. Immediately after the accident, the cars stopped right where they were. John continued to think about the accident over the next few days. He became so upset, he was no longer able to walk near roads or even drive his own car. John wants to sue the driver of the "red" car for his emotional distress. In states that had not adopted the modern negligent infliction of emotional distress, the result would be:

A. John would have no claim since there was no intent.

B. John would have no claim since there was no impact between the car and John.

C. John would recover since the driver of the "red" car was negligent.

D. John would recover since the driver of the "red" car was reckless.

33. Use the facts from Question 32. Assume, however, that after the two cars had run together, the "red" car continued to careen wildly down the street out of control. As it got close to John, the "red" car jumped the curb, ran on the sidewalk and almost hit John. John had to jump out of the way to avoid the impact. If the state has not adopted the modern negligent infliction of emotional distress, the result would be:

A. John would have no claim since there was no intent.

B. John would have no claim since there was no impact between the car and John.

C. John would recover since the driver of the "red" car was negligent.

D. John would recover since the driver of the "red" car was reckless.

34. Use the facts from Question 32. Assume, however, that after the two cars had run together, the "red" car continued to careen wildly down the street out of control. As it got close to John, the "red" car jumped the curb, ran on the sidewalk and almost hit John. John had to jump out of the way to avoid the impact. If the state has adopted the modern negligent infliction of emotional distress, the result would be:

A. John would have no claim since there was no intent.

B. John would have no claim since there was no impact between the car and John.

C. John would recover since the driver of the "red" car was negligent.

D. John would recover since the driver of the "red" car was reckless.

35. Use the facts from Question 32. Assume, however, that after the two cars had run together, the "red" car continued to careen

wildly down the street out of control. As it got close to John, the "red" car jumped the curb, ran on the sidewalk and hit John. John was seriously injured by the impact. John's wife was walking along the sidewalk close to John. John's wife was far enough away not to be threatened by the car, but she saw John being hit. John's wife wants to sue the driver of the red car for the emotional distress she has suffered by watching John get hit. If the state has adopted the modern negligent infliction of emotional distress, the result would be:

A.   The wife would have no claim since there was no intent.

B.   The wife would have no claim since there was no impact between the car and her.

C.   The wife would recover since the driver of the "red" car was negligent.

D.   The wife would recover since the driver of the "red" car was reckless.

5.   Negligence per se

36.   Use the following facts for Questions 36 through 38. Jane was driving down the street at approximately 40 miles per hour. The posted speed limit was 35 miles per hour. Another car pulled out from a side street in front of Jane and Jane's car hit the other car. The driver of the other car, Sam, was injured. Sam wants to sue Jane for his injuries. In that litigation, the fact that Jane was exceeding the speed limit will:

A.   Be irrelevant.

B.   Result in Jane being automatically held at fault.

C.   Result in the speed limit of 35 miles per hour being used as the duty in the negligence case.

D.   Be used as the issue to determine whether Jane's negligence was the cause of the accident.

37.   Use the facts from Question 36. Jane wants to claim that she was using reasonable care in driving her car. Even though she was exceeding the speed limit, she believes that the road and weather conditions were such that a mere 5 miles per hour over the limit was reasonable. Her attorney asks the judge to allow the jury to determine whether exceeding the speed limit by 5 miles per hour is reasonable. The judge should:

A.   Allow the jury to decide whether Jane should be held to the standard of the statute or just using reasonable care.

    B.   Decide that the duty is compliance with the statute and then let the jury decide if Jane violated the statute.

    C.   Allow the jury to decide what the appropriate standard for driving is and then decide who is responsible for the accident.

    D.   Enter a directed verdict for the plaintiff.

38.   Use the facts from Question 36. Jane's attorney wants to argue that Jane's action of driving in excess of the speed limit was not what caused the accident to occur. Jane's attorney wants to argue that the real cause of the accident was the fact that Sam pulled out of a side road in front of Jane. Due to the conduct of Sam, Jane couldn't avoid the accident. According to Jane and her attorney, the accident would have happened whether Jane was driving at 40 miles per hour or 20 miles per hour. What impact should these facts and arguments have on the case.

    A.   They will be considered by the jury in determining the causation issue.

    B.   They will be considered by the jury in determining whether Jane breached a duty.

    C.   They will be considered by the judge in determining whether there was a duty.

    D.   They will be irrelevant.

B. Breach

1. Burden of proof

39.   Use the following facts for Questions 39 through 42. Fred was driving along a side street when he came to an intersection. As he entered the intersection, his car way struck by a car being driven by George. The accident caused injuries to Fred, and Fred sued George for those injuries. At the trial, a local police officer named Officer Smith testified that he had done the investigation of the accident. According to Officer Smith, the intersection was a four way stop and had a stop sign on all of the streets. In addition, it was the expert opinion of Officer Smith that Fred had run that stop sign. Fred testifies that he definitely stopped at the stop sign. What should the judge do with Officer Smith's testimony?

    A.   Direct a verdict against Fred since Fred had a statutory duty to stop and did not stop. The case is "negligence per se."

B. Allow the jury to consider the evidence in order to decide whether Fred did or did not stop at the stop sign.

C. Allow the jury to consider the evidence in order to decide whether Fred was the cause of the accident.

D. Strike the evidence from the record as being inappropriate opinion testimony.

40. Use the facts from Question 39. Assume that Officer Smith testifies that there were stop signs at the intersection, but offers no opinion as to who ran the stop sign. In addition, George offers no other testimony as to whether Fred ran the stop sign. Fred testifies that he definitely stopped at the stop sign and brings three eye witnesses to say that he stopped. What should the judge do with the evidence?

A. Direct a verdict on the issue of breach for Fred since George offered no evidence on the issue.

B. Allow the jury to consider all of the evidence in order to decide whether Fred did or did not stop at the stop sign.

C. Declare the trial a tie since the evidence seems confused and allow the appellate courts to decide the issues.

D. Direct a verdict in favor of George since George was the one injured by the accident.

41. Use the facts from Question 39. Assume that Officer Smith testifies that there were stop signs at the intersection. Officer Smith, however, refused to speculate as to who ran the stop sign. George testifies that he is certain that he stopped at the stop sign before proceeding. He then testifies that he is not sure whether Fred stopped or not. George does say that surely Fred must not have stopped for the accident did happen. What should the judge do with this evidence?

A. Direct a verdict for George against Fred since there is evidence that maybe Fred did not stop.

B. Direct a verdict for Fred against George since the evidence that Fred did not stop is very weak.

C. Send the case to the jury and allow the jury to determine whether Fred stopped or did not stop.

D. Since the facts are close, the judge should carefully consider the facts, the demeanor of the witnesses and determine the fact issue of breach.

42. Use the facts from Question 39. Assume that Officer Smith testifies that there were stop signs at all streets. In addition, Officer Smith has carefully measured all of the skid marks and testifies that his opinion is that Fred ran the stop sign. George testifies that he saw Fred coming along the street and assumed that Fred would stop at the stop sign. According to George, Fred did not stop. Three eyewitnesses to the accident testify that Fred did not stop at the stop sign. Fred testifies that the stopped. What should the judge do with this evidence?

   A. Direct a verdict for George against Fred since the evidence seems overwhelmingly in favor of George.

   B. Direct a verdict for George against Fred because regardless of what all of the other witnesses said, the police officer testified that Fred did not stop. A police officer's testimony is conclusive on the case.

   C. Direct a verdict for Fred against George since although George's evidence is strong, it does not prove the case beyond a reasonable doubt.

   D. Send the case to the jury and allow the jury to determine whether Fred stopped or did not stop.

2. Res ipsa loquitur

43. Use the following facts for Questions 43 through 44. Carl was walking along a side walk when he was suddenly struck by a delivery truck. The delivery truck was owned an operated by Acme Delivery. The driver of the truck was the authorized driver and he was on his regular and routine delivery route. Carl was injured and sued Acme for the injuries. Carl testifies that he doesn't know what happened. He was just walking along the sidewalk and was suddenly hit from the rear. Several eyewitnesses testify that the truck just seemed to suddenly jump the curb and hit Carl. The driver of the truck testifies that everything was going well when the truck just suddenly seemed to jump the curb and hit Carl. Based upon that evidence what should the judge do with the trial case?

   A. Direct a verdict in the case for Carl since this sort of thing does not happen in the absence of negligence.

   B. Direct a verdict for Acme since Carl failed to meet his burden of going forward on the issue of breach of the duty.

   C. Direct a verdict on the issue of breach of the duty for Carl, but send the other issues to the jury.

D. Direct a verdict for Carl on the issue of causation since the truck obviously caused the injuries to Carl.

44. Use the facts from Question 43. When the case goes to trial, Acme brings their head of maintenance to the trial. The head of maintenance gives complete testimony about the usual mainte-nance procedures in Acme and the full records of all of the regular maintenance that had been done on the truck that was involved in the accident. Based upon that evidence, what should the judge do with the trial case?

A. Direct a verdict for Carl on the issue of breach of the duty.

B. Direct a verdict for Acme on the issue of breach of the duty since they offered evidence that no negligence had occurred.

C. Send the case to the jury on the issue of breach of the duty.

D. Decide that the case is a tie and declare a mistrial.

45. Jane went to her doctor and was told she would need minor surgery. Her doctor sent her to see Dr. Sue. Dr. Sue was going to do the surgery. The surgery was done in the morning and Jane remained in the hospital for 3 days. After that, Jane went home. Jane was supposed to report back to the doctor on a regular basis and she did so. Jane was worried about the surgery because it did not appear to heal. The surgery location remained red, swelling, and oozed fluid. After about 4 weeks, Dr. Sue suggested that maybe they ought to reopen the surgery location and take a look. Upon reopen-ing the surgery location, Dr. Sue discovered that a surgery sponge had been left inside Jane's body. The sponge was removed and the surgery closed. After the removal of the sponge, the surgery location healed promptly and properly. Jane would like to bring an action against Dr. Sue. Although the surgery finally healed properly, Jane wants to recover for the additional missed work and pain and suffering of the extended recovery time. In Jane's action against Dr. Sue:

A. Jane can rely on res ipsa loquitur to prove that Dr. Sue breached the duty owed by a physician.

B. Jane will have to introduce expert testimony to prove that Dr. Sue breached the duty owed by a physician.

C. Jane can rely on res ipsa loquitur to prove that Dr. Sue caused the extended recovery time from the surgery.

D. Jane has no claim since leaving a sponge in a patient is a normal risk of surgery.

C. Injury

46. Use the following facts for Questions 46 through 47. Bill was walking home from a movie theater around 10:00 p.m. one evening when he realized that he needed to use a restroom. He saw a gasoline station nearby and walked over to it. Bill noticed that the restroom was to be entered from the back of the station. Since it did not require walking into the station to enter the restroom, Bill did not say anything to the station attendant before entering the restroom. Bill did not realize that it was actually time for the attendant to close the station and lock up. While Bill was in the restroom, the attendant came around to the restroom and put a padlock on the outside of the door. The station attendant then left the scene. When Bill got ready to leave the restroom, he suddenly realized that he could not get out. He began to scream and yell for help. No one heard him. Bill had to stay in the locked restroom until 7:00 a.m. the next morning. At that time, the station attendant arrived at the station and unlocked the door. The attendant found Bill lying on the floor of the restroom. It had been very cold that evening and Bill was suffering from the effects of that cold. An ambulance had to take Bill to the hospital. Bill had to remain in the hospital for 3 days to recover. If Bill wants to sue the station and the attendant for his injuries, he could claim:

    A. The intentional tort of false imprisonment.

    B. Negligence for his injuries.

    C. Both A and B.

    D. Bill has no claim since the cold weather caused the injury.

47. Use the facts from Question 46. Assume that Bill does not remain in the locked restroom the entire evening. In fact, just a few minutes after the attendant locks the door and Bill begins to scream for help, a police officer hears the screams. The police officer quickly understands what the problem is and breaks open the padlock. Bill is released within minutes of being locked inside the restroom. Bill is completely unharmed, but he is very angry. He wants to sue the station and the attendant for this incident. If Bill wants to sue the station and the attendant, he could claim:

    A. The intentional tort of False imprisonment.

    B. Negligence for his injuries.

    C. Both A and B.

    D. Bill has no claim since he had no injury.

D. Causation

1. Cause in fact

48. Professor Mary was a law professor at a major national law school. Among the courses she taught, Torts was her favorite. She enjoys the opportunity to work with first year students and introduce them to the most important course in law school. One day, Professor Mary was teaching the section on "cause in fact." Unfortunately, Professor Mary had gotten it all wrong. It seems that she was having a bad day and had carelessly failed to review her notes before class started. Everyone knows that a law professor, acting as a reasonable law professor must review his or her notes before class. Since Professor Mary had not reviewed her notes, she was negligently teaching Torts. At that very moment, a strange thing occurred outside of the classroom. A third year law student, John, was driving his car along the main road in front of the law school and ran a red light. John then hit the car of another law student, Bill. Bill, of course, sued John for damage to Bill's car. While Bill was talking to some other law students, he discovered the strange fact that Professor Mary was negligently teaching torts at the very instant that his automobile accident occurred out on the main street. Bill added Professor Mary as another defendant in the lawsuit for the damaged automobile. What is the likely outcome of the negligence action against Professor Mary for the damage to Bill's automobile?

   A. Professor Mary will not be liable since she did not cause the injury.

   B. Professor Mary will not be liable since law professors are, by law, not reasonable people.

   C. Professor Mary will be liable since she was negligent.

   D. Professor Mary will be liable since law professors are strictly liable.

49. Carly was driving her automobile along Main Street. She was in a hurry to get to work so she was driving at 40 miles per hour. The posted speed limit on Main Street is 35 mile per hour. Suddenly, without any warning a small child ran into the middle of the lane in which Carly was driving. The child had darted into the street from behind another automobile that was parked on Main Street. The child and the child's parents sued Carly for the injuries to the child. The likely result of that action would be:

   A. Carly will be liable since violating a statute is negligent per se.

B.   Carly will be liable if the accident would not have happen in the absence of Carly's violating the spend limit.

C.   Carly will not be liable since the speed limit laws assume a 5 mile per hour allowance.

D.   Carly will not be liable since parents are responsible for their own children.

50.   Dr. Smith performed surgery on Mr. Brown. The surgery was very dangerous but was thought to be necessary to save Mr. Brown's life. Mr. Brown's chance of survival without the surgery was about 5%. If the surgery went well, Mr. Brown's chance of survival was about 10%. Having all of the facts explained to him, Mr. Brown decided to have the surgery. The surgery went as well as could be expected, but Mr. Brown died. If the family of Mr. Brown wishes to sue Dr. Smith for Mr. Brown's death, which of the following is the best statement of the nature of the action.

A.   Dr. Smith will probably lose the case since surgeons are responsible for the life of their patients.

B.   Dr. Smith will probably lose the case since the surgeons actions were the last circumstances in Mr. Brown's life.

C.   Dr. Smith will probably win the case since the surgeon did not cause the death.

D.   Dr. Smith will probably win the case since everyone will die at some point.

51.   Jane went to her regular doctor, Dr. Fred, with some heath complaints. Jane told her doctor that she was a little short of breath and had a bad cough. Her doctor told her it was probably just a cold or the flu and to take it easy. Jane called or went to see her doctor several times over the next six months with the same complaint. She admitted that it felt better at times and worse at time. Her doctor continued to tell her it was just a nagging cold or flu. After the six month period, Jane found another doctor, Dr. Bill. Dr. Bill did a complete examination, and then immediately put Jane in the hospital. After running a series of test on Jane, he told her that she had cancer. Dr. Bill brought in several of the area's leading experts on Jane's illness, but it was too late. Jane died from the cancer. Jane's family began to investigate and talked to several of the experts. The experts say that Dr. Bill did everything that a qualified physician could do, but the disease had become too advanced. The experts say that had Dr. Fred properly diagnosed the cancer when Jane initially went to him, Jane would have had a 45% chance of

surviving the illness. By the time Dr. Bill saw Jane her chance of survival had dropped to 10%. The family sued Dr. Bill and Dr. Fred. Which of the following is the best statement of the likely outcome of the action?

    A.   Dr. Fred and Dr. Bill will be liable for the death of Jane.

    B.   Neither doctor will be liable for Jane's death since she only had a 45% chance of survival when she first went to Dr. Fred.

    C.   Dr. Fred will be liable for Jane's death since he failed to use reasonable care in the diagnosis but Dr. Bill will not be liable.

    D.   Dr. Fred will be liable for the drop of the chance of survival from 45% to 10% but Dr. Bill will not be liable.

52.   Use the following facts for Questions 52 through 53. John was walking through the woods on a cloudy summer afternoon. John was a smoker, so he lit up a cigarette to enjoy while on his walk. John had used a match to light the cigarette. Without giving it much thought, John dropped the burning match in the woods and walked away. Suddenly, a thunderstorm arose and lightning began to strike all around John. He ran for his car and drove away. A bolt of lightning hit a tree and started a major fire. The fire from the burning tree began to sweep through the forest. It swept over John's burning match and the forest was completely engulfed in flames. If people happen to hear about John dropping the match, could John be held liable for burning down the forest?

    A.   Yes. John's negligence in the forest should be punished by making him pay for all of the harm.

    B.   Yes. All of the possible fire circumstances must be held liable for the ultimate fire.

    C.   Only if the fire would not have happened but for John's negligence.

    D.   Only if the John's negligence was a substantial factor in bringing about the ultimate injury.

53.   Use the facts from Question 52. It appears that some may notice that one of the factors in bringing about the ultimate injury was the lightning. Lightning may be classified as an "act of God." Should the fact that an act of God was a partial cause of this injury relieve John of liability?

    A. Not if John's negligence was still a substantial factor in the injury.

    B. Yes, since acts of God are the primary cause of an injury when they are present at an accident.

    C. No. Since God cannot be sued and held liable, the law will look for someone to pay for damages.

    D. Yes. Acts of God relieve all other actors of liability.

54. Sally was driving towards an intersection that was controlled by four stop signs. Sally was in a hurry and had no intention of stopping. Coming from Sally's right, Jane was also approaching the four way stop. Jane was also in a hurry and had no intention of stopping. Unfortunately, Bill was walking across one of the streets on the intersection, but was unseen by either Jane or Sally. Jane's car entered the intersection, was struck by Sally's car and both cars then hit Bill. Since both Sally and Jane ran stop signs, Bill wants to sue them both for his injuries. What is the most likely result of such an action?

    A. Neither Sally nor Jane will be liable since there was more than one actor in the incident.

    B. Bill must prove which one of the drivers was the cause of the accident or neither one of the drivers is liable.

    C. Both will be liable unless either Sally or Jane can prove they were not the cause of the accident.

    D. Since both Sally and Jane were negligent, they will both be liable if Bill can prove they were both substantial factors in bringing about his injuries.

55. Use the following facts for Questions 55 through 56. Fred was walking along the sidewalk on a quiet street. He was suddenly, and unexpectedly, hit by a car. There was no driver in the car. Fred was injured and taken to the hospital. Fred later discovered that the car was owned by Sally. Sally admitted that she had failed to set the emergency brake when she parked her car. Sally said that it was common practice in that area to leave the car parked without the emergency brake set. In fact, Sally said that her friend Jane never sets her emergency brake either. Jane admits that on the day that Fred was hit by Sally's car, Jane's own car was parked near the scene of the accident without the emergency brake being set. You may assume that the failure to set the emergency brake is a failure to use reasonable care. From whom can Fred recover?

A. Sally since Sally was negligent and her negligence caused the injury.

B. Jane since Jane was negligent and her negligence could cause injuries.

C. Both Sally and Jane under the doctrine of "Summers v. Tice."

D. Neither Sally nor Jane.

56. Use the facts from Question 55. If Fred's attorney uses the doctrine of "res ipsa loquitur," will that assist Fred in winning this case?

A. Only if Fred needs help proving who caused the injury.

B. Only if Fred needs help proving breach of the duty.

C. Only if Fred needs help proving the nature of the duty.

D. Only if Fred needs help proving the injury.

57. Use the following facts for Questions 57 through 58. Joan bought a mattress from a discount mattress store. She had it delivered to the house the following day. Joan and her husband Jim were very pleased with the mattress. According to them, they got the best night sleep in a long time. Joan liked to light a few small candles in the bedroom for about an hour before they went to bed. About a week after having the mattress delivered, Joan lit a candle that was on the nightstand near the bed. Just after lighting the candle, a small spark flew out onto the mattress. The mattress immediately burst into flame and the flames destroyed the house. An expert reviewed the fire and studied the charred remains of the mattress. According to the expert, the mattress was made of material that was extremely flammable. It should never have been used for a mattress. Unfortunately, the labels on the mattress were destroyed by the fire, and no one can tell which manufacturer made the mattress. Assume there are about 6 mattress manufacturers and none of them will admit to having made the mattress that caused the fire. The expert, however, is willing to testify that all of the manufactures make mattress in exactly the same way. Joan and Jim sue all 6 mattress manufacturers. Which of the following doctrines would be most helpful to Joan and her husband to recover?

A. Res ipsa loquitur

B. "Summers v. Tice"

C. Enterprise liability

D.   Market share liability.

58.   Use the facts from Question 57. Assume, however, that there are 200 mattress manufacturers. They all use the same materials and design to make mattresses. Some have gone out of business and others have merged. There are currently 187 manufactures. After careful study, Joan and Jim have learned that about 10 of those manufactures account for 95% of the mattresses sold in their area. Joan and Jim sue those 10 manufacturers. Which doctrine would help Joan and Jim recover?

A.   Res ipsa loquitur

B.   "Summers v. Tice"

C.   Enterprise liability

D.   Market share liability.

2.   Proximate cause

59.   Legend has it that Mrs. O'Leary was responsible for the Great Chicago Fire. According to the story, she went out to milk her cow on the evening of October 8, 1871. She took a kerosene lantern with her to provide light for the barn. The cow kicked the lantern over, the lantern set the straw on fire and the fire spread. First the barn burned down and the fire spread to other buildings. Before the fire would be extinguished approximately three days later, most of the city of Chicago had burned down. Assume that Mrs. O'Leary was negligent in her placement of the lantern by setting it too closely to the cow. Should Mrs. O'Leary be liable for all of the damages that resulted from the Chicago fire?

A.   Yes. She was negligent and her negligence was the cause in fact of the injury.

B.   Yes. Policy dictates that someone must pay compensation.

C.   No. Mrs. O'Leary had no insurance so the law would not impose liability.

D.   No. Policy dictates that liability for injury should extend only so far. This extreme result from this simple negligence is too great to hold Mrs. O'Leary liable.

60.   Use the following facts for Questions 60 through 62. A Gas Company Inc. employee was transferring gasoline from a tanker truck to the underground storage tanks at a gasoline station. The employee knew that if he didn't properly attach a grounding wire

from the truck to the ground, a static electricity spark could fly when he started to fill up the underground tank. The employee also knew that sparks and gasoline vapors were not a good thing to have together. He knew that sparks could ignite the vapors and cause and explosion. The employee did not attach the ground wire, a spark occurred and an explosion erupted. The explosion damaged a customer's car nearby. The customer would like to sue Gas Company for the damage to the car?

    A.   If the law only requires foreseeability of the type of harm, the Gas Company is liable.

    B.   If the law requires foreseeability of the type and full extent of the harm, then the Gas Company is liable.

    C.   The Gas Company will be liable for all damages regardless of the extent of foreseeability.

    D.   The Gas Company is not liable since the employee did not intend the harm.

61.   Use the same facts from Question 60. In this case, assume that the explosion caused a major fire that spread throughout the neighborhood. A homeowner some 2 blocks away suffered a total loss from that fire. That homeowner would like to sue the Gas Company for the harm.

    A.   The homeowner can recover even if the law requires that the defendant foresee the type and extent of injury.

    B.   The homeowner can recover only if the law allows recovery when the harm is within the type foreseen.

    C.   The homeowner cannot recover since the employee did not intend the harm.

    D.   The homeowner cannot recover unless strict liability is imposed.

62.   Use the same facts from Question 60. In this case, however, the employee did attach the ground wire between the truck and the storage tank. Unknown to the employee, however, a stranger saw what was happening and thought he would pull a joke. While the employee was filling the tank, the stranger unattached the ground wire. A spark occurred and caused an explosion. The customers car was damaged by the explosion and the customer wishes to sue the Gas Company.

    A.   The Gas Company is liable if the employee knew the ground wire had been unattached.

B. The Gas Company is liable only if the employee took the ground wire loose.

C. The Gas Company is liable if the employee could have foreseen that someone would take the ground wire off.

D. The Gas Company is not liable since a third party intervened.

E. Defenses

1. Contributory/Comparative Fault

63. Use the following facts for Questions 63 through 67. Assume that Jane was negligently driving her automobile along a residential street. She was driving 35 miles per hour in a 25 mile per hour zone. Professor Rex Legal, a well known but slightly absent minded law professor, was walking along the sidewalk beside the street. Professor Legal was thinking about a particularly tricky proximate cause issue when he turned to cross the street. Since his mind was thinking about the wonders of law, he didn't look both ways before crossing. He was hit and injured by the car that Jane was driving. Who has the burden of proving the defenses that might be applicable in this case?

A. Jane, the defendant, must prove the elements of the defense.

B. Professor Legal, the plaintiff, must disprove the elements of the defense.

C. Jane must introduce elements of the defense and then the burden shifts to Professor Legal to disprove them.

D. Professor Legal must introduce evidence of his due care and then the burden shifts to Jane to disprove those elements.

64. Use the facts from Question 63. If contributory negligence is the defense to be used, what are the elements of that defense?

A. The plaintiff failed to use reasonable care for his/her own safety and knew there was a risk of injury.

B. The plaintiff failed to use reasonable care for his/her own safety and the injury was within the risk created by that failure to use reasonable care.

C. The plaintiff knew there was a risk of injury and the injury was within the risk created by that knowledge.

D. The plaintiff knew there was a risk of injury and voluntarily encountered that risk.

65. Use the facts from Question 63. The jury returns a verdict showing that Jane was 80% at fault and Professor Legal was 20% at fault. Professor Legal's damages are set at $10,000. The jurisdiction still uses the traditional, common law contributory negligence. How much will Professor Legal recover?

A. $10,000.

B. $8,000.

C. $2,000.

D. 0

66. Use the facts from Question 63. The jury returns a verdict showing that Jane was 80% at fault and Professor Legal was 20% at fault. Professor Legal's damages are set at $10,000. The jurisdiction has adopted pure comparative fault. How much will Professor Legal recover?

A. $10,000.

B. $8,000.

C. $2,000.

D. 0

67. Use the facts from Question 63. The jury returns a verdict showing Jane was 80% at fault and Professor Legal was 20% at fault. Professor Legal's damages are set at $10,000. The jurisdiction has adopted one of the modified forms of comparative fault. Under this jury verdict, does it matter which form of modified comparative fault was adopted?

A. No. Any percentage of fault under the modified forms of comparative fault will result in a complete bar to recovery.

B. Yes. Only one form of modified comparative fault will allow recovery of damages by a Plaintiff whose fault is at 20%.

C. No. Both forms of modified comparative fault would allow recovery of 80% of the damages when the plaintiff's fault is 20%.

D. Yes. One form of modified comparative fault would only allow the plaintiff to recover 20% of the damages while the other form would allow the plaintiff to recover 80%.

2. Assumption of Risk

68. Use the following facts for Questions 68 through 71. Pam was 38 years old and a very good automobile driver. He had never had an accident and never had a traffic ticket. Because of her outstanding driving skills, she was frequently asked to teach people to drive. She usually agreed to help. One day she agreed to teach Fred, the 16 year old son of a friend, how to drive. Fred showed up first lesson and admitted that he had never been behind the steering wheel of a car. Pam told him to get into the drivers seat and get ready for the first lesson. Pam went over the basics, had Fred buckle the seat belt and then started the car. They had only driven about 3 blocks when Fred got scared, tried to stop, pushed on the accelerator rather then the brake and hit a tree. Pam was injured. If Pam sues Fred for the injuries, who would have the burden of proving the elements of the defenses that might apply in this case.

A. Fred, the defendant, must prove the elements of the defense.

B. Pam, the plaintiff, must disprove the elements of any defense.

C. Pam must introduce elements of her own due care and then the burden of defenses shifts to Fred.

D. There are no defenses. Driving by teenagers is a strict liability tort and Fred is liable for all injuries.

69. Use the facts from Question 68. Assume that this jurisdictions still uses common law defenses. When Pam sues Fred for the injuries she suffers, what would be the best defense for Fred to use?

A. Contributory negligence.

B. Comparative fault.

C. Assumption of Risk.

D. Unreasonable assumption of risk.

70. Use the facts from Question 68. If Fred uses the defense of reasonable assumption of risk, which of the following is the best statement of the elements of that defense?

A. The plaintiff failed to use reasonable care for his/her own safety.

B. The plaintiff knew and understood the unreasonableness of the risk and voluntarily encountered it.

C. The plaintiff knew and understood the risk and voluntarily encountered it.

D. There is no defense appropriate to this claim.

71. Use the facts from Question 68. Assume that the jurisdiction has adopted pure comparative fault. Which defense would be the best one to apply in this case?

A. Pure comparative fault

B. Contributory negligence.

C. Assumption of Risk.

D. Last clear chance.

3. Statutes of limitations

72. Bill had a car accident where his car was hit by Fred's car. Bill was driving within the posted speed limit and went through a traffic intersection with the green light. Fred was coming from the left side of Bill, over the speed limit and ran the red light. Bill and his car were injured. This jurisdiction had a two year statute of limitations on such accidents. The accident happened on June 4, 1998. Bill's attorney filled the lawsuit against Fred on July 1, 2000. What is the likely result if Fred's attorney raises the issue of the statute of limitations?

A. The action will go forward since the statute of limitations requires that the action be brought after the period of time specified in the action.

B. The action will go forward if Bill's attorney has a very good reason for missing the time period.

C. The action will go even though Bill's attorney filled after the time period. Multiple types of negligence are an exemption to the statute of limitations.

D. The action will be dismissed since Bill's attorney did not file the action within the time allowed.

73. Jane went to a surgeon, Dr. Smith. Dr. Smith had to remove Jane's appendix since it had become inflamed. Before finishing the surgery, Dr. Smith negligently left a small sponge in Jane's abdomen. The surgery was done on February 12, 2000. After the surgery, Jane did not heal properly. She continued to go to Dr. Smith for treatment, but the surgery site remained an infected wound. Fi-

nally, on March 13, 2002, Jane went to another surgeon, Dr. Jones. Dr. Jones immediately recognized the problem, did surgery on Jane the following day and removed the sponge. The surgery site began to heal properly. Jane went to see a lawyer about the issue and asked the lawyer to sue Dr. Smith. The lawyer was concerned since the statute of limitations for this type of action was two years. If the lawyer sues Dr. Smith in June, 2002, what is the likely outcome?

A. The action will be allowed to go forward since the action was filled within two years of the time that Jane discovered the negligence.

B. The action will be allowed to go forward since the time the action is filled is not that late.

C. The action will be barred since the attorney filled after the date of the statute of limitations.

D. The action will go forward since statutes of limitation against medical malpractice actions are unconstitutional.

4. Immunities

74.   John went to the City Charity Hospital to have surgery. The hospital was a non-profit charity that was supported by the churches and other benevolent societies in town. While John was recovering from surgery, the staff of the hospital negligently left the bed rails in a lowered position. John fell out of bed and was injured. When John sued the Hospital, the Hospital claimed that they could not be sued since they were a charity. What is the likely outcome of that claim?

A. The action will be barred since all charities have a charitable immunity to tort claims.

B. The action will probably be allowed to proceed. Although charities once enjoyed charitable immunity, most jurisdictions have abolished that defense.

C. The action will be barred since churches have a constitutional charitable immunity.

D. The action will probably be allowed to proceed since charitable hospitals never enjoyed charitable immunity.

75.   Fred and Anna were married. They had been married for three years. For their anniversary, they went out to dinner. Fred had too much to drink, but drove them home anyway. Fred ran off the road, wrecked the car and injured Anna who was riding in the passenger

seat. Anna sued Fred for the injuries. The insurance company that covered Fred, Anna and the car claimed spousal immunity. What is the likely outcome of that defense?

    A.   The action will be barred since there is a spousal immunity that prohibits actions among members of the family.

    B.   The action will be barred due to a fear that the law has that there will be fraud and collusion among family members.

    C.   The action will probably be allowed to go forward. Although there was once a family immunity that prohibited actions among any family member, those immunities are generally abolished.

    D.   The action will probably be allowed to go forward since driving while intoxicated is a special exception to spousal immunity.

76. Jim and Joan are the loving parents of two children. The children, Jack and Jill, are delightful children. At least they were delightful until they became teenagers. Upon reaching the teen years, Jack and Jill became difficult. Jim and Joan are hard working parents but they are not wealthy. Jack and Jill, however, demand that they be provided with a large allowance so they can buy music online, eat at fast food restaurants, and have the latest electronic gadgets. Jack and Jill also feel that the most important issue is the name brand of their clothes. The teenagers demand that their clothes have only the most popular brand names. When Jim and Joan are financially unable and realistically unwilling to meet those demands, Jack and Jill want to sue Jim and Joan. When the teenagers go to an attorney and ask if they can sue their parents, what legally appropriate answer should that attorney give?

    A.   Family immunities have been abolished and the children can sue their parents for the claims they seek.

    B.   Family immunities still remain in full force and family members can never sue each other.

    C.   Although family immunities have been generally abolished, there still remains immunity for parents exercising parental discretion in discipline, providing care and general household control.

    D.   Spousal immunity has been abolished so that a husband or wife can sue the other spouse, but family immunity still remains and children cannot sue parents.

77. Carl was driving along a state maintained highway when he had an accident. His car left the road and hit a tree. An expert has told Carl that the recent road word done by the state was negligently done. The work caused Carl to lose control of his car even though Carl was driving within the posted speed limit. If Carl sues the state, what is the likely result?

A.   The action may go forward. Although states enjoy a sovereign immunity most have waived that immunity for negligent acts by the state.

B.   The action will be barred since states enjoy sovereign immunity.

C.   The action will be barred. Although most states have waived sovereign immunity, it remains for discretionary functions. Road work is a discretionary function.

D.   The action may go forward. Although states once enjoyed sovereign immunity, such immunity is currently viewed as unconstitutional.

ANSWERS:

A. Duty

1. Adults

1.   The answer is B. A person's own best judgment is not sufficient in negligence cases. A person is expected to act as a reasonable person. It is also important to note that a person is not expected to act with some knowledge of an expert. Society only expects the conduct of reasonable people.

2.   The answer is A. Negligence assumes that a person must be held to the ordinary prudence and understanding of other members of the community. A person may not claim that "I didn't know." In a crowded society, the law expects people to know what other members of the community know.

3.   The answer is D. In a negligence case, the reasonable care that springs from ordinary prudence may be considered in light of the circumstances of the event. It is common, for example, for courts to state that the negligence duty is to act as a reasonable person of ordinary prudence under similar circumstances. It seems unlikely that lack of financial ability to properly build the barn would be considered an appropriate circumstance.

4.   The answer is A. This answer actually states the typical rule in tort cases. The existence of the duty and the nature of that duty is a question of law for the court. In negligence cases the court will determine that the duty is one of a reasonable person of ordinary prudence in similar circumstances. The court will then instruct the jury on that duty. The jury must then determine whether that duty has been breached.

5.   The answer is B. The duty that is owed is that of a reasonable person of ordinary prudence under similar circumstances. Normal acts of God are those types of circumstances that reasonable people of ordinary prudence must plan for. In this example, the neighbors seemed to be aware of high winds in the area. Although wind is an "Act of God," builders of structures must take the normal winds into consideration.

6.   The answer is A. Negligence does not allow a defendant to use their own best judgment or skills. Negligence requires that a defendant use the care and skill of a reasonable person of ordinary prudence under similar circumstances.

7.   The answer is B. Negligence requires that defendants have ordinary prudence. This means that a defendant will be held to the level of knowledge or understanding that other ordinary people in the community will have. If Bill chooses to have a boat, he will be held to the level of knowledge that other boaters have.

8.   The answer is C. The emergency situation will be treated as a circumstance about which the jury may be told. The jury will still have to decide whether Bill acted as a reasonable person under that emergency situation. The existence of the emergency does not automatically relieve Bill of liability.

9.   The answer is D. Intoxication is not a circumstance that reduces the standard for the defendant. The defendant must still use the care and skill of reasonable people of ordinary prudence.

10.   The answer is A. The standard of care is a reasonable person of ordinary prudence under similar circumstances. The loss of consciousness will be considered under that standard. If Ms. Smith was truly unaware of the possibility of the unconsciousness, then it would seem unlikely that a reasonable person could plan for such an event. Ms. Smith will probably not be liable.

11.   The answer is B. The standard of care is that of a reasonable person of ordinary prudence under similar circumstances. A reasonable person would have followed the instructions.

12.   The correct answer is C. Although there are a few jurisdictions that may allow some use of mental illness in negligence cases where that mental illness is unexpected, most jurisdictions do not allow an insanity defense in torts. Mr. Davis will be held to the standard of a reasonable person of ordinary prudence under similar circumstances. Reasonable people do not throw chairs through windows.

13.   The answer is D. Although some physical impairment may be used as a circumstance to consider in the negligence standard, voluntary intoxication is not allowed to affect conduct.

14.   The best answer is B. Although Mr. Hawk intended to shoot the gun, that would not be sufficient intent for an intentional tort. He would have needed the intent to bring about the contact. There is nothing in the facts that indicate that Mr. Hawk knew that Mr. Klim was substantially certain to be hit. The best claim would be negligence.

2.   Children

15.   The answer is C. The usually standard for a child is a child of like age, intelligence and experience. Children are usually not held

to the adult reasonable person standard. There are exceptions to that rule. Some of the additional questions will address those exceptions.

16.   The answer is A. Although Suzie is still a child, there are exceptions as to when the child standard will apply. This set of facts meets those exceptional circumstances. Additional questions will help point out the basis for this exception. It is interesting to note, however, that as a child gets older, the conduct expected from the child standard begins to approach that expected of an adult. From a practical matter, for the 17 year old, it may not matter whether there is a child standard or an adult standard being applied.

17.   The answer is D. That response states the usual principle for applying an adult standard to a child. The adult standard will be applied when the activity is one normally engaged in by adults and is dangerous. Driving an automobile fits those circumstances. Interestingly enough, many jurisdictions have statutes that require adult standards be applied to children when they drive automobiles. In addition, most jurisdictions require parents to agree to be liable for minors engaged in driving automobiles. Response A to this question raises an interesting point. At common law, the courts would have made a decision based upon whether the child was younger than 7, between 7 and 14, or older than 14. If younger than 7, then the child would have been presumed not capable of negligence. If between 7 and 14, the courts would have to review the case on an individual basis. If older than 14, the law would have assumed the child capable of negligence and applied an adult standard. That is no longer the law.

3.   Professionals

18.   The answer is B. A professional holds himself or herself out as having higher levels of skill and training than the ordinary person. The law will hold such professionals to that higher standard. Some courts may articulate this rule as a reasonable person who happens to be under the circumstances of being a professional. That would have suggested that answer A was a better answer. Most jurisdictions, however, would have used language closer to answer B.

19.   The answer is C. Professional malpractice cases usually require the use of expert witnesses. Jurors would not be able to determine the proper conduct of professionals without the assistance of such experts. The experts will usually tell the jury what the care and skill required of the professional and give an opinion on whether the defendant met the usual standard. It would then be up to the jury to decide the case. There may, of course, be cases where

the facts are so clear that the jury does not need the expert witness to decide the case. It is usually better for the attorneys to use experts to make sure the jury has adequate information.

20. The correct answer is C. The appropriate standard of care of a professional is the care and skill of a qualified professional. Since this professional is a surgeon, he would be held to the surgeon level of training skill and experience.

21. The answer is D. Doctors do not guarantee results. Doctors are held to the care and skill of other professionals. The fact that unfortunate, and at times fatal, circumstances may arise does not prove negligence. The plaintiff must prove that the doctor failed to use the care and skill of other professionals.

22. The answer is A. This is one of the types of exceptional cases that may not need experts. To leave a sponge in a patient is usually considered negligence without the proof of expert testimony. From a practical standpoint, the plaintiff's lawyer ought to bring expert testimony anyway. It would be the safer route.

23. The answer is A. There was a time when courts applied a community standard. Physicians were only held to the care and skill of other physicians in their community. Most jurisdictions have, however, gone to a national standard.

24. The best answer is B. Will specifically said not to amputate the leg. In the absence of consent, the "offensive touching" of amputation is a battery. For a more detailed discussion of the intentional torts and the issue of consent, review the material on intentional torts. There is a negligence action of informed consent also. In those examples, the patient did consent to the doctor's conduct but did not fully understand the circumstances. In this example, Will did not consent.

25. The answer is C. Sandy can sue for the negligence tort of informed consent. Before a patient consents to a treatment, the physician must inform the patient of the treatment, the risks, and the alternatives. In this case, the physician did not inform the patient of the risks.

26. The answer is C. Although this set of facts seems to suggest that the physician was acting the patient's best interest, the law still allows the patient to decide a course of treatment. Sandy should have been given full information and allowed to make the decision about the best course of treatment.

27. The answer is D. It appears in this set of facts that Dr. Pam fully informed Sandy of the treatments, risks, and alternatives.

Sandy was allowed to make her own choice. Physicians do not guarantee results. The side effect of the medication was well known and explained to Sandy.

28. The correct answer is A. Physician have a duty to use the skill and training of other physicians. In addition, physicians must inform patients of treatments, risks and alternatives before getting consent to proceed. Physicians do not have a duty to make decisions for the patients. In fact, the law is just the opposite. The patient has the right to make the decision.

29. The correct answer is B. Although it is usually assumed that national standards of care apply to professionals, attorneys must use the appropriate law of the case. Tort law would require the application of state law.

30. The answer is D. Lawyers do not guarantee results by taking a case. The only duty of a lawyer is to use the care and skill of other qualified lawyers.

4. Negligent emotional distress

31. The answer is D. None of the intentional torts would apply since the newscaster had no intent as to Bill. Negligent infliction of emotional distress would not apply for numerous reasons. The tort of negligent infliction of emotional distress is relatively new and not favored. The newscaster appeared to use due care to warn people not to watch. The newscaster probably had a First Amendment right to show the newsworthy event. Bill was such a remote plaintiff, that no recovery would be allowed. Negligent infliction of emotional distress does require a degree of fault. That degree of fault is the failure to use reasonable care. In addition, the courts usually require a more direct connection between the plaintiff and the defendant. That need for a connection is discussed in the following questions.

32. The answer is B. Prior to the adoption of modern negligent infliction of emotional distress; the courts applied an "impact" rule. It appears that some states may still apply that rule. In such a jurisdiction, negligence can only be used as a basis of liability if the plaintiff received some impact from the defendant. After proof of the impact, any emotional distress to could added as "parasitic" damages to the basic negligence claim and would be called "pain and suffering." Using the "impact" rule, John would not be able to recover anything. He was not "impacted."

33. The answer is B. This question is actually the same as the question immediately above. Although John was almost hit, the "impact" rule would have required actual impact. A close call would not be enough.

34.   The answer is C. The modern adoption of negligent infliction of emotional distress allows recovery by the plaintiff for the emotional harm if the plaintiff was within the "zone of danger." In this case it appears that John was almost hit by the car. He was, therefore, within the "zone of danger."

35.   The answer is C. Although John's wife was not within the "zone of danger" a few jurisdictions have expanded the area of recovery. The rule that those states apply may be called the "Dillon Rule." That rule allows recovery if the person who sues was within close proximity to the accident, was a family member of the person who was actually hit and suffered emotional distress. This set of facts meets those elements.

5.   Negligence per se

36.   The answer is C. The existence of a regulatory statute is used as the duty in negligence cases. The courts have the authority to adopt that statute as the duty and then leave it as a question of fact as to whether the defendant breached that duty. The application of the statute as the duty is sometimes referred to as "negligence per se." In this case, the duty would be to drive at 35 miles per hour. Issues of statutes and causation will be discussed in some of the following questions.

37.   The answer is B. The issue of the proper standard of care is a question of law for the courts. The judge must determine whether the standard is one of reasonable care or whether to apply the statute as the duty. The jury cannot be allowed to determine the duty. Once the court decides the duty, the jury will determine whether that duty has been breached and whether the breach was the cause of the injury.

38.   The answer is A. Although a statute may give rise to a duty, the issue of causation remains a question of fact for the jury. Jane's argument that the accident would have happened anyway is a valid argument. The jury will have to determine the factual cause of the injuries to Sam.

B. Breach

1.   Burden of proof

39.   The answer is B. The existence of the stop sign and statutes regulating such signs would raise the issue of negligence per se. That doctrine, however, would only allow the judge to determine that the duty to comply with the stop sign was the duty in the case.

There is still a question of fact as to whether there was a breach of that duty. Where there is conflicting evidence from which the jury could draw one of two valid decisions, the issue must be sent to the jury.

40.   The answer is A. The issue of breach of the duty is ordinarily a question of fact for the jury. In presenting that issue, the plaintiff has the burden to prove that fact. The plaintiff must introduce sufficient evidence of that issue to get the case to the jury. If a defendant makes a motion for directed verdict, the judge has to decide whether there is sufficient evidence to get past the directed verdict. The burden to get past the directed verdict is called the "burden of going forward" or the "burden of production." In deciding that issue, the judge will look at all of the evidence in the light most favorable to the non-moving party. The judge will then ask whether reasonable jurors could find for the plaintiff by a preponderance of the evidence. This example is actually easy. The plaintiff offered no evidence on the issue of who ran the stop sign. Since there is no evidence of who ran the stop sign, there is no evidence on the issue of breach of the duty. The judge must, therefore, issue a directed verdict on that issue. Since breach of the duty is one of the required elements of a negligence case, the judge would ultimately have to issue a directed verdict for the defendant on the whole case. Answer C requires a little statement. That answer would suggest that some cases might end in a tie. Litigation cannot end in a tie. One of the parties will win, and the other party will lose. Burdens of proof help assist the courts and litigants to determine who will win and who will lose when the facts are close or confused. Since the plaintiff is seeking to change the status quo, that is, the plaintiff is seeking to make the defendant pay a judgment; the law requires that the plaintiff have the burden of proof. The plaintiff must move the case past even balance or the plaintiff will lose. The trial court is not allowed to just give up and send the case to the appellate courts.

41.   The answer is B. There are some facts that the plaintiff has introduced to show that the defendant breached the duty. The test for the directed verdict, however, is that the judge must be able to determine that "reasonable jurors" could find in favor of the plaintiff by a preponderance of the evidence. In this case, the facts for the plaintiff are so weak that a decision in the plaintiff's favor by the jury would be a mere guess. The judge must issue a directed verdict for the defendant. Notice that the judge is not carefully considering the demeanor of the witnesses to determine who to believe. The judge is considering the quantity and the quality of the evidence to determine whether there is enough to allow the jury to reach those decisions reasonably.

42.   The answer is D. Once the judge has decided that the evidence is strong enough to get past a motion for directed verdict, the case will usually go to the jury. The jury must decide whether the plaintiff has proven the case by a preponderance of the evidence. It would be rare, if ever, for the evidence to be strong enough for a judge to direct a verdict for the plaintiff. In addition, the "beyond a reasonable doubt" burden of proof is used in criminal cases and not civil cases. It has no application here.

2.   Res ipsa loquitur

43.   The answer is C. This question raises the doctrine of "res ipsa loquitur." Roughly translated, that means "the thing speaks for itself." The doctrine is nothing more than a form of circumstantial evidence that helps the plaintiff prove the issue of breach of the duty. In order to use the doctrine the plaintiff must show that the defendant had exclusive custody and control of the instrumentality of the injury and the type of accident that occurred is one that does not normally occur in the absence of negligence. In this case the doctrine of res ipsa loquitur would apply. The truck was owned and operated by Acme and their authorized agent was driving the truck. In addition, trucks do not jump the curb unless there is some negligence. The application of this doctrine is that it helps the plaintiff prove breach. Since it helps prove breach, and there is no conflicting evidence on that issue, the court can direct a verdict on the issue of breach. Other issues such as injury and causation must go to the jury.

44.   The answer is C. The majority rule is that the doctrine of res ipsa loquitur creates a presumption of breach of the duty. In the absence of evidence to rebut the presumption, the plaintiff is entitled to a directed verdict on the issue. If the defendant offers rebuttal evidence, however, then the presumptions disappears. The evidence, however, will go to the jury and allow the jury to decide the issue of breach.

45.   The answer is A. The surgeon has exclusive custody or control of the surgery and leaving in a sponge is something that does not normally occur in the absence of negligence. This is a classic example of res ipsa loquitur. It is also one of the few examples where a plaintiff does not have to introduce expert testimony in a medical malpractice case. Leaving in a sponge is so obviously negligent that a jury does not need the expert testimony to reach a decision.

C. Injury

46.   The answer is B. Bill could claim negligence, but he could not claim the intentional tort of false imprisonment. For false impris-

onment, the element of intent to confine is missing, since the attendant did not in fact know that Bill was inside. On the other hand, it appears that the attendant may have been negligent. A reasonable attendant should have at least asked if anyone was in the restroom before locking it up. Some brief check of that condition would have been sufficient. One of the elements of negligence is that the plaintiff must have suffered an injury. In this example, Bill suffered personal injury.

47. The answer is D. As noted above, the lack of intent to confine would rule out false imprisonment. In addition, injury is an element of negligence, and in the absence of proof of some injury, the judge would direct a verdict for the defendant. So neither claim would be successful. The case would not go to the jury. For a discussion of the types of injuries that allow recovery and the measure of loss for such injuries, see the chapter on damages.

D. Causation

1. Cause in fact

48. The answer is A. This intended to be a simple, introductory question to the issue of cause in fact. Although Professor Mary may have failed to use reasonable care in teaching and the plaintiff suffered an injury, a negligence action requires that the plaintiff prove that the failure to use reasonable care was the "cause" of the injury. Professor Mary was not the "cause" of the traffic accident outside of the law school. The following questions in this section will help illustrate the proper test to apply for "cause in fact." Keep in mind that causation actually has two parts. The plaintiff must be able to prove that the defendant was the "cause in fact" of the injury and that the defendant was the "proximate cause" of the injury. This section will deal with "cause in fact." The next section will deal with "proximate cause."

49. The best answer is B. That response actually states a variation of the "but for" test. The "but for" test is one of the tests that is used for cause in fact. The test requires that the plaintiff be able to prove that the injury would not have occurred "but for" the negligence of the defendant. In this case, therefore, the plaintiffs would have to prove several things. There would have to be proof that Carly had a duty and breached it. That could be proven by showing the speed limit laws and that Carly was exceeding the posted speed. That evidence, however, would only prove duty and breach. The plaintiffs would still have to prove causation. Using the "but for" test, the plaintiffs could try to show that the injury to the child would not have occurred "but for" Carly's negligence. That may be a difficult

proof problem. The sudden appearance of the child in the middle of the road may have made it impossible for Carly to stop, regardless of her speed. That issue of causation would be one of fact for the jury.

50.   The answer is C. Using the "but for" test, there is no evidence that Mr. Brown would not have died "but for" Dr. Smith's negligence. In fact, there does not appear to be any negligence on the part of Dr. Smith.

51.   The best answer is D. This question raises a difficult issue in causation and there is not universal agreement among jurisdictions. It is clear that Dr. Bill will not be liable for anything. Dr. Bill used the proper care and skill of a physician. In addition, his conduct did not cause the injury. Jane lost her chance of survival and ultimately died due to the course of the illness. In some jurisdictions, however, Dr. Fred will have some liability. It does not appear that Dr. Fred was the "but for" cause of the death. Jane only had a 45% chance of survival even if Dr. Fred had made a proper diagnosis when Jane first went to Dr. Fred. It is clear that the "but for" cause of Jane's death could well be the cancer. Some jurisdictions, however, will find Dr. Fred liable for something. It is clear that Dr. Fred failed to use the proper degree of care. The experts are willing to testify that when Jane initially went to Dr. Fred she would have had a 45% chance of survival. By the time Jane went to Dr. Bill, her chance of survival had dropped to 10%. Some jurisdictions would say that Dr. Fred was clearly the "but for" cause of that drop in the chance of survival. As such, Dr. Fred would be liable for that percentage of lost chance of survival.

52.   The answer is D. Where there is one possible cause of the injury, the courts usually use the "but for" test. Where there are multiple possible causes of the injury, many jurisdictions use a "substantial factor" test. There must be some proof that the defendant was a substantial factor in bringing about the injury.

53.   The answer is A. The test is whether John's conduct was a substantial factor in bringing about the injury. Whether the other acts were by other people or and act of God, the test is the same.

54.   The answer is D. The facts indicate that both of the defendants were negligent. It also appears fairly obvious that both of them were substantial factors in bringing about the injury. Bill should have no problem proving his case. Answer C in the question suggests there might be another alternative. That answer raises the issue of "Summers v. Tice." This question is not a "Summers v. Tice" problem. In "Summers v. Tice," both defendants were negligent, but only one defendant could have caused the accident. In this question, it

appears that it took both defendants to cause Bill's injury. In this question, the defendants are concurrent tortfeasors. "Summers v. Tice" is covered in the next question.

55. The answer is A. Sally was negligent and her negligence was the "but for" cause of the injury. Although Jane was negligent, her negligence was not a cause of the injury. "Summers v. Tice" only applies when two or more of a small group of defendants are negligent and only one of the defendants could have caused the injury. In addition, that doctrine applies when the plaintiff cannot know who caused the injury. In this case, the evidence of the cause of the injury is clear.

56. The answer is B. Res ipsa loquitur is used to prove breach of the duty. The doctrine looks somewhat like "Summers v. Tice" but they are substantially different. Whereas res ipsa loquitur is used to prove breach, "Summers v. Tice" helps prove causation.

57. The answer is C. Res ipsa loquitur is used to prove breach. The expert in this example will testify that the material used in the mattress was inappropriate. That will be evidence of breach. Enterprise liability is used when there are a small number of defendants, they all breached a duty, they appear to be acting in concert and only one could have caused the injury. This is the best description of this case. The manufactures all make identical mattresses and appear to be working in concert. They would all be liable unless individual defendants could prove he or she was not the cause. Market share liability assumes a much larger number of defendants.

58. The best answer is D. Market share liability is used when there are a large number of defendants and the plaintiffs cannot get them all into court. Keep in mind, however, that market share liability has only been adopted in a very small number of jurisdictions. In addition, it appears to having been used only for drug litigation. Unfortunately for Joan and Jim, they probably would not be able to recover under this set of facts.

2. Proximate cause

59. The answer is D. That simple example and answer choice is designed to illustrate the underlying themes of proximate cause. The question clearly shows most of the elements of negligence. Mrs. O'Leary failed to use reasonable care by placing the lantern too closely to the cow. This negligence was the cause in fact of the burning of the city of Chicago. If Mrs. O'Leary had not placed the lantern where she did, the city would not have burned down. Clearly the destruction of the city is an injury. Looking at those circum-

stances there is a duty, it was breached, there was an injury and the breach was the cause in fact of that injury. Proximate cause acts as a policy limit on liability. The law will allow the liability to extend only so far and no farther. In this case, it would seem that the doctrines of proximate cause would not have held Mrs. O'Leary liable for the whole city. The following questions will illustrate some of the tests that courts have used to apply proximate cause.

60. The best answer is A. The modern issue of proximate cause uses foreseeability as the key element. Different jurisdictions require different levels of foreseeability. Some allow liability only where the defendant could foresee the full type and extent of injury. Here, the employee could have foreseen the explosion, but the facts do not tell us whether he could have foreseen cars being damaged. Some jurisdictions allow liability where the harm is within the general type of harm that was foreseen, even if to a greater extent. Here, the employee could foresee explosions, and the car was damaged by the explosion. That would be sufficient. Obviously, intending the harm was not necessary for a negligence claim.

61. The best answer is B. This shows and example of allowing recovery when the defendant could foresee the type of harm, but not the extent of harm. The issue of proximate cause uses the idea of foreseeability as the key. Different jurisdictions, however, explain the test differently. Some jurisdictions even note that liability will attach if the harm was the "natural and probable consequences of the act."

62. The best answer is C. When the conduct of a third party intervenes and helps to cause the injury, the issue is still one of foreseeability. The test is whether the defendant could have foreseen the intervening act. As a rule of thumb, courts will usually rule that the intentional acts of others are not foreseeable. Such courts may also rule that the negligent acts of others are foreseeable. The test, however, is always to ask whether the intervening conduct was foreseeable.

E. Defenses

1. Contributory/Comparative Fault

63. The answer is A. Contributory negligence, comparative fault and assumption of risk are "affirmative defenses" that the plaintiff must plead and prove.

64. The answer is B. That answer correctly states the elements that must be proven for Contributory negligence and comparative

fault. As a matter of interest, answer D comes very close to stating the elements of assumption of risk.

65. The answer is D. Under traditional, common law contributory negligence, any fault on the part of the plaintiff was a complete bar to recovery.

66. The answer is B. In a pure comparative fault jurisdiction, the plaintiff recovers the full amount of damages less the percentage that the plaintiff was at fault.

67. The answer is C. Both forms of modified comparative fault would allow recovery of 80% of the damages under the facts given. The critical point on modified comparative fault is when the fault is allocated as 50% for both the plaintiff and defendant. Under one form of modified comparative fault the plaintiff would recover 50%, while under the other, the plaintiff would recover zero.

2. Assumption of Risk

68. The answer is A. Assumption of risk is an "affirmative defense" that the defendant must plead and prove.

69. The best answer is C. The conduct on the part of Pam was not unreasonable. It is reasonable to offer to teach new drivers how to drive cars. It does raise the issue of reasonable assumption of risk. The next question addresses the elements of that claim.

70. The best answer is C. The elements of reasonable assumption of risk are stated by that answer. There is no element of unreasonableness. Even if the risk being assumed is reasonable, assumption of risk is available.

71. The answer is A. In jurisdictions that have adopted comparative fault, the defense of assumption of risk is usually merged with comparative fault. Although the facts look like assumption of risk, the courts treat it as a comparative fault defenses.

3. Statutes of limitations

72. The answer is D. Since Bill's attorney filled after the statute of limitations, the action is barred.

73. The answer is A. Most jurisdictions recognize a time of discovery rule for medical malpractice actions. The running of the statute is tolled until the patient knew or in the exercise of reasonable care should have discovered the negligence.

4. Immunities

74.   The best answer is B. Although charities once enjoyed immunity from tort claims, most jurisdictions have abolished those immunities. Charitable organizations may now be sued like other organizations.

75.   The answer is C. Like many immunities, family immunities are being abolished.

76.   The answer is C. Family immunity has been generally abolished. As this question should make clear, however the courts are not going to hear such claims. Parents still retain some control over making family decisions. Of course, at the point such things as discipline reach the level of child abuse, the immunity is abolished.

77.   The answer is A. This is the most difficult immunity. Most states have sovereign immunity, but have waived that immunity. The immunity is still seen to exist for such things as discretionary functions. Such functions are usually viewed as the exercise of discretional in the distribution of resources. The road work example is a good one. The decision to spend money to repair a road is probably a discretionary function. Once, however, the state has decided to spend the money and the repairs are done, the work is ministerial. It must be done correctly.

CHAPTER 4
VICARIOUS LIABILITY

QUESTIONS:

1. Use the following facts for Questions 1 through 4. Carl was a plumber. He found an advertisement for a new job with Acme Plumbing Company. Acme Plumbing would do all of the advertising for new customers, would set up a phone line to take calls for jobs and then contact a plumber to go out to do repairs for the new customers. Acme would also have the contracts with credit card companies so customers could pay with credit cards. When Carl asked about working for Acme, he was told that he would have to be "on call" three days a week and one weekend a month. He would have to furnish all of his own tools, his own transportation to jobs, and maintain his own plumbing certification and license. Carl would be expected to follow local plumbing codes when doing repairs, but he would be responsible to make sure he carried out the work properly. He would charge customers at the rate of $65 an hour for labor, plus the cost of any parts. He would turn all of the money over to Acme Plumbing. On the first of each month, Acme would reimburse Carl for all of the cost of parts plus 60% of the money brought in for labor for the previous month. In addition to all of the above details, the contract stated, "All plumbers are to understand that they are Independent Contractors." Carl signs up with Acme Plumbing and takes his first assignment. When he gets to the home of Mr. and Mrs. Smith, he is asked to repair a hot water heater. While doing the repairs, Carl negligently connects the gas line and an explosion occurs just as Carl is leaving the house. There is no doubt that Carl's negligence caused the explosion. If the Smith family wants to sue Carl for the damage:

    A. Carl will be liable for his own negligence.

    B. Carl will not be liable since he is an independent contractor.

    C. The Smith family must sue the employer and may not sue the actual worker.

D. Neither Carl nor Acme would be liable since Carl is an independent contractor.

2. Using the same set of facts as Question 1, the Smith family decides that it would also like to sue Acme Plumbing for the negligence of Carl. Acme Plumbing will claim that the first issue to decide is whether Carl is a servant or an independent contractor. The most likely outcome is:

A. Carl is an independent contractor since the contract says that he is an independent contractor.

B. Carl is a servant since he receives pay from Acme Plumbing.

C. Carl is an independent contractor since he supplies his own tools.

D. The court would have to review all of the details of the relationship between Carl and Acme to determine whether Carl is an independent contractor.

3. Using the same set of facts as Question 1, assume that the court determines that Carl was an independent contractor. The Smith family would still like to hold Acme liable for the damages. The court would rule:

A. The action against Acme would be dismissed since an employer is never liable for the conduct of an independent contractor.

B. The action against Acme can continue if the conduct of Carl concerned a "non-delegable" duty.

C. The action against Acme can continue if Acme was negligent in allowing Carl to be out on the job.

D. Both B and C.

4. Using the same set of facts as Question 1, assume that Carl is an independent contractor but the family still wants to hold Acme liable. Assume that the Smith Family is able to show that in hiring Carl, Acme Plumbing did no background check. If Acme had done a background check it would have found out that Carl had been fired from two previous plumbing jobs. It seems that Carl never learned to properly install natural gas lines in hooking up hot water heaters. Under those circumstances:

A. Acme would not be liable since the conditions do not fall under negligence of the employer or a "non-delegable duty."

B. Acme may be liable for its own negligence for failing to use reasonable care in doing a sufficient background check of Carl.

C. Acme may be liable since doing background checks is a "non-delegable duty."

D. Acme would not be liable since no employer does background checks anymore.

5. Use the following facts for Questions 5 through 8. Bill was having trouble with his automobile. It was about 6 years old and had around 50,000 miles on it. He noticed that when he tried to stop, the brakes did not seem to hold real well and they made a screeching noise. Bill took his car to the First Rate Automobile Dealership where he had originally bought the car when it was new. He felt that the dealership would be the best place to have it repaired. He took the car in and the service manager said they would take care of it. Bill left the car for the entire day and returned to pick it up around 4:30 in the afternoon. The service manager said the car had needed a full brake job and it had been completed. Bill paid for the repairs and drove away. As Bill approached the first stop sign on the road out in front of the dealership, he put his foot on the brake pedal to stop. The pedal went all the way to the floor and the car kept moving right into the intersection. Another car had already entered the intersection and Bills car hit the other automobile. The driver of the other automobile, Sarah, wants to recover from Bill for the injuries to herself and her car. The most likely result of an action against Bill is:

A. Bill is not liable since he did not do the repairs to his car.

B. Bill is not liable since he had the repairs done by a reputable dealership.

C. Bill is liable for the damages since maintaining working brakes on an automobile is a "non-delegable duty."

D. Bill is liable in strict liability since automobiles are abnormally dangerous instrumentalities.

6. Using the same facts as Question 5, Sarah would also like to include the dealership that repaired Bill's automobile as a defendant. The court would rule that:

A. The dealership may be liable if negligence on the part of the repairs can be shown.

B. The dealership may be liable since maintaining brakes is a statutory duty.

C.   The dealership is not liable if Bill is liable.

D.   The dealership is not liable because the duty to repair brakes was a non-delegable duty for Bill.

7.   Using the same facts as Question 5, Bill's attorney tells him he will probably have to pay Sarah for the personal injuries and property damages. The attorney suggests that Bill sue the Dealership that did the repairs to try to recover all of the damages that Bill has to pay. If Bill decides to sue the Dealership, the court would rule:

A.   The dealership may be liable if negligence on the part of the repairs can be shown.

B.   The dealership may be liable since maintaining brakes is a statutory duty.

C.   The dealership is not liable if Bill is liable.

D.   The dealership is not liable because the duty to repair brakes was a non-delegable duty for Bill.

8.   Using the same facts as Question 5, assume that after the accident, Bill must again have his automobile repaired. After the bad experience with the dealership, Bill begins to look for another option. A friend tells him about another repair place. Bill has his wrecked car taken to a repair facility called, "Shade Tree Mechanics." When Bill arrives with his car in tow, he discovers that the facility is actually the front yard of a farm house. There are a few men standing around the yard who agree to do the repairs. After talking with them a few minutes, they quote Bill a price that is unbelievable low. Since he had lost so much money already, he thought that sounded great. He left his car to be repaired. He had to leave the car for two weeks, but then was called to come pick it up. The damage to the car had been repaired and the men assured Bill that everything was in working order. Bill paid the originally quoted repair cost and left the "Shade Tree Mechanics." While driving along the road, Bill approached an intersection controlled by a stop sign. When Bill put his foot on the brake pedal to stop the car, the pedal went all the way to the floor and the car went into the intersection. Bill hit a car being driven by Fred. Fred suffered personal injury and property damage to his car. Fred wants to sue Bill for the damages. In addition to the allegation that that keeping the brakes in working order are a non-delegable duty for Bill, Fred's attorney will make an additional allegation in the complaint. That allegation is:

A.   Bill is strictly liable for the abnormally dangerous automobile.

    B.   Bill failed to use reasonable care in selecting the car repair facility.

    C.   Bill's conduct was intentional since he knew the repair facility was not adequate.

    D.   Bill is a known reckless driver since he had two accidents in such a short period of time.

9. Use the following facts for Questions 9 through 17. Acme Delivery Company needed to hire a new driver for in city deliveries. They advertised and got 10 applicants for one position. They interviewed the applicants, reviewed resumes, and checked backgrounds. They hired Susie as the new driver. She had truck driver training and 10 years experience driving the types of trucks that Acme used. In addition, she was familiar with the city and could make deliveries in a reasonable time. Susie was required to come to work five days a week from 7 a.m. until 4 p.m. She was allowed to take one hour for lunch. She would be assigned a truck that was already loaded when she arrived at work and given a route to follow in making deliveries for that day. Susie would be paid a weekly salary. She would get two weeks vacation and 10 days sick leave every year. Susie had been working as a driver for about a year when she had an accident. It was a normal day and Susie was on her scheduled route. Susie had come up to an intersection that was controlled as a four way stop. There were stop signs on all four of the roads entering the intersection. Susie stopped, looked both ways and then proceeded into the intersection. A car coming from the left, being driven by Margie, did not stop, ran her stop sign and hit the truck being driven by Susie. Margie wants to sue Acme trucking for the damage to her car. The likely result will be:

    A.   Acme will be liable as the employer of Susie.

    B.   Acme will be liable in strict liability for placing the truck on the road.

    C.   Acme will be liable as the owner of the truck that Susie was driving.

    D.   No liability for Acme.

10. Using the same facts as Question 9, assume that the actual accident occurred differently. This time, Susie did not stop at her stop sign. In fact, Susie did not slow down. She came up to the stop sign, kept going and went into the intersection. It was Margie that had stopped at her stop sign and only entered the intersection after using due care for her own safety. Susie's truck hit Margie's Car. Margie wants to sue Susie for the injuries. What is the likely result?

    A.   Susie will not be liable since she is merely an employee.

    B.   Susie will be liable only if Acme is not liable.

    C.   Susie may be liable for her own negligence.

    D.   Susie would be liable since all truck drivers are liable for accidents.

11.   Using the same facts as Question 9, and continuing to assume that Susie ran the stop sign, Margie wants to sue Acme Delivery Company. Acme wants to allege that Susie is an independent contractor.

    A.   Susie is an independent contractor based on the nature of the working relationship.

    B.   Susie is an independent contractor since all delivery truck drivers are independent contractors.

    C.   Susie is not an independent contractor, but is, instead, a servant, based on the nature of the working relationship.

    D.   Susie may be an independent contractor but driving a truck is a non-delegable duty.

12.   Using the same facts as Question 9, and continuing to assume that Susie ran the stop sign, Acme Delivery still wants to raise a defense to Margie's claim. Acme will want to claim that even though Susie was a "servant" they should not be liable for her accidents. To hold Acme vicariously liable for Susie's conduct, Margie will need to plead and prove that:

    A.   Susie's conduct was gross, willful and wanton.

    B.   Susie was acting within the scope of her employment when the accident occurred.

    C.   Truck driving is a non-delegable duty.

    D.   Acme was negligent in hiring Susie.

13.   Using the same set of facts as Question 9, Margie will be trying to prove that Susie was acting with the scope of her employment. In order to show that fact, Margie will have to prove:

    A.   The employer exercised some control over Susie's conduct.

    B.   Susie was acting in furtherance of her employer's business.

    C.   Susie was not on a frolic or detour of her own.

    D.   All of the above.

14.   Using the same set of facts as Question 9, Acme will try to claim that it cannot control truck drivers. Each driver of the truck must maintain control over the truck while driving it. It would be absurd to assume that the company controls the truck. Acme will further allege that since it cannot control the truck, the claim lacks the control element for vicarious liability. That allegation is:

    A.   True since a company cannot drive a truck and only the driver can drive the truck.

    B.   False since the law will assume that the company set the working hours and routes.

    C.   True since the law looks at actual control and not theoretical control.

    D.   False since Acme will be strictly liable.

15.   Using the same set of facts as Question 9, assume that just before the accident; Susie remembered that she had promised to help her brother move a little furniture. She knew she was going to be able to finish her route on time that day, so she decided to leave her prescribed route. Rather than following the route she had received that day, she drove three blocks out of the way to go to her brother's apartment. She was planning on picking up some furniture in the truck, delivering it to her brother's new apartment. Before she reached her brother's apartment, however, the accident occurred. If Margie sues Acme for this accident:

    A.   Acme will escape liability since Susie was not in the scope of her employment.

    B.   Acme will escape liability since Susie violated work rules by leaving the prescribed route.

    C.   Acme will still be liable since Susie was still in an Acme Delivery Company truck.

    D.   Acme will still be liable since ownership of a truck is a non-delegable duty.

16.   Using the same set of facts as Question 9, assume that on the morning of the accident, Susie was assigned to a new truck that Acme had just purchased. Susie looked at the truck and told her supervisor that she had never driven a truck like that one. The new truck was larger and more difficult to maneuver then the one she was use to driving. The supervisor told Susie that she could either

drive the new truck or be fired. Susie took the new truck out for the deliveries and had the accident. She did not want to run the stop sign, but was just not able to stop a truck with which she was unfamiliar. Margie will sue Acme for vicarious liability. Her attorney would like to add another allegation. Which of the following would be the best allegation to add?

    A. Acme breached a non-delegable duty by assigning a new truck to a driver without training on that truck.

    B. Acme is liable for punitive damages for assigning a new truck to Susie.

    C. Acme is liable for its own negligence for failing to use reasonable care to train Susie for the new truck.

    D. Acme is strictly liable for assigning Susie to the new truck.

17. Using the same set of facts as Question 9, Susie had been having some problems at work. It seemed that Acme kept adding more deliveries to the usual work day and Susie was having trouble finishing. When she questioned her supervisor about the additional deliveries, she was told that she would make the deliveries that were assigned in the time of the normal work day. If she was not able to make those deliveries, they would find someone who could. Susie clearly felt her job was being threatened. The next day, she decided that she would have to make the deliveries regardless. The accident occurred because Susie was intentionally exceeding the speed limit in an effort to make all of her deliveries. Acme had a work rule that clearly stated that drivers must driver the truck at or below the posted speed limits. When Margie sues Acme, what is the likely result?

    A. Acme will escape liability since Susie violated a work rule.

    B. Acme will escape liability since Susie was engaged in intentional conduct.

    C. Acme will be liable since the supervisor engaged in outrageous conduct.

    D. Acme will be liable in vicarious liability even though Susie was engaged in intentional conduct.

18. The doctrine that allows the employer to be held liable for the torts of employees is frequently referred to as:

A. Respondeat superior

B. Res ipsa loquitur

C. Habeas corpus

D. Mandamus

19. Use the following facts for Questions 19 through 24. Pam was walking along the street going back to her office after lunch. She noticed that the time on the parking meter by her car had expired, so she put a little more money into the meter. Pam was going to have to go to an appointment away from the office in a short time, so she did not need to leave the car there very long. Without any warning, Pam was suddenly tackled from behind by Police Officer Carol. Officer Carol was a relatively new officer having just finished police academy two months earlier. She was still on a probationary status and assigned to handle traffic matters in a quiet section of town. Officer Carol had noticed the car with the expired meter and had planned on writing a ticket for overtime parking. Carol had not had the opportunity to write many tickets and was looking forward to the experience. She also wanted to look good to her supervising Police Sergeant. Just that morning the Sergeant had read a note from the Mayor to all of the shift patrol officers. The note had said, "Traffic in the city is getting to be a problem. Our tourists in town have no place to park and enjoy the city because local residents take all of the street parking. Overtime parking must stop. Use whatever tactics are necessary to stop it." It was signed, Mayor Smith. She was so angry that Pam had placed money in the meter that Carol decided to arrest Pam. Rather than saying anything to Pam; Carol just ran forward and tackled Pam from behind. Carol then picked Pam up off the sidewalk, put handcuffs on her and placed her in a patrol car. Carol took Pam to the station and brought her into the arrest area of the station. Carol then explained to the supervising Police Sergeant the nature of the arrest. The Police Sergeant knew there was no basis for that arrest and told Pam to sit on a bench while the Sergeant and Carol had a little talk. The sergeant explained to Carol that her conduct had been a little overboard. It would have been proper to go ahead and ticket the car, but not to arrest Pam. In fact, the Sergeant explained that it was possible that Pam could cause them a lot of trouble. The Sergeant then released Pam from the handcuffs told her that they would let it go this time, and that she was free to go. Pam asked if she could get a ride back to her office and the Sergeant said, "No, we aren't a limousine service. You'll have to get your own way back." Pam caught a taxi and had it take her to the hospital emergency room. Pam's Knees and hands were terribly scrapped from being knocked to the sidewalk. She was treated at the hospital and released. Rather then going to her afternoon appointment, Pam went straight to her lawyer's office. Pam first wants to sue Carol for the injuries. If she sues Officer Carol:

A. Officer Carol may be liable for her own torts.

B. Officer Carol will not be liable since she was merely acting under orders from the Mayor.

C. Officer Carol will not be liable since she is an employee of the city. Pam will have to sue the city.

D. Officer Carol will not be liable since she has a supervisor. Pam will have to sue the supervisor.

20. Using the same set of facts as Question 19, Pam's attorney mentions that there may be some issues as to whether Officer Carol is an independent contractor or a servant. If that issue arises:

A. Carol is a servant since all public employees are "servants of the people."

B. Carol is a servant since the city supplies the tool of her trade, assigns work hours, controls the nature of her work, and generally sets the conditions of daily activity.

C. Carol is an independent contractor since she must exercise independent thought while on the job.

D. Carol is an independent contractor since she is expected to maintain and purchase new uniforms after her initial allocation begin to wear out.

21. Using the same set of facts as Question 19, Pam would also like to sue the Supervising Sergeant. If Pam decides to sue the Sergeant, her best claim would be:

A. The Sergeant is vicariously liable under the doctrine of respondeat superior. In fact, the Sergeant was the immediate "respondeat superior."

B. The Sergeant allowed Carol to exercise a non-delegable duty.

C. The Sergeant may be liable for his own negligence or other tort.

D. The Sergeant will not be liable in this example.

22. Using the same set of facts as Question 19, Pam continues to have a discussion with her attorney. They decide they would like to also sue the primary supervisor of the training academy where Carol did her officer training. What claim would have the best chance of recovery against that training supervisor?

A. No claim would be appropriate against the training supervisor.

B. The allocation of a non-delegable duty to Carol by the training supervisor.

C. Vicarious liability under the doctrine of respondeat superior.

D. The training supervisor may be liable for his or her own negligence or other tort.

23. Using the same set of facts as Question 19, Pam's attorney finds out about the note that the Mayor wrote and had read to the officers. Pam would like to sue the Mayor for her injuries. What claim against the Mayor would have the best chance of recovery?

A. No claim against the Mayor would be appropriate.

B. The Mayor would be liable under respondeat superior. A mayor is the "respondeat superior" of the whole city.

C. The Mayor may be liable for his own negligence.

D. The Mayor would only be liable if no other defendants were liable.

24. Using the same set of facts as Question 19, Pam and her attorney decide that they also want to sue the city itself for the injuries that Pam suffered. If they sue the city, the best chance of recovery would fall under which claim?

A. Cities are not liable for torts of police officers.

B. The city may be vicariously liable for the torts of Carol, the Supervising Sergeant, the training supervisor and the Mayor.

C. The city may be liable for the breach of non-delegable duties.

D. The city may be liable for its own negligence.

25. John purchased 100 shares of Acme Delivery Corporation stock. He was quite please with his investment and enjoyed watching the stock prices rise. One day, John was notified that a driver for Acme Delivery Corporation had run a red light, hit another car and injured the driver of the other car. John went to his attorney and asked whether he personally would be liable for that accident. The best advice the attorney could give is:

A. Shareholders are not vicariously liable for the torts of employees of the corporation.

B. Shareholders are vicariously liable for the torts of the employees of the corporation if the employee was acting within the scope of his or her employment.

C. Shareholders are vicariously liable for the torts of the employees of the corporation if the employee was engaged in the performance of a non-delegable duty.

D. Either B or C can be correct.

26. Use the following facts for Questions 26 through 28. Jack and Jill enter into a partnership to run a delivery service. The company is called "Jack and Jill Deliveries." Jack and Jill hire Bob to be the primary driver for the delivery service. While making a delivery, Bob runs a stop sign and causes an accident. If other injured parties seek to sue "Jack and Jill Deliveries" for the damages, the likely result would be:

A. The Partnership cannot be held vicariously liable for the torts of employees.

B. The Partnership can be held liable for the torts of employees if the driver was acting in the scope of his or her employment.

C. The Partnership can be held liable for the conduct of employees if the partnership was negligent in hiring the employee.

D. Either B or C may be correct.

27. Using the same set of facts as Question 26, the injured parties seek to sue Jack and Jill personally for the damages from the accident. The probable outcome of such litigation would be:

A. Partners, just like investors in a corporation, cannot be held personally liable for acts of employees.

B. Partners may be held personally liable for acts of employees acting within the scope of their employment.

C. Partners may be held liable for acts of employees only if the partner is actually negligent in hiring that employee.

D. Partners may be held liable for acts of employees only if the partner allows the employee to perform a non-delegable duty.

28. Using the same set of facts as Question 26, further investigation reveals that the brakes had failed on the "Jack and Jill" truck and that was what caused the accident. Jill was the partner who was responsible for doing maintenance on the trucks. It appears that she was negligent in that maintenance. The injured parties would like to sue both Jack and Jill for the damages. What is the possibility that Jack would be liable for those damages?

A. One partner is not liable for the acts of other partners.

B. One partner is only liable when he or she is personally negligent.

C. One partner is only liable for the conduct of other partners if the first partner attempted to delegate non-delegable duties to other partners.

D. One partner may be vicariously liable for the conduct of other partners.

29. Use the following facts for Questions 29 through 31. Fred, Jane, Bill, and Sue all decided to purchase a truck. They thought that they could use the truck to do a little hauling for the community and make a little extra money. In addition, they thought they could take turns using the truck for their own personal needs around each of their homes. They all pitched in equal shares of money and designated Sue to buy the truck. Sue was the most knowledgeable about trucks so that decision only made sense. After they purchased the truck, they advertised for hauling jobs in the local paper. The response was amazing. They had more jobs then they could handle. Each of the four took turns handling the jobs. When each of them would get paid for a job, that person would split the money with the other three. None of the four ever wrote any of this agreement on paper. The only record of the agreement was that the truck title showed ownership in all four names. One day, Fred was driving the truck to make a delivery that had been contracted for by a local furniture store. On the way to the delivery, Fred ran a stop sign and caused an accident. The people in the other car were injured. If the injured people seek to sue all four of the truck owners for the damages, what would be the best claim to make?

A. The truck ownership was a joint venture by the four people

B. The truck ownership was an implied corporation by the four people.

C. The truck ownership was an implied partnership by the four people.

D.   The truck ownership was an implied limited partnership by the four people.

30.   Using the facts from Question 29, the injured parties want to claim that the agreement among the four people was a joint venture. In order to prove that relationship, the plaintiffs must show:

A.   That the four people had an agreement, a business purpose, and all four had the right to control the use of the truck.

B.   That the four had an agreement, a business purpose, and all four were controlling the truck at the time of the accident.

C.   That the four had agreed to be liable for the each other torts.

D.   Members of a joint venture are not vicariously liable for the torts of other members of the venture.

31.   Using the same set of facts as Question 29, assume that Fred had not been using the truck to make a delivery for pay. Instead, Fred had borrowed the truck to run some personal errands. While running those personal errands, the accident occurs. If the plaintiffs seek to sue all four members of the joint venture, the likely result is what?

A.   Members of a joint venture all liable for the torts of a fellow member of that venture.

B.   Members of a joint venture are not vicariously liable for the torts of a fellow member of that venture.

C.   Members of a joint venture are only vicariously liable for torts of a fellow member of that venture if that fellow member is acting within the scope of the venture.

D.   Members of a joint venture are not vicariously liable for torts of a fellow member of that venture unless riding in the truck at the time of the accident.

32.   Jim and Carol are husband and wife. They are a "two car" family. Just for convenience, Jim and Carol each have one of the cars titled in only one name. Jim and Carol usually only drive the car that is titled in their own names. Occasionally, however, Jim or Carol will find it necessary to drive the other car. One day, Carol was driving the car actually titled in Jim's name. Carol had an automobile accident. Jim is wondering if he may also be liable for the accident that happened in his car. If he comes to you with this question, what is your answer?

A. One spouse is not liable for the torts of the other spouse.

B. One spouse may be liable for the torts of the other spouse while driving a car under the Family Purpose Doctrine.

C. One spouse may be liable for the torts of the other spouse while driving a car if the first spouse knows the second spouse is a bad driver.

D. One spouse may be liable for the torts of the other spouse while driving a car only if the spouse driving the car does not have a driver's license.

33.   Use the following facts for Questions 33 and 34. Jim and Carol have a car that is titled in both of their names. They have a son who recently turned 16 years old and got a drivers license. Jim and Carol let the son drive the car. He is allowed to drive to the mall, drive to school one day a week, and drive the car to his summer job at the fast food restaurant. One day, while driving to the mall, the son has an accident. Jim and Carol want to know if they can be held liable for their son's accident.

A. Parents are not liable for the torts of their children.

B. More than likely the parents would be liable under an Automobile Consent Statute.

C. Parents are only liable for the car accidents of their children if they know the children are bad drivers.

D. Since automobiles are very dangerous, parents are strictly liable for accidents happening in their cars.

34.   Using the same set of facts as Question 33, assume that at the time the accident happened, Jim and Carol's son was not actually driving the car. Before the son went to the mall, he stopped to pick up his girl friend Mary. Mary is also 16 and has a driver's license. Mary asked the son if she could drive the car and he agreed. Mary was driving the car when the accident happened. Under those circumstances, Jim and Carol would like to know if they would still be liable.

A. The parents would be liable only if the trip to the mall was still a "family purpose."

B. The parents would be liable only if they knew Mary was a bad driver.

C. The parents would not be liable since they did not give consent to Mary to drive the car.

   D. The parents would be liable under the Automobile Consent
       statutes.

35.   Jim and Joan were husband and wife. They were out for a drive
on a Saturday afternoon in their family car. Joan was driving the car
and Jim was riding in the passenger seat. Joan was driving at a
speed in excess of the posted speed limit. As she entered an
intersection, an automobile from the right ran a stop sign and hit
Jim and Joan's car on the passenger side door. Jim was injured. The
automobile that hit Jim's side of the car was driven by Mike. Jim
wants to sue Mike for his own injuries. Mike would like to be able to
use Joan's negligence to reduce or bar the recovery by Jim. What is
the likely result of Mike's attempt to do that?

   A. A plaintiff may not impute the negligence of one spouse to
       another in order to use contributory negligence or compara-
       tive fault against the injured spouse.

   B. The negligence of one spouse may be imputed to another in
       order to use contributory negligence or comparative fault
       against an injured spouse.

   C. Negligence of a driver of a car may not be imputed to
       passengers in order to use contributory negligence or com-
       parative fault against a passenger.

   D. Negligence of a driver of a car is always imputed to
       passengers in order to use contributory negligence or com-
       parative fault against the passengers.

36.   Super Star Sam was a rich pop singer. He had millions of fans
and millions of dollars. He rode around in a long limousine. Sam did
not drive his own limousine, but had hired a reliable person to be his
driver. The driver was a well trained, properly licensed professional
driver. One day, the driver was exceeding the posted speed limit and
entered an intersection. A car being driven by Mike entered the
same intersection from the right, ran a red light and hit the
limousine. Super Star Sam was injured in the accident. If Sam
wants to sue Mike for the damages, can Mike impute the negligence
of the driver to Sam?

   A. No. The negligence of a driver may not be imputed to a
       passenger in order to impose contributory negligence or
       comparative fault.

   B. Yes. Under these circumstances, the negligence of the
       driver may be imputed to Sam since it meets the "both
       ways" test.

    C.   No. Under these circumstances, the negligence of the driver may not be imputed to Sam since it does not meet the "both ways" test.

    D.   Yes. The negligence of a driver is imputed to passengers in order to impose contributory negligence or comparative fault.

37.   Use the following facts for Questions 37 through 40. Acme Tree Company needed to hire some new tree trimmers. They put advertisements in the newspapers and hired Betty Sue. Betty Sue had five years of experience and an excellent work record. Her contract with Acme provided that she would work a minimum of 35 hours a week and a maximum of 45 hours a week. She would be paid $15 an hour. She would receive full benefits of employment. Acme would provide all tools and the truck that she would drive to job locations. Betty Sue would report to work each morning at 7:30 am and receive a list of jobs to be completed that day. She would return to the office when she completed that work. After working for some time, Betty Sue had an accident while at work. While cutting tree limbs, one fell and hit the roof of a nearby house. The owners of the house would like to sue Betty Sue for the damage to the house. What is the likely result of the action against Betty Sue?

    A.   An employee may be held liable for his or her own torts.

    B.   An employee may not be held liable for his or her own torts. Only the employer may be held liable for the torts of employees.

    C.   An employee may be held liable for his or her own torts only if the act is a non-delegable duty.

    D.   An employee may not be held liable for his or her own torts while acting in the scope of employment.

38.   Using the same facts as Question 37, the owners of the house would also like to sue Acme Tree Company. The president of Acme Tree Company would like to know if Betty Sue is an independent contractor or a servant. Which of the following is the best answer?

    A.   The determination of that question will depend on an analysis of all of the circumstances of the employment, but she appears to be an independent contractor.

    B.   The determination of that question will depend on an analysis of all of the circumstances of employment, but she appears to be a servant.

    C. The determination of that question will depend on what her status is stated to be in her employment contract.

    D. The determination of that question will depend on whether Betty Sue was acting in the scope of employment at the time of the accident.

39. Using the same facts as Question 37, the president of Acme Tree Company wants to claim that the company cannot be liable for limb damage done by employees. The president will point out that the employee handbook clearly states, "Employees must not let limbs fall on houses." Will that violation of work rules render the employer not liable?

    A. Yes. Violation of work rules bars the use of vicarious liability against an employer.

    B. No. Although Betty Sue may have violated a work rule that alone is not the conclusive factor in determining whether the employer is liable.

    C. Yes. If it can be shown that Betty Sue knew of the work rule that would bar the use of vicarious liability against an employer.

    D. No. If an employee is a servant, the employer is liable regardless of the nature or circumstances surrounding the accident.

40. Using the same facts as Question 37, Betty Sue is not exactly doing a job assigned by the employer. While completing a task assigned by the employer, a person living close by asks Betty Sue if she could do a little trimming on some additional trees. This new persons shows Betty Sue what needs to be done and asks how much would it cost. Betty Sue realizes she is finished with all assigned tasks for the day and is a little early. She could do the extra job, not tell her employer and pocket a little extra money. Betty Sue quotes the new person a price, the person accepts and Betty Sue begins work. It is while working on this new project that the accident happens. This new person would like to sue Acme Tree Company. What is the likely hood of success in that action?

    A. Acme will probably be liable since they allowed Betty Sue to sue its truck and tools.

    B. Acme will probably be liable since tree cutting is a non-delegable duty.

    C. Acme will probably not be liable since Betty Sue is violating work rules.

D. Acme will probably not be liable since Betty Sue is not acting in the further of the employer's business.

ANSWERS:

1.   The answer is A. In any employment situation the person who was negligent may be sued for the damage. The usual problem is whether the employer may also be held liable for the harm. In this question, the problem of whether the employee is actually an independent contractor would be the first major issue in determining whether Acme Plumbing is also liable.

2.   The best answer is D. The mere fact that the contract states that Carl is an independent contractor is not controlling. In fact, no one fact in the relationship is controlling. The law will usually assume that the nature of the job, the method of payment, who supplies the tools, the nature of the hours of work, the supervision, and other job details, must all be reviewed to determine whether the employee is a servant or independent contractor.

3.   The best answer is D. Although some liability is relaxed for the employer of an independent contractor, there are still times when such an employer may be liable for the acts of such an employee. The best examples of when an employer of an independent contractor may still be liable are when the employee is engaged in a "non-delegable duty" or where the employer was also negligent. Examples of those conditions will be explored in other questions.

4.   The best answer is B. An employer has some duty to do a background check before sending employees into the homes of people. In this case, a routine check would have discovered that Carl had difficulty with the very type of job that Acme was to send him to repair. It appears, therefore, that Acme failed to use reasonable care in the hiring of Carl. This type of liability is called negligent entrustment. Employers may be held liable for their own negligence for failing to use reasonable care in hiring, training, supervising, or placement on a job.

5.   The correct answer is C. This set of facts is one to consider the issues of vicarious liability. Bill is the "employer" of the dealership. The dealership, however, is clearly an independent contractor. They supply their own tools, determine the method of work, hire assistants, and have the appearance of independent contractors. Maintaining brakes on an automobile, however, would be considered a non-delegable duty. Such duties usually arise where there is a statutory duty by the person or the activity creates a high risk of harm. Most states have statutes which require the owner of a car to maintain working brakes. In addition, the failure to maintain working brakes creates a great risk of harm. Although vicarious

liability looks like strict liability, the answer that relies upon strict liability in incorrect. Bill would only be liability for the non-delegable duty if negligence on the part of the repair company could be shown. Bill is, in fact, being held liability for the negligence of another.

6. The answer is A. Although Bill may be liable for the non-delegable duty of maintaining proper brakes, the repair firm may also be liable if negligence can be proven.

7. The correct answer is A. Bill may have an action against the dealership for any damages that Bill must pay. The action would be one of indemnity. Where Bill was not negligent but the dealership was negligent, Bill could recover.

8. The answer is B. This is another example of negligent entrustment. In this case, Fred would allege that Bill failed to use reasonable care in selecting the repair facility. That allegation would not have worked as well when Bill used the dealership. Car owners are not expected to know how to repair cars, but they are expected to use reasonable care to select the types of repair facilities that other reasonable people would select.

9. The answer is D. Although vicarious liability looks like strict liability, it is not. In order to hold the employer liable for acts of the employee, there must be some fault on the part of the employee. In this set of facts, the plaintiff, and not Susie, was at fault. Since Susie was not at fault, Susie's employer would not be liable.

10. The correct answer is C. Regardless of the issues of vicarious liability; an employee may be liable for his or her own negligence. The employer may also be liable, but the liability of the employer will not relieve the employee.

11. The answer is C. Susie is not an independent contractor. Acme supplies the tools of the job, sets the hours, sets the routes and maintains the status of "master" to Susie's status as a "servant."

12. The correct answer is B. In order to hold Acme vicariously liable Margie will need to prove that Susie was acting within the scope of her employment. The issue of non-delegable duty only arises when the employee is an independent contract. This set of facts assumes that Susie is a servant. If Margie proved the gross, willful or wanton conduct on the part of Susie the action against Acme would be more difficult.

13. The correct answer is D. The first three answers state the elements of proof for scope of employment.

14.   The answer is B. Clearly a company cannot take actual control of truck away from the driver. That is not, however, the issue. For vicarious liability, the law is looking to see if the employer exercises control over such things as hours, times and routes.

15.   The answer is A. By leaving the prescribed route, Susie was no longer in the scope of her employment. She had gone on a frolic of her own, had left control of Acme and was not acting for the furtherance of the employer's business.

16.   The best answer is C. By failing to properly train Susie in the use of the new truck, Acme may be liable for its own negligence. This is another form of negligent entrustment.

17.   The best answer is D. Although it may be thought that employers should escape liability when employees engage in intentional conduct, that is not always the case. Even intentional conduct may be considered within the scope of employment. That is true even when the intentional conduct violates a work rule. Where the conditions of employment seem to expect or require such conduct, the intentional conduct is part of the scope of employment.

18.   The answer is A. This question is just a little break from the more difficult issues faced in many of the other questions. It is important, however, to know the names and proper terms for the doctrines in law. Knowing the proper names allows easy access to research materials and accurate discussions with other attorneys and judges. In the area of vicarious liability, the doctrine of respondeat superior deals with the issues of holding an employer liable for acts of employees. Another term that may be important is "imputed negligence." The concept of imputed negligence is the broader term that covers all examples of vicarious liability where negligence is involved. It suggests that the way that someone is being held liable is that the negligence of the wrongdoer is being "imputed" to someone else. That "someone else" is then held vicariously liable. The term imputed negligence sometimes suggests that intentional acts may not be imputed to others. Although intentional acts may frequently seem outside the scope of employment, there are times when a person may be held liable for the intentional acts of another. The delivery driver questions gave several examples of those.

19.   The correct answer is A. Just like the other employment vicarious liability issues, the employee may be liable for his or her own torts. In this case, although Officer Carol is a police officer and a public employee, she can and probably will be liable for her improper arrest.

20.   The correct answer is B. The first question for all respondeat superior issues is whether the employee is a servant or an independent contractor. The method of deciding the issues is always the same. The primary issue is the ability of the employer to control the nature of the work. As in this case, courts would look at the details of the employment conditions. Supplying the tools, setting hours, control work times, and controlling condition of work are examples of the factors that are considered. The more control over the work that the employer imposes, the more likely the employee will be considered a servant.

21.   The best answer is C. It may appear that since the Sergeant was the supervisor that vicarious liability ought to apply to him. The Sergeant, however, is not the employer of Carol. In fact, both Carol and the Sergeant are both employees of the same employer. The employer is the city. Fellow employees are not vicariously liable for the torts of other employees. For that reason, there would be no vicarious liability for the Sergeant. The Sergeant, however, has a duty to supervise and continue to instruct officers in his command. As such, the Sergeant may be negligent for failing to properly supervise Carol. This is another example of negligent entrustment. In this case, the Sergeant is probably liable for failing to properly supervise Carol. The Sergeant may also be liable for his own treatment of Pam after the events occurred.

22.   The best answer is D. As the time period between the training and the incident gets longer, the action against the training academy weakens. The best claim, however, would be an allegation that the supervisor of training was negligent in the training of Carol. It should be obvious that this is another example of negligent entrustment. The training supervisor would not be vicariously liable for the same reasons that the supervising sergeant is not vicariously liable. The training supervisor is merely another employee of the same employer.

23.   The best answer is C. As with the Supervising Sergeant and the training supervisor, the Mayor is merely a fellow employee of the city. There would be no vicarious liability between Carol and the Mayor. The Mayor, however, could be liable for his or her own negligence. This action, although a possibility, would appear to be weak on issues of foreseeability.

24.   The best answer is B. This question illustrates the way that actions are brought against law enforcement officers. The officer who commits the initial tort is usually sued for that tort. The officers who act as supervisors, training officers, or other in the command hierarchy are usually sued for their own negligence under the

doctrine of negligent entrustment. There are times that even the city officials may be sued for their own negligence due to statements or policies that have been issued. The city itself is then sued as the employer of all of those people. The liability of the city would be vicarious liability. There are times, of course, that many cities try to avoid liability by using sovereign immunity. That defense does not tend to be useful in actions of police misconduct.

25.   The best answer is A. Shareholders are, of course, the investors in corporations. One of the advantages of incorporation is that investors are not personally liable for the torts of employees. The corporation may, of course, be liable if the other requirements of respondeat superior are met. The only time a shareholder may be liable for the torts of employees is if the corporation is so under funded that the courts would allow the plaintiff to "pierce the corporate veil" and sue individual investors.

26.   The best answer is D. Partnerships, like any other company, may be held vicariously liable for the torts of the employees who are acting within the scope of their employment. In addition, partnerships may be held liable for their own negligence.

27.   The correct answer is B. Partners are liable for acts of employees. That liability may be based on vicarious liability under respondeat superior, negligent entrustment or attempts to delegate non-delegable duties.

28.   The correct answer is D. Partners are vicariously liable for the conduct of other partners. In order to limit that liability, people forming a company should look into forming a "limited partnership" or a corporation.

29.   The best answer is A. Implied business associations like partnerships and corporations do not exist. The best claim would be for joint venture.

30.   The best answer is A. That answer states the basic requirements of a joint venture. The interesting requirement is that of the right of control. Notice that the right of control seems to be more of a right of general control over the instrumentality of the injury. There is no requirement to show that all members of the venture were in control of the truck at the time of the accident. Obviously, only one person can drive a truck at one time.

31.   The correct answer is C. Joint ventures are somewhat like other forms of respondeat superior. The people to be held vicariously liable are only liable when the tortfeasors was acting with the scope of the duties created by the venture. Where a member of the venture is on a personal activity, the other members of the venture would not be liable.

32.   The answer is B. Ordinarily one spouse is not liable for the torts of the other spouse. Due to the high number of traffic accidents, the courts have created doctrines to try to spread liability for such accidents. One such doctrine is the family purpose doctrine. Where a member of the family is driving the car for something like a "family purpose," the titled member of the car is liable.

33.   The answer is B. Most states have automobile consent statutes. These statutes provide that if the automobile is being driven with the consent of the owner, then the owner is liable for accidents that happen with that automobile. These statutes are usually paired with insurance regulations that require that the owners' car insurance also cover any accidents that happen with the automobile while it is being driven with the consent of the owner.

34.   The answer is D. Courts have interpreted the Automobile Consent Statutes broadly. Although the parents did not consent specifically to Mary to drive, the parents did consent to the car being driven. That consent is usually enough to make the statutes applicable. Courts have routinely held that in order to be outside the Automobile Consent statute, the car has to be just about stolen.

35.   The best answer is A. Although it is possible to impute negligence in order to impose contributory negligence or comparative fault against an injury party, the courts are reluctant to do so. The states that still allow that practice may refer to the "both ways" test. If the negligence could have been imputed in order to impose vicarious liability, then the negligence may be imputed to impose contributory negligence or comparative fault. The law does not impose vicarious liability between spouses by the mere nature of the marriage relationship. Since vicarious liability is not imposed between spouses, the negligence would not be imputed to impose contributory negligence or comparative fault between the spouses.

36.   The answer is B. This example is one that meets the "both ways" test. Since the driver is a servant of Sam, Sam can have the negligence of the driver imputed to Sam in order to create vicarious liability. Since the setting is one where vicarious liability could be imposed, it is also one where imputed contributory negligence or comparative fault could be imposed.

37.   The answer is A. This series of questions is in the nature of a review of most of the material in this chapter. Although issues of impute negligence may arise, it is clear that an employee may be held liable for his or her own torts.

38.   The best answer is B. The determination of that question will depend on a series of factors. Those factors include the major issue

of who has general control of the terms and conditions of work. A reading of the terms of her employment, make it appear that Betty Sue in a servant.

39.   The best answer is B. The mere violation of work rules does not bar vicarious liability. The issue is whether the employee was acting in the scope of their employment at the time of the injury. Scope of employment is determined by looking at whether the employer had control over the work, the employee was acting in the further of the employer's business and the employee was not on a frolic or detour of his or her own.

40.   The answer is D. Betty Sue in no longer acting in the further of the employer's business. She is, in fact, on a frolic or detour of her own. Unless the plaintiff could prove that the employer was somehow negligent in its own conduct, there would be no liability on the part of that employer.

CHAPTER 5
STRICT LIABILITY

QUESTIONS:

A. Animals

1.   Use the following facts for Questions 1 through 3. Bill owned four cats. His usual practice was to let them out in the evening just before he went to bed. The cats would roam around the neighborhood for an hour, and then return to the house. After Bill had been doing this for about a year, he got served with a lawsuit from one of the neighbors. It seems that the cats had being going into the neighbor's flower garden and digging up some prized petunias. The neighbor had pictures of the cats doing the damage. The most likely result for the neighbor on this lawsuit on these facts alone is:

   A.   Win since the law provides for strict liability for damage done by roaming animals.

   B.   Win since the law provides for strict liability for damage done by all animals.

   C.   Lose since the law requires proof of intentional conduct for trespass to land.

   D.   Lose unless the neighbor can prove negligence on the part of Bill.

2.   Using the same set of facts as Question 1, prior to filing the lawsuit, the neighbor goes to Bill and explains the problems with the cats digging up the petunias. The neighbor asks Bill to please prevent the cats from doing that. Bill thanks the neighbor for the concern, but does not change his practice at all. Bill continues to let the cats out to roam free at night. After a few days of the cats continuing to dig up the flowers, the neighbor now sues Bill. Under this set of facts, what is the likely result of the lawsuit for the neighbor?

117

A. Win since Bill's failure to act makes the conduct intentional.

B. Win since Bill's failure to act makes the conduct negligent.

C. Win since Bill is strictly liable for his roaming cats.

D. Lose since Bill will not be liable for damage done by cats.

3. Using the same set of facts as Question 1, prior to any of the events occurring, the local government had passed a "leash law." The law provided, "All owners of dogs and cats must keep their animals within an enclosed fenced area. If the animals are allowed outside of a fenced enclosure, the animals must be restrained on a lead or leash not to exceed eight (8) feet in length. Any owner who fails to comply with this statute shall be guilty of a class D misdemeanor. Such violations are punishable by a fine not to exceed $100." The neighbor's lawyer knows of the statute and plans to use it in the litigation concerning the petunias that have been destroyed by the cats. By raising the issue of the statute, the likely outcome of the lawsuit for the neighbor is:

A. Win since the statute will create strict liability for the owner of roaming dogs and cats.

B. Lose since the statute only applies to criminal issues and not civil issues.

C. Win since the neighbor can now use the statute to create a duty using negligence per se.

D. Lose since the neighbor is not strictly liable for roaming cats.

4. Use the following facts for Questions 4 through 7. Clare had a large dog that she kept in the house. She would take the dog for a walk on a leash at least three times a day. One afternoon, while walking the dog, the leash broke and the dog ran loose. The dog ran through a neighbor's yard, knocked over some flower pots, broke the pots and destroyed the plants. The neighbor wants to sue for the harm. The best claim would be:

A. Negligence for allowing the dog to escape the leash.

B. Strict liability for roaming dogs.

C. Strict liability for violation of the common law duty of keeping a dog on a leash.

D. Intent since the dog intentionally ran through the yard.

5. Using the same set of facts as Question 4, assume that the city where Clare lives has a "leash law." The leash law provides, "All owners of dogs and cats must keep their animals within an enclosed fenced area. If the animals are allowed outside of a fenced enclosure, the animals must be restrained on a lead or leash not to exceed eight (8) feet in length. Any owner who fails to comply with this statute shall be guilty of a class D misdemeanor. Such violations are punishable by a fine not to exceed $100." When Clare's dog damages the flower pots and flowers owned by the neighbor, the neighbor wants to use the leash law as a basis for the claim for the damages. How should the neighbor use that statute?

   A.   The statute can be used to create a negligence duty under the doctrine of negligence per se.

   B.   The statute can be used to create a strict liability duty for roaming dogs.

   C.   The statute can be used in intent for the intentional violation of statutes.

   D.   The statute cannot be used in a civil case since it is a criminal statute.

6. Using the same set of facts as Question 4, additional problems arose when Clare's dog got off the leash. In addition to knocking over some flower pots, the dog bit the neighbor. It seems that while the dog was running through the yard, the neighbor came out of her house and tried to get the dog away by waving a broom at the dog. The dog turned on the neighbor and bit her on the leg. The neighbor would now like to sue Clare for the dog bit. What is the most accurate description of the likely outcome?

   A.   The neighbor will win since there is strict liability for dog bites.

   B.   The neighbor will win an action in strict liability if she can show that Clare had knowledge of the vicious tendencies of the dog.

   C.   The neighbor will win an action in strict liability if she can show that the dog had bitten someone before.

   D.   The neighbor will win an action in negligence if she can show that Clare had knowledge of the vicious tendencies of the dog.

7. Using the same set of facts as Question 4, assume that Clare's dog bit the neighbor. The city where Clare lives has the leash law

which states, "All owners of dogs and cats must keep their animals within an enclosed fenced area. If the animals are allowed outside of a fenced enclosure, the animals must be restrained on a lead or leash not to exceed eight (8) feet in length. Any owner who fails to comply with this statute shall be guilty of a class D misdemeanor. Such violations are punishable by a fine not to exceed $100." The neighbor would like to sue for the dog bite and needs to know what the appropriate action will be.

    A. The neighbor should sue for strict liability if Clare had knowledge of the vicious tendencies of the dog.

    B. The neighbor should sue negligence under the doctrine if negligence per se for violation of the leash law.

    C. Both A and B.

    D. The neighbor should sue for strict liability for roaming dogs.

8. Use the following facts for Questions 8 through 9. Cowboy Bob owns a horse. The horse is young and fairly active. Bob is the only one that seems to be able to control the horse. Bob is well aware of how rowdy the horse is and does not let other people ride him. Bob's friend Phil came to Bob's farm to talk about some farming business. While walking through the barn, the Bob's horse came out of his stall and bit Phil. Phil was injured by the bite and wants to sue. The best basis for a claim against Bob would be:

    A. Intent for intentionally keeping a dangerous horse.

    B. Negligence for failing to use reasonable care to control the horse.

    C. Strict liability for attacking animals.

    D. Strict liability for an attacking animal for which the owner had knowledge of the vicious tendency.

9. Using the same set of facts as Question 8, Bob has another friend named Tom. Tom came to visit Bob and asked to ride the horse. Bob said, "Tom, I don't think that is a good idea. You know how crazy my horse is. I think he'll throw you." Tom was adamant and wanted to ride the horse. Bob let Tom ride the horse and the obvious thing happened. Tom had not been on the horse for 5 minutes when the horse started to buck and threw Tom to the ground. If Tom sues Bob for the injuries, what is the likely outcome? You may assume this jurisdiction uses common law defenses.

    A. Tom will lose since he was contributorily negligent.

    B.   Tom will lose since he knowingly and unreasonably assumed a risk.

    C.   Tom will win since there are no defenses to strict liability.

    D.   Tom will win since only consent is a defense to strict liability.

10.   Use the following facts for Questions 10 through 11. George owns a large dog that is used as a watch dog around his house. The dog is kept in the back yard and the yard has a high fence. There are signs on the fence that say, "Danger—Vicious Watch Dog." Fred lives down the street from George and feels like the dog is really not necessary for the area in which they live. Fred likes to irritate George by aggravating the dog. Fred will get near the fence where the dog is kept and call out to the dog. The dog will run to the fence, bark, jump, and snarl. Fred thinks this is very funny. After a while Fred began to poke stick through the fence just to irritate the dog further. One day, Fred got a little carried away. In his excitement to irritate the dog, Fred reached through the fence to hit the dog on the head. The dog avoided the hit, and then bit Fred's hand. The dog did substantial injury to Fred's hand. Fred would like to sue George for keeping a vicious dog. What would George's best claim be to avoid substantial liability? You may assume that this jurisdiction uses modern comparative fault.

    A.   George may claim that he was not aware of the vicious tendency of the dog.

    B.   George may allege comparative fault on the part of Fred.

    C.   George may allege consent on the part of Fred.

    D.   George is going to lose this case since there are no defenses to dog bites by vicious dogs.

11.   Using the same facts as Question 10, George's large vicious dog got out from the fence one day. The dog began to run around the neighborhood. Interestingly enough, once out from the fence, the dog was not quite certain what to do. The dog just seemed to run up and down the streets. The dog saw a small child playing on the sidewalk and the dog ran up to the child. The child began to play with the dog. The dog did not bite the child, but after several minutes of play, the dog happened to bump into the child. The dog was so large and the child so small, the dog knocked the child down. The child was injured by the fall and there has been a lawsuit brought to recover for the child's injuries. The best basis of the claim would be:

    A.   Negligence for not restraining a large dog.

   B.   Strict liability since the owner had knowledge of the vicious
        tendency of the dog.

   C.   Strict liability for roaming dogs.

   D.   Intent since the owner intentionally kept a vicious dog.

12.   Use the following facts for Questions 12 through 14. Dora
wanted to own an exotic pet. She went to a pet store and bought an
iguana. It was a small pet and she was delighted. Dora kept the
iguana in a warm, moist terrarium and fed it well. Needless to say
it grew to a very large size over the course of several years. Dora was
visited by her best friend Clare one afternoon. Although Clare had
heard about the iguana for years, she had never seen it. Clare
begged Dora to show her the pet. Dora finally agreed and took Clare
to the room where the iguana's terrarium was kept. Clare was
amazed at the color and size of the iguana. Clare asked if she could
touch the back of the iguana to see what the skin felt like. Dora said,
"Oh sure. Go ahead and touch it. He is very gentle." Clare carefully
placed her hand in the terrarium, but before she could touch the
back of the iguana, the pet bit her hand. The bite was severe and
caused substantial pain and injury. Clare had to go to the hospital
emergency room for stitches. Clare wants to sue Dora for the injury.
What would be the best claim for Clare to bring?

   A.   Strict liability for an attacking wild animal.

   B.   Strict liability for an attacking animal with known vicious
        tendencies.

   C.   Negligence for failing to use reasonable care in monitoring
        a wild animal.

   D.   Misrepresentation for not warning of the danger of the bite.

13.   Use the same facts as Question 12. If Dora is sued for the
iguana bite to her friend Clare, she would seek ways to avoid
liability. What facts would be most helpful for Dora to avoid
liability?

   A.   Dora did not know the iguana was vicious.

   B.   Clare did not know the iguana was vicious.

   C.   Dora encouraged Clare to touch the iguana.

   D.   Clare voluntarily touched the iguana.

14.   Use the same facts as Question 12. If Dora is sued for the
iguana bite and seeks to show that her friend Clare voluntarily tried
to touch the iguana what is the likely outcome of the litigation?

A. Clare would win since Dora was negligent in not knowing of the dangerous tendency of the iguana.

B. Dora would win since she did not know of the dangerous tendency of the iguana.

C. Clare would win since liability for attacking wild animals is base on strict liability.

D. Dora would win since Clare's conduct would bar recovery under assumption of risk.

15. Use the following facts for Questions 15 through 17. William Roberts lived in rural Arkansas. All of his friends called him Billy Bob. Since Billy Bob was a great University of Arkansas fan, he wanted to own a razorback hog. In addition to being the University of Arkansas mascot, that animal is a species of hog that lives in the forests of Arkansas. They are most common in the Ozark Mountains. Since Billy Bob lives in the Ozark Mountains, he knew how to catch a razorback. Billy Bob was very successful in finding and catching a small, baby male razorback. He kept the hog for about three years, fed it well and watched it grow. When it got to full size, he put it in a pen behind the local general store and would charge tourists $1 to see and photograph the hog. Tourists from the big city of Memphis, Tennessee would drive into the Ozark Mountains in the fall to see the leaves change color. They would see a sign for the live razorback and stop to take a picture. One such tourist was named Fred. Fred stopped at the General Store and asked to see the razorback. Billy Bob was there, explained it would cost $1, collected the money and led Fred out the back door. Fred was a little disappointed in the razorback. Fred had imagined something much different. To Fred, the animal just looked like a large, dark version of a pig that just happened to have tusks. Fred commented on his disappointment. Fred said, "That doesn't look like much. Just looks like a brown pig." Billy Bob said, "Oh you are wrong there. That is a real razorback hog. I caught him myself when he was just a little thing." Before Billy Bob could react, Fred stuck his hand in the pen and said, "See. That thing is just a pig." The razorback gored Fred's hand with a tusk and then bit off two fingers. Fred had to be rushed to a community medical center. It took lengthy surgery to close up the cuts. The fingers could not be saved. If Fred wants to sue Billy Bob for the injuries, what would be the best claim?

A. Negligence for failing to use reasonable care in keeping a wild animal.

B. Strict liability for injury caused by the attacking wild animal.

    C.   Intent for intentionally keeping a wild animal.

    D.   Negligence for failing to use reasonable care in warning Fred.

16.   Use the facts from Question 15. If Billy Bob is sued he would like to defeat the claim as not being appropriately based on strict liability. Billy Bob would like to claim that the razorback is a domestic rather than a wild animal. Are the razorbacks likely to be designated wild or domestic?

    A.   Wild, since they are currently treated as wild animals even in Arkansas.

    B.   Domestic since they are the mascot of the University of Arkansas.

    C.   Domestic since they were once livestock brought over by Hernando De Soto. They escaped and are now classified as feral animals.

    D.   Domestic since the look so much like pigs.

17.   Use the following facts for Questions 17 through 20. Farmer Brown was a pig farmer. She had a very large number of pigs on the farm. She raised the pigs and then sold them to a local slaughter house. She did quite well in the business. She was, in fact, one of the more prosperous farmers in the area. Some of the other farmers felt a little envy at her success. One day, Farmer Brown made a mistake and left the gate to the main pig sty open. Two large pigs wandered out of the sty and began to roam. One was a male (boar) and the other was a female (sow). The two pigs ran to the neighboring farm and found a vegetable garden growing there. The neighboring farm was owned by Farmer Smith. For about an hour, the two pigs rooted around in that neighboring vegetable garden. When Farmer Smith discovered the pigs in his vegetable garden, he was very upset. Those pigs had done substantial damage to the crops growing in the garden. If Farmer Smith wants to sue Farmer Brown for the damage to the vegetable garden, which of the following would be the best claim. Assume for this portion of the question that the jurisdiction has no fencing statutes.

    A.   Negligence for the failure of Farmer Brown to use reasonable care in keeping the gate closed.

    B.   Strict liability for roaming farm animals.

    C.   Intent for Farmer Brown knowing that it was important to keep the gate closed.

    D.   There is no claim for roaming farm animals.

18. Using the same facts from Question 17, assume that the jurisdiction had a "fencing out" statute. Neither Farmer Brown nor Farmer Smith had built a fence. When Farmer Smith sues Farmer Brown for the damage to the vegetable garden, the basis of the claim would be:

    A.   Strict liability since Farmer Brown failed to build a fence to fence the pigs out of Farmer Smith's garden.

    B.   Strict liability since Farmer Smith failed to build a fence to fence the pigs out of his own garden.

    C.   Negligence for the failure of Farmer Brown to use reasonable care to keep the gate closed.

    D.   Negligence for the failure of Farmer Brown to build a fence.

19. Using the same facts from Question 17, assume that the jurisdiction had a "fencing in" statute. Neither Farmer Brown nor Farmer Smith had built a fence. When Farmer Smith sues Farmer Brown for the damage to the vegetable garden, the basis of the claim would be:

    A.   Strict liability since Farmer Brown failed to build a fence to fence the pigs out of Farmer Smith's garden.

    B.   Strict liability since Farmer Smith failed to build a fence to fence the pigs out of his own garden.

    C.   Negligence for the failure of Farmer Brown to use reasonable care to keep the gate closed.

    D.   Negligence for the failure of Farmer Brown to build a fence.

20. Use the same facts from Question 17. When the pigs come onto Farmer Smith's farm, Smith sees the pigs rooting in the garden. He tries to force the pigs out of the garden by yelling at them and throwing some small stones at them. This conduct merely aggravates the pigs and they attack Farmer Smith. They knock him down and butt him with their heads. They also begin to bite him. The worst of the injury is that Farmer Smith suffers a broken leg. If Smith sues Brown for the broken leg, the likely basis of liability would be:

    A.   There is no liability for attacking farm animals.

    B.   Strict liability.

C. Intent.

D. Negligence.

21.   Farmer Brown needs to take some of the pigs to market. The easiest way for her to get them there is to let the pigs walk along the "Farm to Market Road" that goes through the county. Farmer Brown rides on her ATV and "drives" the pigs along the road much like an old western cattle drive. The pigs seem to walk along the road at a casual walk with the expectation by Brown that it would take about 3 hours to get to the slaughter house. While going along the road, the pigs suddenly turn off the road and enter a corn field owned by Farmer Jones. It takes Brown about 30 minutes to get all of the pigs out of the corn field. During that period, the pigs do substantial damage to the corn crop. When Farmer Jones sees what has happened, he wants to sue Farmer Brown for the damage. The best basis of that claim would be:

A. There is no liability for farm animals that wander from a public way onto the fields of another.

B. Strict liability for roaming animals.

C. Negligence for failing to use reasonable care by Farmer Brown.

D. Intent since Farmer Brown knew there was a risk of the pigs entering the fields of others while on the way to the slaughter house.

B. Ultrahazardous and abnormally dangerous activities

22.   Use the following facts for Questions 22 through 23. Assume that these facts are to be decided under the English rule of Rylands v. Fletcher. Mill owner Jones needed to build a small dam on a stream that ran through his property. By building the dam, Jones could cause the water to back up and then have a longer drop as it went across the water wheel that he used for the Mill. Jones built the dam out of large stones that he found on his property. He stacked them up in the stream and caused the water to begin to back up. Several neighbors suggested that Jones should seek the help of knowledgeable dam builders in preparing this dam. It appeared to the neighbors that the stones were unstable and likely to move. Jones assured his neighbors that he knew what he was doing and did not want to pay a huge sum of money for such a simple task. After the dam was built, the water backed up and created a pond behind the dam that was 15 feet deep. During the next heavy rain,

the disaster stuck. The surge of water caused the stones to move, become dislodged from the dam and wash downstream. Water and stones ran down the stream and washed up on neighbor Smith's land. The water and stones did substantial damage to some small buildings on that land. Smith wants to sue Jones for the damage. The basis of the claim would be:

   A.   Strict liability since the dam was not naturally there.

   B.   Negligence since Jones used his own best judgment and not reasonable care.

   C.   Strict liability since the dam was an abnormally dangerous activity.

   D.   Negligence since England has rejected strict liability.

23.   Use the facts from Question 22. Jones recognizes that the rule in Rylands v. Fletcher will apply. Jones argues, however, that stones and water are natural items. Since the stones and water were natural to his land, and he merely rearranged them, Jones believes that he should not be strictly liable. After hearing that argument, the court should rule:

   A.   Jones is correct. His stones and water were natural to the area.

   B.   Jones is mistaken. Although the stones and water were natural to the area, the building of the dam was a non-natural use.

   C.   Jones is correct. Stones and water are naturally occurring items and can never be the basis of strict liability. Only artificially created items can lead to strict liability.

   D.   Jones is mistaken. Although stones and water are natural items, any attempt to move them at all will create strict liability.

24.   Assume that the English rule of Rylands v. Fletcher will apply to the following facts. It was war time in England and it was necessary to build an ammunition plant. The plant was built by a commercial enterprise in an industrial area of England. Unfortunately, after the plant was operating, an accident occurred. Due to an unknown mishap, the plant exploded. With so much explosive material in the plant, substantial damage was done over a broad area. Several of the owners of nearby plants sought to sue the owners of the ammunition plant for the damage done to the property. The basis of liability for this claim would be:

    A.   Strict liability since ammunition is a non-natural use of land.

    B.   Strict liability since ammunition plants are an ultrahazardous activity.

    C.   Negligence since ammunition plants are a natural use of commercial land.

    D.   Negligence since the case could only be proven by res ipsa loquitur.

25.   Use the following facts for Questions 25 through 26. Also assume that the First Restatement of Torts section on strict liability will apply to this series of questions. Daredevil Dan was a stunt pilot. He owned several planes and flew them in county fairs around the country. During the off season, he wanted to make a little extra money. He had noticed that "crop dusting" by airplanes was a common practice in the Mississippi River delta. Pilots would load up small airplanes with fertilizers, fly over the crops and spray the fertilizers from the air. It was necessary to fly within about 10 feet of the ground for this to work. Dan thought this would be exciting and could make a lot of money by expanding the practice to other areas of the country. Dan moved his airplanes to California and offered crop dusting to the wine region. Several wineries hired Dan to spray some fertilizers on their vines. The first day up for Dan in this new job did not go well. On his second pass over the vineyard, Dan did not have his plane climb fast enough after finishing the spraying. The plane hit a very nice visitor center and tasting room building that was just on the edge of the vineyard. Fortunately there was no one in the building and Dan did survive the crash. Unfortunately, the building burned down. The owners of the building want to sue Dan for the loss of the building. The best basis for the claim would be:

    A.   Negligence since Dan failed to use reasonable care in selecting the correct type of airplane for crop dusting.

    B.   Negligence since Dan failed to use reasonable care in getting adequate training for crop dusting.

    C.   Strict liability since crop dusting is a non-natural use of airplanes.

    D.   Strict liability since the risk of harm from crop dusting cannot be eliminated with the use of utmost care.

26.   Use the same facts as Question 25. Dan realizes that the crop dusting is extremely hazardous. In fact, Dan enjoys the thrill. He

claims, however, that he should still not be strictly liable for the harm. Which of the following answers best addresses Dan's concern?

A. Negligence should apply since crop dusting is a common means of fertilizer application.

B. Negligence should apply since a risk/utility analysis will always be the best method of deciding tort cases.

C. Strict liability should apply since crop dusting in California vineyards is not natural.

D. Strict liability should apply since crop dusting, although of common usage in the Mississippi River delta, it is not of common usage in California vineyards.

27. Use the following facts for Questions 27 through 29. Assume the Second Restatement of Torts section on strict liability applies to this series of questions. Pete the Pest Killer ran a fumigation business. He would go into homes and businesses that had bug problems. He could do a little light spraying around the floors on a monthly basis to get rid of common bugs. If a home or office had a serious bug infestation, Pete would offer his special plan. He would go into the home or office on a Friday evening, spray a super strength bug spray and set off several "bug bombs." The "bug bombs" would emit a poison gas that would kill anything in the building. Pete would return to the home or building on Sunday afternoon to open the windows, clean up dead bugs and make sure the area was safe. Other people would have to remain out of the home or building until Monday morning. Pete got a contract to clear bugs from the home of the Baker family. After a few routine sprayings, Pete informed the Baker family that they needed the special plan. Agreeing to Pete's terms, the Baker family left their house on Friday morning, taking the children and all of the pets on a short vacation. The Baker family talked to Pete on Sunday evening and he assured them they could return on Monday. The Baker family returned to their house on Monday evening. The family got home late so they went right to bed. On Tuesday morning, there was chaos. A pet rabbit had died during the evening and the Baker daughter, was terribly ill. The Baker family took the daughter to the emergency room. She remained in the hospital for about a week and ultimately recovered. She had suffered vomiting, diarrhea and dehydration. The long stay in the hospital was to make sure she had fully recovered. It did appear that she recovered fully and would have no lasting injury. Tests showed that the daughter got sick and the rabbit died as a result of inhaling some lingering amounts of one of

the poisons that Pete had used for the special treatment over the weekend. If the family sues Pete for the injuries, the likely basis of the claim will be:

A. Strict liability

B. Negligence

C. Intent

D. Contract

28. Use the facts from Question 27. Since there appears to be some question as to the proper basis of liability, the issue may arise as to which is the appropriate person or body to decide the different issues in the case. Which of the following is the best summary of the role of the judge and jury in such a case?

A. The Jury will decide whether strict liability or negligence will apply and then decide whether the defendant breached the appropriate duty.

B. The judge will decide whether strict liability or negligence will apply and then decide whether the defendant breached the appropriate duty.

C. The jury will decide whether strict liability or negligence will apply and then the judge will decide whether the defendant breached the appropriate duty.

D. The judge will decide whether strict liability or negligence will apply and then the jury will decide whether the defendant breached the appropriate duty.

29. Use the facts from Question 27. In running tests on both the daughter and the rabbit, the experts learned some interesting things. It appears that rabbits are peculiarly allergic to the type of poison that Pete had used. Other pets are not affected. In addition, the daughter had that same peculiar allergy. In the absence of that rare allergy, the daughter would not have suffered any harm from the residual gas in the house. Considering that the injuries were a result of a rare allergy, what should the court consider in reviewing the case?

A. When strict liability applies, the defendant is liable regardless of other related causes to the injury.

B. The court and jury will have to consider the allergy as one possible cause of the injuries and ask whether the injury was still within the risks created by the poisons used.

C.   When there is a possible intervening cause, strict liability does not apply and the case must be one of negligence.

D.   When there is a possible intervening cause, that breaks the chain of cause in all strict liability cases and there is no liability.

30.   Use the following facts for Questions 30 through 33. Acme Construction Company was primarily engaged in road building. As with most road builders, it used dynamite in its work. One day while blasting away a hill side in order to build a road, the dynamite shook the ground around the blast location. About one-half mile away, the home of Farmer Sue was severely shaken. After the tremor, Sue noticed that she had cracks in the walls and cracks in her driveway. It didn't take long to figure out why the cracks occurred or who caused them. Sue wants to bring a claim against Acme. Which if the following is most accurate?

A.   Sue should base the claim in negligence since Acme failed to use reasonable care.

B.   Sue should base the claim in intent since Acme intentionally set off the dynamite.

C.   Sue should base the claim on strict liability since blasting is routinely seen as both an ultrahazardous activity and an abnormally dangerous activity.

D.   Sue cannot use strict liability since dynamite is "of common usage" among road builders.

31.   Use the facts from Question 30. Acme wants to claim that the tremor that went all the way to Farmer Sue's house was the result of a underground fault. The dynamite would not have caused the damage to Sue's house without the existence of that fault. The most likely result of this argument will be:

A.   The existence of an intervening cause will break the chain of causation and result in a verdict for Acme.

B.   The existence of an intervening cause will result in the case being based in negligence rather than strict liability.

C.   The existence of the fault is probably a foreseeable risk and within the risks created by blasting. Acme would still be liable for the injury.

D.   The existence of an intervening cause is irrelevant to a claim for Strict Liability.

32. Use the facts from Question 30. After the initial trouble with the house, Sue took an interest in what Acme was doing. On a day when Acme was going to be doing some additional blasting, Sue went over to watch. Acme tried to get everyone out of the way, but Sue sneaked in close to the blast location. She had brought her camera with her and wanted to get some pictures of Acme's work. When the dynamite went off, Sue got hit by flying rock. She lived but was severely injured. If Sue wants to bring an action for her personal injuries, which of the following is most likely to be accurate?

   A. Acme can raise the defenses of contributory negligence, assumption of risk or comparative fault depending on the defense recognized by the jurisdiction. If Sue is found to have failed to use reasonable care for her own safety and voluntarily encountered a known risk that may reduce or bar her recovery in Strict Liability.

   B. Acme may raise the defenses of contributory negligence, assumption of risk or comparative fault depending on the defense recognized by the jurisdiction. If Sue is found to have failed to use reasonable care for her own safety and voluntarily encountered a known risk that may reduce or bar her recovery but only if the court bases the claim on negligence.

   C. Acme may not raise Sue's conduct as a defense to Strict Liability.

   D. Sue's conduct would completely bar her recovery in Strict Liability. Such conduct defeats all claim in that basis.

33. Use the facts from Question 30. After all of the news about the issues with Acme's use of dynamite, Sneaky Sam decided to go and steal some dynamite. Sam, at night, went to the location where the dynamite was kept. He dismantled the alarm system and broke in the multiple locks on the doors. He found a few sticks of dynamite and carried them outside. Sam just wanted to blow them up. While outside, Sam attached a few blasting caps that he had also stolen, moved off a good distance and then set off the dynamite. Damage was done to several neighboring buildings. The owners of the neighboring buildings want to sue Acme. Which of the following is accurate?

   A. Acme cannot be liable since the damage was the result of a theft.

   B. The theft will be treated as an intervening cause and the jury will have to determine whether the injury was within the risk created. In short, could Acme foresee the possibility of theft?

C. Blasting leads to strict liability for the owner of the dynamite. The issue of theft is irrelevant to the case.

D. The issue of theft will change the case from one of strict liability to one of negligence.

ANSWERS:

A. Animals

1.   The best answer is D. There is strict liability for roaming farm animals, but not for roaming household animals. In the absence of some statute, the plaintiff in this case would have to prove negligence on the part of the owner of the animals. In addition, although intent is usually a requirement for the old common law tort of trespass to land, there is always a claim for negligence for doing injury to another's person or property. If a person or some instrumentality of that person goes on the land of another and causes harm, there would be a claim for negligence.

2.   The best answer is B. Much like the previous question, Bill's only possible liability would be based on negligence. Clearly if Bill was intentionally having the cats dig up the flower bed, there would be a claim for intent. It seems unlikely that the neighbor would be able to prove that Bill was intentionally having the cats do anything. Cats are not known for following the instructions and dictates of owners. The better claim would still be negligence. Since Bill is now on notice of the conduct of the cats, the neighbor may allege that a reasonable person would do something to avoid having the injury occur. Strict liability is still not appropriate for roaming household animals.

3.   The best answer is C. A close reading of the statute does indicate that it is a minor criminal statute. It does not provide for civil recovery. It is clear, however, that using minor criminal statutes to create duties in negligence is a traditional concept in tort law. The neighbor can use the statute to create a duty under the doctrine of negligence per se. It should be noted that the leash law created for the question is not typical of community leash laws. Most leash laws do not include cats. Communities tend to pass leash laws to control dogs but allow cats to run free.

4.   The correct answer is A. The only possible claim that is available in the list of answer is the possibility of negligence. There was no strict liability for roaming dogs nor was there a common law leash duty. The law of intent deals with the intent of humans and does not try to determine the mental state of animals. Since the only possible claim here is negligence, recovery will be difficult. The neighbor will have to prove that Clare failed to use reasonable care in keeping her dog under control.

5.   The correct answer is A. As with other examples of minor criminal statutes, this statute could be used to create a negligence duty under the doctrine of negligence per se.

6.   The best answer is B. There is a form of strict liability for dog bites, but it is not an absolute liability. In order to use the strict liability, the plaintiff must prove that the dog owner had knowledge of the vicious tendencies of the animal. This element of proof is called "scienter." This element of proof is sometimes referred to as the "one bite rule." The theory is that if the dog has bitten someone before, then the owner will have knowledge of the vicious tendency. It is sometimes mistakenly believed that the rule means that "every dog is entitled to one free bite." That is not true. Although a prior bite will clearly place the owner on notice that the dog is vicious, it does not take a prior bite to prove that. A dog owner may be knowledgeable about the vicious tendencies of a dog without the dog having bitten anyone before. As such, a prior bite may be evidence of vicious tendency, but evidence of the prior bite is not necessary to prove the element of "scienter." If, of course, the neighbor could show that Clare had knowledge of the vicious tendencies of the dog and failed to use reasonable care to keep the dog on a leash, then an action in negligence might also be appropriate. The claim for strict liability, however, would be easier to prove since there is no requirement of proving the failure to use reasonable care.

7.   The best answer is C. It is possible to sue for strict liability if Clare had knowledge of the vicious tendency of the dog. If, however, Clare did not have knowledge of that vicious tendency, then the action will not lie. The leash law does provide an easy secondary remedy in negligence. The neighbor should sue on both bases in order to make sure of recovery.

8.   The answer is D. Although the rule that allows strict liability for knowledge of the vicious tendency of animals is usually found to apply to dogs, it does apply to all domestic animals. In this case, it appears that Bob was aware of the vicious tendencies of the horse. As such, there would be strict liability for the attack upon proof of that scienter.

9.   The best answer is B. Simple contributory negligence has not been a defense to strict liability. Where, for example, a person fails to use reasonable care to discover a dangerous risk that would not be a defense. Courts have felt, however, that where a plaintiff knew and understood a risk and then failed to use reasonable care in encountering that risk, that conduct should be a defense. Traditionally such conduct would be viewed as a form of unreasonable assumption of risk. Since a majority of courts today use comparative fault, the law is less clear. It does appear that the conduct of the plaintiff in encountering a dangerous risk would be allowed into evidence to reduce the recovery.

10.   The best answer is B. George should not try to claim that he was unaware of the vicious tendencies of the dog. He posted signs saying that he had "scienter." The best defense would be to raise comparative fault. Jurisdictions that use comparative fault are allowing such a defense to claims for strict liability.

11.   The answer is A. Although the owner has knowledge of the vicious tendency of the dog, the knowledge relates to biting. There is no causal connection between the known vicious tendencies and the injury that occurred. Because of that absence of connection, the best claim for relief would be negligence.

12.   The answer is A. There is strict liability for attacking wild animals. There is no need to prove the element of scienter, or knowledge, as there is with attacking domestic animals. Misrepresentation would be inappropriate since there is no indication that Dora knew the animal was vicious.

13.   The answer is D. The best way to avoid liability would be to prove a defense. Since this is strict liability for attacking wild animals, the best defense would be something like unreasonable assumption of risk. Even in comparative fault jurisdictions, the proof that Clare voluntarily tried to touch the iguana would help prove that she failed to use reasonable care for her own safety. Such evidence would be admissible for comparative fault. The fact that Dora did not know of the vicious tendency of the animal is irrelevant to the claim or defense. The fact that Clare did not know that the animal was dangerous would not help Dora. In fact, such evidence would reduce the degree of fault on the part of the Clare. The fact that Dora encouraged Clare to touch the animal does not seem important.

14.   The best answer is C. Liability for attacking wild animals is based on strict liability. Answer D does have some attraction. It appears that Clare's conduct would have met traditional rules of assumption of risk. As strict liability arose, however, courts were not inclined to allow simple assumption of risk to bar recovery. Courts were more likely to require something like unreasonable assumption of risk before recovery was barred. In this case, Clare had no knowledge of the dangerous tendency of the animal. In addition, most jurisdictions have adopted comparative fault. As a part of that adoption, many jurisdictions have merged the traditional rules of assumption of risk into comparative fault. The traditional behavior of assuming the risk may now reduce but not bar recovery. The most likely outcome of this litigation is that Clare would win. The jury may reduce her damages by some percentage because of her voluntary action of trying to touch the iguana.

15.   The answer is B. There is strict liability for injuries caused by attacking wild animals. In this part of the question, it appears that the razorback is a wild animal.

16.   The answer is A. Razorbacks would be treated as wild animals. The issue is actually a difficult one. In the British Empire, there were animals that may have been considered domestic in some places, but wild in others. An elephant would have been considered a domestic beast of burden in India, but a wild animal in London. In addition, llamas are considered beasts of burden in some parts of South America but would probably be considered wild in the United States.

17.   The best answer is B. At common law, in the absence of fencing statutes, there was strict liability for roaming farm animals.

18.   The best answer is C. A "fencing out" statute would place the burden on the injured farmer to keep other's livestock out of his or her own field. If Farmer Smith had built that fence, the Smith could have sued Brown in strict liability when the pigs came through the fence. Since there was no fence the appropriate remedy would be in negligence.

19.   The answer is A. Where there is a "fencing in" statute, an owner of livestock has a duty to build a fence to keep the livestock contained. If the livestock escape, then there is strict liability.

20.   The best answer is D. Strict liability applies to attacking wild animals. For domestic animals, there would need to be proof of knowledge of the vicious tendency of the animals in order for strict liability to apply. Since these facts do not suggest any such knowledge, the best claim would be in negligence.

21.   The best answer is C. There is no strict liability for farm animals that leave a public way and enter the fields of another. If the animals went through that field and entered yet another farmer's field, there would be strict liability. For entry onto the first field off a public way, however, the only claim would be negligence.

B. Ultrahazardous and abnormally dangerous activities

22.   The answer is A. This rule reflects the use of strict liability in England under Rylands v. Fletcher. The rule has been interpreted to allow strict liability where someone brings something on the land that was not naturally there, that instrumentality escapes and causes harm.

23.   The answer is B. Although stones and water are naturally occurring items, the building of a dam is a non-natural use. It is not, however, any movement of items that creates the non-natural use. In fact, the natural—non-natural distinction that England has used creates some difficulty. The courts have had to review numerous cases to try to figure out whether items are natural or non-natural. The next question raises that issue again.

24.   The answer is C. As odd as this answer seems, it reflects a ruling from an actual case in England. The ruling also reflects the difficulty in applying the natural—non-natural distinction. It may seem that studying a rule from England, especially one that seems impossible to apply, would make little sense for a law student in the United States. The reality of the situation is, however, that the natural—non-natural distinction has found some use in the United States. As states in the U.S. began to adopt a form of strict liability, those states would routinely reject the theories of Rylands v. Fletcher. The states would, however, adopt some form of abnormal or ultrahazardous use. As a part of those doctrines, the states would look to see where the activity under scrutiny in the litigation was "of a common use." It was thought that things that were of a "common use" should only be subject to negligence. Things that were of "uncommon use" could possibly be subject to strict liability. The problem with the "common use" doctrine is that the courts would begin to look to see where the activity was "common" to the area. In some ways, "common use" began to take on some of the analysis ideas of "natural—non-natural" uses. Studying the English cases helps to see the background to the modern abnormally dangerous or ultrahazardous activity doctrine.

25.   The best answer is D. The First Restatement of Torts saw the necessity of use strict liability for "Ultrahazardous Activities." These were activities that the risk of harm could not be eliminated even with the use of utmost care. It would appear that crop dusting is so dangerous that it fits this definition. The rule in the First Restatement, however, had a second element that is not presented in the possible answers to this question. Look at the next question for that issue.

26.   The answer is D. This question highlights the second element of strict liability under the First Restatement of Torts. Strict liability applies only if the activity is "not of common usage." The "common usage" element has some of the same problems as the "natural use" element of Rylands v. Fletcher. Courts may reach different conclusions about the nature of a common use. It would appear that crop dusting would probably be found to be a common use in the Mississippi River delta, but not in California. One of the

other possible answers suggested negligence since risk/utility is a common analysis technique in torts. Notice that the use of strict liability is actually a continuation of a form of risk/utility. In strict liability examples, the risk of the activity has reached such a high level, as compared to its utility, that the courts have increased the likelihood of liability on the part of the defendant. As such, strict liability can be viewed as merely another part of using risk/utility to reach an answer in a tort case.

27. The answer is A. This appears to be a question that would be appropriate for strict liability under the Second Restatement. Unlike the First Restatement which used two elements to determine whether strict liability ought to apply, the Second Restatement used a balancing test of applying six factors. This factor analysis is more like a risk/utility analysis than the First Restatement. The court would have to review such factors as the risk of harm as compared to the commonality of the use. Those two major issues were broken down into the six factors. It is interesting that the Third Restatement of Torts has shown a return to the use of elements in a manner much like the First Restatement. It will take some time and research into particular jurisdictions to see which of the analysis techniques will become the majority rule.

28. The answer is D. Strict liability and negligence cases are, in fact, handled the same way in the courts. The judge will review the basic facts and decide whether strict liability or negligence is appropriate. In determining whether strict liability will apply, the judge will have to use the elements of the first restatement or the factors of the second restatement. If strict liability is to apply, the jury will decide the remaining fact questions. Those fact questions will include whether the defendant engaged in the particular conduct, whether there was an injury, and causation.

29. The best answer is B. Causation remains a troubling issue in strict liability just as it is in negligence. Just because the case is in strict liability does not mean that it is one of absolute liability. The court must still submit the issue of causation to the jury. The causation issue does not appear to be as complex in strict liability as it does in negligence. The courts would appear to use some test of does the injury appear to have been within the risk created. In the alternative, the courts may ask if the injury was one that was generally foreseeable from the conduct. It would seem that an allergy to poisons would be a foreseeable risk of using poison.

30. The correct answer is C. Blasting has routinely been seen as an appropriate activity for strict liability. It is the type of activity that creates a risk that cannot be eliminated with the use of utmost care.

In addition, although dynamite is of common usage among road builders, it is not of common usage in the community at large. Even using the second Restatement, courts have assumed that applying the risk/utility balancing has left the risk of dynamite high enough to create strict liability.

31.   The answer is C. Intervening causes must be considered in strict liability cases. The test is whether the injury was within the risk created. The court may also seek to determine if the risk was foreseeable within the conduct being done. It would appear that underground faults are sufficiently common to require companies using dynamite to be aware of the issue. The intervening cause of the underground fault will not defeat liability.

32.   The answer is A. Most jurisdictions allow the conduct of the plaintiff to be introduced in cases of strict liability as a way to reduce or bar recovery. It appears that getting in close to a blasting location, especially after having suffered some harm from blasting would be relevant evidence. It seems that Sue knew and understood the risk and voluntarily and unreasonably encountered it.

33.   The answer is B. This again raises the issue of causation and strict liability. The issue would be treated the same way as the other causation issues. It does seem that Acme may have taken all reasonable precautions to avoid this theft. Acme may escape liability for this series of injuries.

CHAPTER 6
NUISANCE

QUESTIONS:

A. Public

1.   Acme Chemical Company was discovered to be dumping a toxic chemical into a river that ran near its plant. The state's attorney general wants to bring an action against the company to force it to stop dumping the chemical into the river. The best claim for relief would be:

    A.   Nuisance

    B.   Negligence

    C.   Trespass to land

    D.   Strict liability

2.   When a chemical company dumps toxic chemicals in a river, the action in public nuisance is appropriate since the chemicals will cause:

    A.   the river to smell bad.

    B.   the river to be polluted.

    C.   the fish in the river to die.

    D.   all of the above.

3.   John Jones opens a small café where he sells sodas, candy, and newspapers. He also runs an illegal gambling game known as "the numbers." When the police find out about the gambling, John is arrested. If the local public prosecutor also wants to sue John for public nuisance to recover damages, what is the likely result?

A. The nuisance action will be barred since the criminal action supersedes it.

B. The nuisance action will be barred since allowing the civil action would be double jeopardy.

C. The nuisance action can proceed as a protection of the public rights.

D. The nuisance action can proceed only if the criminal action fails.

4. Jane Smith was driving a truck along a state highway. The truck was loaded with dirt. The loaded portion of the truck failed and dumped the whole load of dirt right in the middle of the highway. Jane was able to move her truck out of the highway, but the state police had to close the highway for several hours. A truck and a front end loader had to be brought from the state department of highways to clear the highway. The state wants to sue Jane for the cost of clearing the highway. If the state brings a nuisance action for that cost, the likely result would be:

A. The action will proceed since interference with a public highway is a public nuisance.

B. The action will proceed only if the highway can prove that Jane's conduct was intentional.

C. The action will be barred since the state highway department is supported by tax money and Jane is a taxpayer. Jane has, therefore, already paid for the work of the highway department.

D. The action will be barred unless an individual was hurt and that individual wants to sue Jane for a negligent automobile action.

5. Joan Roe wants to open as small grocery/convenience store near an area that appears to be primarily residential. She figures that the residents will come to her store since there are no other commercial properties in the area. Joan discovers that this area happens to have no zoning laws, so she opens her business. The state attorney general brings a nuisance action and seeks to close her business. The best answer would be:

A. The state must pass zoning laws for this area or anyone can feel free to make any use of the property.

B. An action in nuisance is the best way to resolve the dispute. Prior to zoning laws, nuisance actions were the way to resolve land use issues.

C. Zoning is necessary since an action to close the business would be a taking without just compensation.

D. Although there are no zoning laws, the state attorney general will need to find some other criminal law that Joan Roe is violating in order to close her down.

6. A company is releasing toxic chemicals in the air. John Smith wants to sue the company for a public nuisance. John claims that the chemicals in the air make his eyes burn. Can John sue the company for a public nuisance?

A. Yes. Anyone injured by a public nuisance can sue.

B. Yes. If John's injury is greater in degree of harm then other people's injury by this private nuisance.

C. No. The action should be brought by a representative of the public like an attorney general.

D. No. A private individual can never bring an action for public nuisance.

7. Use the following facts for Questions 7 through 10. Logging Company was hauling logs along a state highway. One of their trucks dropped a full load of logs on the highway. The highway had to be closed for three days in order to get the logs cleared. Can a state attorney general bring an action for public nuisance for the damages caused by the accident?

A. No. The state has a duty to maintain highways and cannot shift that burden to others by way of lawsuits.

B. No. Only specifically injured people can sue for harm for interference with a public highway.

C. Yes. If the state can prove that the driver of the truck or the company was violating some other law, the state can also sue for the damages caused by the blocked highway.

D. Yes. Blocking a public road is a public nuisance which may be brought by a public representative.

8. Use the facts from Question 7. Carl drove to and from work using that public road. For the three days that the road was blocked, Carl had to driver an extra 25 miles a day to get to and from work. Carl wants to sue the Logging Company for the additional mileage. What is the likely result of his lawsuit?

A. Carl cannot recover since his injury is merely different in degree from the general public.

    B. Carl cannot recover since his injury is merely different in kind from the general public.

    C. Carl can recover for a private nuisance for the harm he has suffered.

    D. Carl can recover since his injury is different in kind from the general public.

9. Use the facts from Question 7. Betty was driving along the same highway as the logging truck, just as the truck lost its load of logs. Betty was right behind the logging truck and the logs hit Betty's car. Betty wants to sue for the injuries she suffered to her car. What is the likely result of that lawsuit?

    A. Betty cannot recover since her injury is merely different in degree from the general public.

    B. Betty cannot recover since her injury is merely different in kind from the general public.

    C. Betty can recover for a private nuisance for the harm she has suffered.

    D. Betty can recover since her injury is different in kind from the general public.

10. Use the facts from Question 7. Linda owns real property (a farm) along the highway where the logging truck dropped a load of logs. On the day it happened, Linda needed to get to her farm. When she got near the gate, she discovered that the highway was closed and she could not get to her farm. Although she explained her problem to the police and they were very sympathetic, there was no way that Linda could get past the logs to her farm gate. Linda wants to sue the Logging Company for the damages she suffered by being unable to get to her farm for three days. What is the likely result of that lawsuit?

    A. Linda cannot recover since her injury is merely different in degree from the general public.

    B. Linda cannot recover since her injury is merely different in kind from the general public.

    C. Linda can recover for a private nuisance for the harm she has suffered.

    D. Linda can recover since her injury is different in kind from the general public.

B. Private

11.   Carol wants to sue her next door neighbor for making noise very late at night. Carol goes to an attorney in order to see what can be done. The attorney tells Carol that she can sue the neighbor for a private nuisance. What will Carol need to proof in order to bring the private nuisance action?

>   A.   The neighbor is creating a harm to the public's health or safety.

>   B.   The neighbor is creating interfering with Carol's use and enjoyment of her land.

>   C.   The neighbor is interfering with Carol's exclusive possession of her land.

>   D.   Carol cannot bring an action for private nuisance. It must be brought by the public representative.

12.   Fred owns a large farm in a rural area. He primarily raises cattle and pigs. His farm has substantial road frontage along a state highway. Sarah owns a small lot where she lives in a small house. That lot is on the corner of the state highway and the county highway intersection. This lot and house is the only lot that Fred does not own along the highway. If he could buy this lot, he would have continuous ownership of land along the state highway all the way to the intersection of the county highway. Fred has offered to purchase the land from Sarah numerous times, but she refuses. Fred has even offered more than the property is worth, but Sarah still refuses. Fred decided to put a feed lot right up beside the property owned by Sarah. A feed lot is a small plot that is fenced and holds a substantial number of livestock. The livestock are kept in the enclosed area in order to gain weight rapidly before taking to market. With a small number of livestock in a small area, the odor is horrible. Sarah asked Fred to move the feedlot, but Fred claims he has a right to put the feedlot anywhere he wants. If Sarah sues Fred for having to endure the odor, her best claim would be:

>   A.   Private nuisance.

>   B.   Pubic nuisance with an injury different in kind.

>   C.   To convince the local attorney general to bring an action for public nuisance.

>   D.   Strict liability.

13.   Bob and Carol own a house in a residential area. Their home is a short distance from the corner. The corner lot remained vacant for

some years. A corporation bought the corner lot and had it rezoned for a commercial use. The corporation then built a large grocery store on the lot. The grocery store is open 24 hours a day. The increased traffic around the store has started to cause noise in the area. In addition, the store employees do not do a good job of cleaning up the parking lot. Bob and Carol constantly have to pick up debris that is left in the grocery store parking lot and then blows into their yard. If Bob and Carol want to get some recovery, the likelihood of success is:

A. Good, if they can get the local attorney general to sue for public nuisance.

B. Bad, since the zoning change bars any action against the grocery store.

C. Good, if they sue for the blowing debris as a private nuisance.

D. Bad, since zoning is a non-reviewable governmental function.

14. Ted and Alice live in a residential area. They have had some problems with their neighbor, Carl. Carl is difficult to live near. Carl likes to play loud music all night long. Ted and Alice finally got tired of being kept awake and asked Carl if he would please turn off the music earlier in the evening or use ear plugs to listen to his music after ten in the evening. Carl got terribly mad at Ted and Alice for even suggesting such a thing. Carl began to use ear plugs to listen to music, but began to put flood lights in his back yard. Once a week, Carl would purchase and mount another flood light in his back yard. After about a month, the whole neighbor seemed to glow from the amount of light shining from Carl's yard. Needless to say, Ted and Alice now had a problem with all of the light coming into their area. They tried heavier shades with thick curtains. Carl just added more floodlights. After a while, Ted and Alice wanted to sue. What would be their best claim?

A. Trespass to land.

B. Trespass to chattels.

C. Public nuisance with an injury different in kind.

D. Private nuisance.

C. Substantial harm

15. Bill grows a rare strain of violets in his yard. They are very rare because of their vulnerability to almost everything. They are

one of the most difficult plants to grow. One day Bill notices that his violets are beginning to wilt and die. He takes several soil and air samples before realizing what is causing the problem. It appears that Bill's neighbor, Carl, is cooking out on a grill approximately two Saturday nights a month. Although this does not seem like much, the small amount of smoke put in the air by the home grill is enough to harm the very rare type of violet. When Carl refuses to stop cooking hamburgers on his grill twice a month, Bill sues for private nuisance. What is the likelihood of success for Bill?

A. Bad. The harm to the rare violets is not sufficiently substantial to force Carl to give up grilling twice a month.

B. Good. Causing any disruption of the use and enjoyment of land is a private nuisance.

C. Bad. Grilling hamburgers on a Saturday evening is a Constitutional right.

D. Good, since this is a public nuisance and Bill suffers an injury different in kind.

16. Acme Chemical Company was dumping chemicals in a local stream. The chemicals were getting into the local water supply. It became obvious that people in the town were coming down with a greater than average percentage of cancers. The attorney general sued to get an injunction to stop the pollution by Acme Chemical. Should the attorney general be successful in the action?

A. Yes. If, but only if, there is a specific federal regulation that prohibits the pollution of the specific chemical that the company dumped in the stream.

B. No. Some incidence of cancer in a small community is not sufficient harm to justify a nuisance action.

C. Yes. The increased risk of cancer is sufficient harm for an action for public nuisance.

D. No. Although there is some increase in cancer, there is no interference with anyone's use and enjoyment of land.

D. Bases of liability

17. Fred noticed that the small factory that was next to his warehouse, would, occasionally, emit a foul smelling smoke. Fred mentioned this to the owner of the factory. The factory owner was concerned and noted that the presence of the foul smell would

indicate a particularly corrosive chemical was escaping. The owner promised to look into it. Fred didn't say anything for about a year, until he noticed that the shingles on his roof were falling apart. A chemical expert came to look at Fred's roof and identified the damage as caused by a corrosive chemical probably being emitted by the nearby factory. Fred wants to sue for the damage to his roof. In order to win, he must prove which of the following?

A.   The elements of private nuisance.

B.   The elements of private nuisance and negligence.

C.   The elements of private nuisance and intent.

D.   The elements of private nuisance and strict liability.

18.   Pam owned a small home in a rural area. A developer bought up a large tract of land and started making plans to build a large residential neighborhood on that tract. In order to put in streets, sidewalks and utilities, the developer had to do some blasting with dynamite. After a particularly long day of blasting about three miles from Pam's house, Pam noticed cracks had developed in the foundation of her house. An expert told Pam the cracks would have been caused by the blasting. When Pam asked the developer to help her pay for the damage to her home, he refused. He said that he was following all appropriate industry standards in using the explosives. He did nothing wrong. He was sorry her house foundations had cracks, but that was not his problem. Can Pam recovery for a private nuisance against the developer.

A.   No. It does not appear that the developer was negligent.

B.   Yes. This is a private nuisance and a private nuisance may be based on intent, negligence and strict liability.

C.   No. There was no intent to harm Pam's house.

D.   Yes. Developers are absolutely liable for harm they cause.

19.   A road building company was working to widen a major highway. In order to complete the work, it was necessary to use dynamite to remove some of the rock and stone in the way of the project. During the first day of blasting, a farmer that lived 2 miles away from the blasting zone, felt his house tremble every time the explosions went off. Before the blasting started on the second day, the farmer notified the company of the problem with the blasting and the shock of the blast. The company owner realized that the workers had been a little careless the day before, but really didn't care. The owner decided that the work was a little behind schedule

and he wasn't going to do anything to slow it down. The blasting from the second day's work caused structural damage to the farmer's home. If the farmer sues the company for private nuisance for the interference to the use and enjoyment of his land, what would be an appropriate basis of liability?

    A. Intent.

    B. Negligence.

    C. Strict liability.

    D. Any of the above.

E. Remedy

20. A factory owned by Joyce allowed toxic chemicals to escape from a smokestack. A nearby warehouse owned by Fred suffered roof damage due to the corrosive nature of the chemical. Joyce has remedied the problem to make sure that the factory no longer allows the chemical to escape. Fred would like to recovery sufficient money in damages to repair his warehouse roof. Can he recovery that money in a nuisance action?

    A. No. Nuisance claims are only designed to stop the continuation of the nuisance. No damages are allowed.

    B. Yes. If Fred can prove that the escape of the chemical was due to the intentional conduct of Joyce, damages are recoverable.

    C. No. Nuisance claims only allow recovery by the representative of the public, not by individual members of the public.

    D. Yes. Nuisance claims allow recovery of damages for harm caused.

21. Joan and Tom own a home in a neighborhood that has some houses and some small stores. One of the stores, a small grocery, has flood lights in their parking lot. Some of the lights have, over time, shifted so that a substantial amount of the light shines in the windows of the house of Joan and Tom. Joan and Tom asked the store owner to please turn the lights back towards his own parking lot, but he responded, "That is too much trouble and will cost me money. I'm not going to do it." Joan and Tom would like to bring an action to get an injunction to force the store owner to redirect the floodlights. Will Joan and Tom be successful?

   A. Yes. Since a private nuisance protects a right in land, injunctive relief is available.

   B. No. Injunction are equitable remedies. Such remedies are only available when damages at law are inadequate. Since damages may be recovered in a nuisance action, that is the only recovery allowed for private nuisance.

   C. Yes. It will, however, require that the local attorney general decide that the lights are a public nuisance.

   D. No. Zoning laws must be consulted to determine if an injunction is allowed.

22.   The corporation owns a factory in a town. The factory has discharged chemicals into the local river for approximately 30 years. Unfortunately, the chemicals have also gotten into the town's water supply. Recently the state health department has determined that the chemicals have polluted the river, caused deformities in the fish in that river and cancer in a large number of the town's residents. The state attorney general has brought an action for pubic nuisance to seek an injunction to force the factory to stop dumping the chemical in the river. Can the state get that injunction?

   A. No. Injunctive relief is available for private nuisance but not public nuisance.

   B. Yes. Injunctive relief is available for private nuisance and public nuisance.

   C. No. Damages to clean up the water supply can be awarded, but there is nothing unique about public health to allow the use of equitable remedies.

   D. Yes. Injunctive relief is available if the chemical is on the Federal Banned Substances lists.

23.   A small town has a factory that employs most of the residents of the town. The factory is also the largest tax paying entity in the town. The owners of the factory estimate that it cost several millions of dollars to build the factory 20 years ago and still require around two hundred thousand dollars a year for maintenance. The factory, unfortunately, is noisy. The humming and banging from the factory can be heard all over town. Fred worked at the factory for 10 years until he was fired about a year ago. Fred sued the owners of the factory for firing him, but his case was dismissed. The owners had the right to fire Fred under the employment contract. Since Fred still lives in the town, Fred now wants to sue the factory owners for

private nuisance. Fred wants to claim that the noise is an interference with the use and enjoyment of his home. Fred wants an injunction to force the factory to be quiet. Can Fred get that injunction?

A. Probably no. Fred could only get an injunction if he could prove that the noise was conduct that would lead to strict liability.

B. Probably yes. A private nuisance is an interference with an interest in land. Injunctions are available to protect the natural resource.

C. Probably no. The "balance of the equities" favors the factory over Fred.

D. Probably yes. The courts must protect the individual over large corporations.

F. Defenses

24. Bill and Edna had lived in a city for their whole lives. Upon retirement, they wanted to move to a rural area. It was a dream they had always had. They drove out into the country looking for a new home. They found a small house on a one acre lot in the country. They loved the setting. The house was situated between two farms. Bill and Edna bought the house and went back into town to begin preparations to move. Bill and Edna retired from their jobs, sold their condo in the town, and had all of their belongings moved to the country home. It did not take long before Bill and Edna got upset. It appears that one farm near them was a pig farm and the other farm was a chicken farm. The pig farm would tend to give off a bad odor on warm days and the roosters on the other farm would begin to crow around 5:00 each morning. Bill and Edna could not get any sleep because of the chickens and they felt the odor from the pigs was unbearable. When no one else in the area seemed to even understand what their concern was, they wanted to sue to stop the odor and the chickens. If they consulted a lawyer about the matter, which of the following is the most accurate advice the lawyer could give them?

A. "Moving to a nuisance" is a form of assumption of risk. It will bar any recovery for nuisance.

B. "Moving to a nuisance" is a form of assumption of risk. It will bar injunctive relief but allow the plaintiffs to get damages.

    C.   "Moving to a nuisance" is a form of assumption of risk. It will bar money damages but allow plaintiffs to get an injunction.

    D.   "Moving to a nuisance" is not a bar to recovery, but will be a factor to determine whether there is substantial harm and where the "balances of the equities" lie.

25.   Farmer Joan knew that the county garbage and debris clean up service would be around the following morning picking up debris. She cut up several logs and placed them just on the road in front of her farm. During the night, Fred was trying to drive home along that same road. Unfortunately, a fog had settled in and it was hard to see the road. Fred hit the logs that Joan had left in the road and had an accident. Fred wants to sue Joan. This appears to be a public nuisance with Fred suffering an injury different in kind. Joan believes she should have a defense since Fred should have been more careful. Which is the best answer?

    A.   Joan would have to prove that Fred consented to the contact since Joan's conduct was intentional.

    B.   Joan can bar Fred's recovery since his conduct was contributorily negligent.

    C.   Since Joan's conduct is subject to strict liability there is no defense.

    D.   Fred's conduct will bar recovery since he knew or in the exercise of reasonable care should have known of the garbage and debris collection in the county the next morning.

ANSWERS:

A. Public

1.   The answer is A. The best claim for relief is in nuisance. It would actually be a public nuisance. Negligence is a basis of liability that may be used in nuisance, but nuisance would be the claim. The same holds true for strict liability. The nuisance claim may be based on strict liability. Trespass to land is an intentional tort to be brought by the person with the right of possession to the land. The attorney general would be the wrong party for such a claim.

2.   The answer is D. An action for public nuisance can be brought to protect the public from an interference with the public's right to health, safety, convenience, or morals. The pollution of the river, together with the smell and dead fish, would qualify.

3.   The answer is C. Public nuisance claims are to protect the public's right to health and safety. Many public nuisance claims are based on the violation of minor criminal laws. Bringing the criminal action to punish the wrongdoer and seeking civil damages for the harm to the public would be appropriate.

4.   The answer is A. Interference with a public highway is a public nuisance. Nuisance can be based on intent, negligence or strict liability, so there is no need to require proof of intent.

5.   The answer is B. Prior to the enactment of zoning laws, actions in nuisance were used to resolve land use disputes. It is frequently said that a nuisance is merely a thing in the wrong place. It is sometimes stated that a nuisance is a "pig in a parlor." Placing a commercial enterprise in a residential area may be placing a thing in the wrong place. The courts will have to resolve the issue in a nuisance action.

6.   The best answer is C. Ordinarily, a public representative should bring an action for public nuisance. There are exceptions to this rule, however. Because of the exception to that rule, answer D is not correct.

7.   The answer is D. Blocking a public road is a public nuisance. A representative of the public can bring an action for damages caused by that conduct.

8.   The answer is A. In order for a private citizen to bring an action for public nuisance, that citizen must suffer an injury different in

kind from the general public. This injury to Carl is merely one of degree. The injury to the public is an inconvenience due to the blocked road. Carl has an injury greater in degree since he travels the road more often than many people.

9.   The answer is D. Betty's injury is different in kind from the general public. Although the public suffered an injury of inconvenience in travel, Betty suffered damage to personal property.

10.   The best answer is C. Linda is prevented from entering her real property. She is suffering and interference with the use and enjoyment of her land. That is a private nuisance. Answer D would also be a good answer. Linda may also be able to claim a public nuisance for an injury different in kind. The interference with her real property rights is different in kind and not merely degree from the general public.

B. Private

11.   The answer is B. A private nuisance is an action to recover for damages for the interference of a person's use and enjoyment of their land.

12.   The answer is A. The best action would be for a private nuisance. By placing the feedlot, with all of its odors, near Sarah's house, Fred is interfering with her use and enjoyment of her real estate. It would be possible to seek a public nuisance with an injury different in kind, but the private nuisance is better. Since Fred intentionally placed his feedlot next to her home, the nuisance action would be based on intent.

13.   The answer is C. After the zoning change, the corporation is allowed to place a commercial use on the property. Bob and Carol cannot sue because of the location of the grocery store. They can, however, sue to protect from inappropriate uses of the property. Although the corporation has the right to run a grocery store, they must run it correctly. Allow garbage to blow around the neighborhood would be a private nuisance.

14.   The answer is D. Trespass to land is a tort that is used to remedy interference with the exclusive right of possession of land. It usually requires some physical invasion of the property. Light would not qualify in law as a physical invasion. Private nuisance is intended to protect against the interference with the use and enjoyment of land. This appears to be a private nuisance.

C. Substantial harm

15.   The answer is A. Nuisance actions, both public and private require proof of "substantial harm." In some ways, this requirement

is a balancing of the rights and obligations of all citizens to behave in a way that does not cause harm to others. Just because Bill opts to grow a very rare type of plant, that does not give him the right to force others in the neighborhood to give up normal activities.

16. The answer is C. Both public and private nuisance actions require some proof of substantial harm. This would be a public nuisance action since it threatens the pubic health. An increased risk of cancer would be a sufficient "substantial harm."

D. Bases of liability

17. The answer is A. Nuisance is an area of the law and not a separate basis of liability. Public and private nuisance claims may be based on intention or negligent conduct. In addition, they may be based on conduct which gives rise to strict liability. The conduct that gives rise to nuisance may start as negligent or strict liability, but become intentional after the wrongdoer is notified of the harm that is being caused. In this question, for example, it appears that the escaping chemicals may be occurring due to negligence or even innocent conduct at the very beginning. Once Fred notified the factory owner of the problem, allowing the chemicals to escape becomes intentional. At that point, the factory owner knows, to a substantial certainty, that the chemicals are escaping.

18. The answer is B. Nuisance actions may be based on intent, negligence or strict liability. Damage from blasting is a classic example of strict liability. This damage from blasting was an interference with Pam's use and enjoyment of her real estate.

19. The answer is D. Nuisance actions can be based on intent, negligence or strict liability. In this case, blasting is a classic example of conduct that may lead to strict liability. Strict liability would, therefore, be an appropriate basis of liability. The facts state, however, that the owner understood that some carelessness had occurred. That appears to allow the use of negligence in this case. When the owner realized that the blasting was causing harm to the farmer's home, the conduct become intentional. Intent would be an appropriate basis of liability.

E. Remedy

20. The answer is D. Nuisance claims, whether based in intent, negligence or strict liability allow recovery of money damages. This is a private nuisance in that Fred suffered an interference with the use and enjoyment of his land. He would be entitled to recovery damages for the harm he suffered.

21.   The answer is A. Injunctive relief is an equitable remedy. The courts will routinely say that equitable remedies are not available unless the remedy at law is inadequate. Since private nuisance protects a right in land, it is assumed that the remedy at law, that is damages, may be inadequate. The law assumes that land is unique and must be protected. All of that being true, an action for private nuisance may allow the plaintiffs to seek an injunction to prohibit the continuation of the nuisance causing behavior.

22.   The answer is B. The use of injunctive relief is available for public nuisance as well as private nuisance.

23.   The answer is C. Before a court will grant an injunction, it must "balance the equities." The court looks to see whether the injunction is justified and will serve the ends of the community. In this case, the factory is the chief employer and financial asset of the community. If the court forces the factory to be quiet, the factory will probably have to close. Closing the factory would mean a substantial financial loss to the factory owners, the employees and the town. The court will probably deny Fred's request for an injunction.

F.   Defenses

24.   The answer is D. A "move to the nuisance" does look like assumption risk. It appears that the plaintiffs knew and understood the nature of the surroundings and chose to live there anyway. In addition, if there is an unpleasant condition near real property, the value and price of the real property for sale will probably reflect, in a lower price, the nature of that unpleasant condition. If the plaintiff is allowed to purchase property at a lower price because of unpleasant conditions and then remove the conditions by an action for nuisance, the plaintiff has gained a windfall. On the other hand, the law will not allow a nuisance to create some type of prescriptive right to continue just because it was there first. In fact, as times and circumstances change, the courts would like to see property uses be able to change to maintain property in its highest and best use. If a person was able to get to an area first, create foul conditions so that no one else could come, there would not be progress. Because of these conflicting issues, the "move to the nuisance" is not a complete bar to recovery. It is a circumstance that the courts will review in determining whether there is a nuisance and the type of remedy that should be available.

25.   The best answer is A. Nuisance actions can be based on intent, negligence or strict liability. Defendants can raise defenses in a nuisance action that is appropriate to the underlying basis of the claim. In this question, the defendant intentionally placed the logs

on the road. Blocking a public road is a public nuisance. Since the underlying basis is intent, defenses appropriate to intent could be used. As an extra comment, many states have moved from contributory negligence to comparative fault. In those states, comparative fault would be used in a nuisance claim that had negligence as the underlying basis of the claim.

CHAPTER 7
WRONGFUL DEATH AND SURVIVAL

QUESTIONS:

1. Use this set of facts for Questions 1 and 2. Carl was cutting grass in his pasture near a railroad track. A train passing nearby threw out a hot piece of coal and struck Carl in the chest. The hot coal caused a trauma injury and a severe burn. Carl lived for three weeks in serious pain and then died. Carl's wife has consulted an attorney to see if there is some remedy for the loss. At common law, the appropriate remedy would be:

    A.   Damages for Carl's death if negligence on the part of the railroad could be proven.

    B.   Damages for Carl's pain and suffering prior to death if negligence on the part of the railroad could be proven.

    C.   Damages could be recovered for death only if intentional conduct on the part of the railroad could be proven.

    D.   No damages could be recovered in this example at common law.

2. Using the same set of facts as Question 1 above, assume that Carl's wife has consulted an attorney in the present day. If that attorney consulted the state's modern statutes, which of the following best represents the likelihood of recovery?

    A.   There should be a recovery for the injuries suffered by Carl prior to his death.

    B.   There should be a recovery for the damages caused by Carl's death.

    C.   There should be a recovery for both A and B above.

    D.   No damages could be recovered in this example.

3.   Use this set of facts for Questions 3 through 8. Leslie was driving her car using all appropriate care along a major street when Mike, while driving another car, rammed the car that Leslie was driving. Mike had run a stop sign just prior to hitting Leslie's car. Leslie was wearing her seat belt, but suffered major injuries due to the crash. The emergency response technicians had to cut open the door to the car to get to Leslie. She was then rushed to the hospital for emergency treatment. The hospital staff had to do emergency first aid in the emergency room and then rush Leslie to the operating room. The staff surgeon performed emergency surgery to repair the internal injuries. Although the whole hospital staff performed excellently, Leslie lived for two weeks and then died of the injuries from the automobile wreck. During that two week period, Leslie was conscious and in great pain. The hospital staff and the doctors had to constantly administer medical treatment to try to keep Leslie alive. Upon Leslie's death, Leslie's husband Fred consulted an attorney to try to determine if there was some way that he could recover damages. It may be important to note that Fred and Leslie had two children. Those children were ages 6 and 8. If Fred sues Mike seeking to recover for all of the medical bills that are now due for the treatment given Leslie, the most likely result is:

    A.   Fred can recover the medical bills if the state has a survival statute.

    B.   Fred can recover the medical bills if the state has a wrongful death statute.

    C.   Fred can recover the medical bills only if it can be proven that Mike's conduct was intentional.

    D.   Fred cannot recover the medical bills.

4.   Using the same set of facts as Question 3 above, assume that Fred also wants to recover for the pain and suffering that Leslie endured during the two weeks that she was alive in the hospital. If Fred wants to recover for the pain and suffering, he will:

    A.   Have to show that the state allows such recovery under the wrongful death statute.

    B.   Have to show that the state allows such recovery under the survival statute.

    C.   Not be allowed to recover for the pain and suffering since that recovery is personal with the injured party and dies with that party.

D. Have to prove that he actually suffered some monetary loss that justifies the pain and suffering damages.

5. Using the same set of facts as Question 3, Fred would like to bring an action for loss of consortium for the loss of his wife and loss of parental care for the loss of the mother of the two children. Fred's attorney should:

   A. Closely check the wrongful death and survival statutes to see if recovery is allowed for those claims in that state.

   B. Assume that loss of consortium and loss of parental services are always recoverable even when the injured party dies.

   C. Assume that loss of consortium and loss of parental services are never recoverable when an injured party dies.

   D. Assume that loss of consortium is recoverable but loss of parental services is not recoverable when an injured party dies.

6. Using the same set of facts as Question 3, when the action is brought to recover for Leslie's injuries under the survival statute, the proper party to name as the plaintiff is:

   A. Most likely Leslie.

   B. Most likely the two children.

   C. Most likely Leslie's parents.

   D. Most likely Fred.

7. Using the same set of facts as Question 3, consider one more possible measure of damages. In addition to some of the losses noted in the above questions, which of the following would be the best measure of loss to also seek recovery under the survival statute?

   A. Future pain and suffering.

   B. Future medical bills.

   C. Future lost wages.

   D. None of the above.

8. Using the same set of facts as Question 3, assume that the litigation under the survival statute produces a substantial judgment based upon the injuries suffered by Leslie during the two weeks between the accident and her death. Who will actually receive the money from that judgment?

A. The money will pass under Leslie's will.

B. Leslie's husband.

C. Leslie's children.

D. Leslie's husband and children.

9. Use the following facts for Questions 9 through 13. Dr. Pam was standing on the street corner across from the hospital. Since she was the chief of surgery in the hospital, she had crossed this street many times. Dr. Pam carefully looked both ways before crossing the street and then started to walk forward. A car pulled around the corner, speeding and running a red light, and hit Dr. Pam. The driver of that automobile was named Jack. Several other doctors saw the accident and immediately ran to Dr. Pam's aid. The automobile had crushed most of her body including her skull. Unfortunately, Dr. Pam appeared to have died instantly from the injuries. Dr. Pam was married to Bill. Bill was a local investment banker and had substantial income of his own. Bill and Dr. Pam had three children. The children were ages 2, 5, and 7. Bill will seek recovery from Jack for medical bills and pain and suffering suffered by Dr. Pam. Most states would hold that:

A. Bill cannot recover medical bills and pain and suffering for Dr. Pam.

B. Bill can recover medical bills but not pain and suffering for Dr. Pam.

C. Bill can recover pain and suffering but not medical bills for Dr. Pam.

D. Bill can recover medical bills and pain and suffering for Dr. Pam.

10. Using the same set of facts as Question 9, Bill would like to recover from Jack for the funeral expenses and the cost of administering the estate of Dr. Pam. What is the likelihood of that recovery?

A. Bill should not be able to recover either of those costs.

B. Bill should be able to recover the funeral expenses but not the cost of administering the estate.

C. Bill should be able to recover the cost of administering the estate but not the funeral expenses.

D. Bill should be able to recover both funeral expenses and the cost of administering the estate.

11. Using the same set of facts as Question 9, it should be obvious that Dr. Pam was earning a substantial income every year. It should also be obvious, however, that her husband bill also earned a substantial income every year. Bill will want to recover from Jack a judgment that includes damages for Dr. Pam's future lost wages. In determining whether those damages ought to be recovered, the court will probably limit those damages to the following:

A. The future lost wages will be limited to one year's wages since the statute of limitations for most torts is usually one year.

B. The future lost wages will be limited to that period of time in which reasonable people would assume that Bill will remarry.

C. The future lost wages will be limited to that period of time from the time of death to the time of the expiration of Dr. Pam's normal life expectancy.

D. Future lost wages are not recoverable in a wrongful death claim.

12. Using the same set of facts as Question 9, Bill will want to consult with his attorney about how the damages for Dr. Pam's future lost wages will be determined. Since Bill earns a substantial annual salary himself, he has not used Dr. Pam's income. Dr. Pam's income was invested to pay for future education expenses for their three children. What advice should Bill's attorney give him?

A. Since Bill earns a substantial income there can be no recovery for Dr. Pam's future lost wages.

B. Some jurisdictions would determine the total amount of future lost wages for the recovery and then divide it among the beneficiaries.

C. Some jurisdictions would determine the amount of damages for future lost wages based upon the amount that individual beneficiaries actually lost. Under such a determination, the children would receive a substantial recovery and Bill would receive nothing.

D. Both B. and C.

13. Using the same set of facts as Question 9, Bill is concerned about who should bring the action for the death of his wife, Dr. Pam. He is concerned that someone might believe that he and his children have a conflict of interest. Who should bring the action?

A. Bill should bring the action if he is appointed under the appropriate state statute.

B. Bill and the children must bring separate actions for the death of Dr. Pam.

C. A third party should be appointed to bring the action to avoid a conflict of interest.

D. Any of the above is correct.

14. Use the following facts for Questions 14 through 18. Jim was in a hurry to get to an appointment and was driving his automobile along a city street. He approached an intersection where the light was yellow so he speeded up to get through that intersection. In fact, by the time he reached the intersection, the light turned red. Jim, however, went through anyway. On the cross street, a car driven by Charles went through the intersection since Charles noted that his light had just turned green. Charles hit Jim's car and caused substantial injury to Jim. Charles was not hurt. An ambulance was called to take Jim to the hospital, but the ambulance got lost on the way to the accident location. The operator taking the call made a few mistakes. The operator did not keep the caller on the line, wrote down the wrong address and did not read the address back to the caller to check that address. By the time that the ambulance found the accident, Jim was in much worse shape from loss of blood. Jim was taken to the hospital where emergency surgery was completed. Although Jim lived for 24 hours, he ultimately died. The evidence will show that Jim would have had a better chance to live if the ambulance had arrived on time. Jim was not married but had lived with the same woman, Jill, for 4 years. Jim and Jill had a son that is now 2 years of age. Jim was an accountant with a major accounting firm. Jill has consulted an attorney and would like to bring an action against Charles for the injury and death of Jim. Who is the proper party to act as plaintiff in the action?

A. Jim will be the named plaintiff.

B. A personal representative will have to be appointed to bring the action.

C. The child will be the named plaintiff.

D. Jill will be the plaintiff since she lived with Jim for 4 years.

15. Using the same set of facts as Question 14, if the action for Jim's death generates a substantial judgment, who will receive the money from that judgment?

A. Jill will receive all of the money and will be expected to share it with the child.

B. Jill and the child will receive the money jointly.

C. The child will receive the money.

D. Since Jim had no spouse, Jim's parents or other next of kin will receive the money.

16. Using the same set of facts as Question 14, a proper plaintiff may bring the action to recover for the death of Jim against Charles. Charles, of course, under this set of facts will want to claim that Jim was contributory negligent in driving through the red light. If the issue of contributory negligence or comparative fault is raised in this action, it will:

A. Be considered to reduce or bar recovery.

B. Be ignored since the award would not go to Jim, but ultimately to a beneficiary of the action.

C. Be considered but only if it can be shown that the beneficiary of the award was also negligent.

D. Be ignored since there are no defenses to wrongful death.

17. Using the same set of facts as Question 14, a proper plaintiff brings an action for the death of Jim against Charles. Charles wants to raise the issue of intervening cause because of the conduct of the ambulance service. The issue of causation will be:

A. Ignored since causation is not an element of wrongful death or survival.

B. Be considered just as in any other tort claim.

C. Be ignored since the conduct of all of the parties was negligent.

D. Be considered only if Charles' conduct was intentional.

18. Using the same set of facts as Question 14, a proper plaintiff brings an action for the death of Jim against Charles and the ambulance company. In order to recover against either Charles or the ambulance company, the plaintiff must prove:

A. The defendants were acting intentionally.

B. The defendants were acting negligently.

C. The defendants were acting in such a way as to be subject to strict liability.

D. Any of the above.

ANSWERS:

1.   The best answer is D. At common law, there was no recovery when the injured partied died. There were two reasons for this result. The law assumed that the personal injury action was personal with the injured partied and died with that person. In addition, it was assumed that the tort and the crime merged at the death. Any action would be a criminal action against the wrongdoer. As a result of this condition at common law, most states have passed statutes to allow recover for the injuries suffered by the injured party prior to his or her death and for damages suffered as a result of the death. Damages for the injuries suffered by the party prior to death are recoverable under a "survival statute." Damages for injuries suffered due to the death are recoverable under a "wrongful death statute."

2.   C is the correct answer. As noted in the answer to the above question, there was no recovery allowed at common law when the injured party died. Modern state statutes, however, have changed that condition. Most states now have both "survival" and "wrongful death" statutes. The survival statutes allow recovery for those injuries suffered by the injured party prior to death. The wrongful death statute allows recovery for those damages caused by the death.

3.   The correct answer is A. Modern survival statutes allow recovery for those damages that the injured party could have recovered had the injured party survived the injuries. Modern survival statutes allow recovery whether the claim is in negligence, intent or strict liability. There is, therefore, no requirement that Mike's conduct be intentional.

4.   B is the correct answer. Recovery for the pain and suffering of the injured party, now deceased, would fall under the state survival statute. In order to recover that loss, the plaintiff would have to show that the state survival statute allowed pain and suffering damages. Many state survival statutes do allow such recovery.

5.   The best answer is A. Since survival and wrongful death is a matter of state law, the law may differ among the many states. Loss of consortium and loss of parental services are two of the areas where the law lacks uniformity. It would be important to closely research the local state law to determine if those measures of loss were recoverable.

6.   The best answer is D. This question raises a problem with state law. Obviously Leslie is probably not going to be the proper party to

name as a plaintiff. She is dead. It is unlikely that the children would be named as plaintiffs since they are minors. The most likely named plaintiff would be the husband, Fred. State law will designate who is the proper party plaintiff in the action. The state law may frequently note that the "personal representative of the estate" is the proper party. The husband could, of course, be named that representative.

7.   The correct answer is D. This is something of a trick question. Survival statutes allow recovery for the damages suffered by the injured party from the time of injury until that person's death. Depending on the local state statute, that may include the medical bills, pain and suffering, or wages lost during that period of injury. Survival statutes, however, will not allow recover for "future" injuries. The person who was injured is dead. The law now allows for recovery based upon suffering or wages after death. The damages for injuries suffered due to the death must be recovered under the wrongful death statute.

8.   The most likely answer to this question is D. The award of damages from a survival action does not usually pass under the deceased's will. The survival statute will usually indicate who is to receive the money. Most statutes will set up a hierarchy of people that should receive the money. Usually the spouse is considered the one to receive the money. If there is a spouse and children, then those people share the proceeds. If there is neither spouse nor children, then usually the parents or next of kin receive the money.

9.   The most likely answer is A. The facts state that Dr. Pam appears to have died instantly from the injury. As such, Dr. Pam did not suffer any injures between the time of the accident and her death. Medical bills and pain and suffering are usually recoverable under a survival statute. Since Dr. Pam did not suffer any losses which can be recovered under such a statute, none can be recovered. Due to the instantaneous nature of Dr. Pam's death, Bill's claim will be limited to a wrongful death claim.

10.   The best answer to the question is D. Again, it should be remembered that wrongful death actions are matter of state statutory law. It would be necessary to research the particular state law to make sure of the correct answer in any particular jurisdictions. Many jurisdictions, however, allow recovery of funeral expenses and the costs to administer the estate.

11.   The correct answer is C. Future lost wages is the primary measure of loss in a wrongful death claim. The beneficiaries are entitled to recoup what they would have enjoyed had the deceased

lived. The normal period for determining the lost wages is to figure the number of years from the date of death to the date of the normal life expectancy of the deceased.

12. The best answer is D. There are two different rules that are applied. The majority of jurisdictions apply a "loss to beneficiary" rule. Under such a rule, the plaintiff must prove what each beneficiary would have enjoyed over a lifetime and the damages are based on those figures. A few jurisdictions apply a "loss to estate" rule. Such jurisdictions determine the total amount of wages that the deceased would have earned over a lifetime and that amount of money is the basis for the award.

13. The correct answer is A. In many states, statutes will designate who is to bring the action. A likely person is the personal representative of the estate. Under this set of facts, it is likely that Bill, as the husband, will serve as the representative of the estate.

14. The correct answer is B. A personal representative will have to be appointed. It is possible that Jill could be appointed the personal representative to bring the action. The law will not assume that appointment, however, just because Jill and Jim lived together and had a child.

15. The answer is C. The distribution of the judgment of a wrongful death action is determined by specific state statutes. The proceeds of such an action do not pass under a will or through the estate. Most of those statutes speak of "spouse" as a possible beneficiary of the award. Most of those statutes do not recognize a right to recovery any portion of the award by a "significant other" that is not married to the deceased. This would mean, therefore, that neither an "opposite sex" nor "same sex" significant other would be able to recover any of the proceeds. In this set of facts, the likely beneficiary of the money would be the biological child of the deceased.

16. The correct answer is A. All of the usual defenses are applied in actions for wrongful death and survival. Although it is true that the deceased will not be enjoying the proceeds of the action, the deceased's conduct will still be used to reduce or bar recovery.

17. The answer is B. Wrongful death and survival claims are just like other tort claims. Issues such as causation must be considered.

18. The correct answer is D. Wrongful death and survival claims are merely ways to assure that normal tort claims are available when the injured party dies. The underlying bases of such claims are still the usual bases of liability that are used in all other tort claims. The plaintiff may recover by using intent, negligence or strict liability.

CHAPTER 8
PRODUCTS LIABILITY

QUESTIONS:

1.   Use the following facts for Questions 1 through 9. Motorco is a manufacturer of automobiles. The lowest priced model manufactured by Motorco, the Flimsey, comes equipped with both driver and passenger front air bags, as well as driver and passenger lap and shoulder seat belts. On the dashboard in front of the driver is a small sign, in small but readable type, which states: "Airbag equipped. Always fasten seat belt when car is in motion." On the sun visor on the passenger side is a sign, of similar size, which says the same thing.

Driver purchased a Flimsey from Motorco. While operating the car, with Pat as a passenger in the front seat, Driver negligently ran a red light. Driver's car was hit on the driver's side by a vehicle driven by Bill, which was going about 45 miles per hour, 15 miles over the speed limit. Driver was not wearing a seat belt, and the force of the impact threw him through the side window of the car, causing severe injuries. The air bag did not open because it was designed to deploy only in head-on collisions. Pat was wearing the lap and shoulder belts, but one of the bolts anchoring the seat belt to the car broke, and she was thrown to the driver's side of the car. The impact with the side of the car caused severe injuries that she would not have suffered if the bolt had held.

Analysis of the bolt that failed showed a defect in the metal that must have occurred during manufacture. Motorco buys these bolts from twenty different suppliers and tests samples from each batch. Motorco's records do not reveal that any defects of the type found in the bolt have ever been discovered during the inspection process. In an action based on strict products liability by Pat against Motorco, Pat will try to prove that her injuries were caused by what type of defect?

   A.   Manufacturing defect.

B. Design defect.

C. Failure to warn.

D. Failure to perform reasonable inspection.

2. Use the same facts as Question 1. In an action based on strict products liability by Pat against Motorco, the proof needed to establish a prima facie case is:

A. Only that a defect existed in the automobile.

B. That a defect existed that was not discovered by reasonable inspection.

C. That a defect existed that was not discovered by reasonable inspection and that her injuries were not contributed to by the negligence of Driver.

D. That a defect existed and that the defect was a cause in fact and proximate cause of her injuries.

3. Use the same facts as Question 1. In an action based on strict products liability by Pat against Motorco, which of the following defenses would be most effective?

A. Proof that Motorco performs reasonable inspections of the bolts used in seat belt anchors.

B. Proof that the defect in the bolt could not have been detected by any known test before it failed.

C. Proof that the bolt that failed was a replacement bolt supplied by an auto repair shop after the car left Motorco's manufacturing plant.

D. Proof that the forces in the accident exceeded the design specifications for the bolt.

4. Use the same facts as Question 1. In an action based on *negligence* by Pat against Motorco, which of the following defenses would be most effective?

A. Proof that Motorco performs reasonable inspections of the bolts used in seat belt anchors.

B. Proof that Motorco relies on the bolt manufacturers to inspect the bolts.

C. Proof that Driver's negligence was a legal cause of Pat's injuries.

D. Proof that the bolts were properly designed.

5. Use the same facts as Question 1. In an action based on strict products liability by Pat against Motorco, what is the effect of the negligence of Driver?

A. It will be a complete defense for Motorco.

B. Motorco will be entitled to complete indemnity from Driver.

C. Motorco and Driver will be jointly liable.

D. Pat <u>must</u> sue both Driver and Motorco in one action.

6. Use the same facts as Question 1. If Driver sues Motorco for failure to warn of the dangers of driving without a seat belt even in a car equipped with an air bag, the sign on the dashboard will have what effect?

A. It will have no effect if Driver never saw it.

B. It will have no effect since Driver did not obey it.

C. It will force Driver to prove that it was inadequate.

D. It will defeat the action as a matter of law.

7. Use the same facts as Question 1. If Driver sues Motorco for a design defect for not equipping the Flimsey with a side curtain air bag in the door to protect against side impact collisions, how would the approach to design defect litigation of the Third Restatement of Torts, Products Liability, affect the cases of plaintiff and defendant?

A. Driver would have the burden of proving that a reasonable alternative design would have reduced or avoided the injury and the failure to adopt the alternative made the product not reasonably safe.

B. Driver would simply have to prove that some aspect of the design contributed to his injuries; Motorco would have the burden of showing that no other design was feasible.

C. Driver would have the burden of proving that the design contributed to his injuries and that another design was technologically possible; Motorco would then have the burden of showing that the change would reduce the utility of the product.

D. Driver would have the burden of proving that the custom in the industry was to put air bags in the doors.

8. Use the same facts as Question 1. Driver sues Motorco for a design defect for not equipping the Flimsey with a side curtain air bag in the door to protect against side impact collisions. Driver then shows that side curtain airbags were technologically feasible at the time the Flimsey was manufactured. Does this proof, by itself, establish that the Flimsey was defectively designed?

    A. Yes, because the failure to incorporate any available safety feature in a product is per se unreasonable.

    B. Yes, because manufacturers must keep up with the state of the art.

    C. No, as long as Driver was aware at the time of purchase that the car lacked side curtain air bags.

    D. No, because the omission of this safety feature does not necessarily mean that the Flimsey was not reasonably safe.

9. Use the same facts as Question 1. If Pat identifies the manufacturer who supplied the defective bolt that caused her seatbelt to fail, can Pat sue the bolt manufacturer in strict products liability?

    A. No, because the bolt manufacturers are not in privity of contract with Pat.

    B. No, because the bolt manufacturer is not a seller of the automobile.

    C. Yes, because the bolt was defective when it was manufactured.

    D. Yes, but only if the contract of sale of the bolt permits such actions.

10. Use the following facts for Questions 10 through 13. Dudley Armaments manufactures cheap, easily concealed handguns. Felon purchased a Dudley handgun from Gunshop, a local retailer, using a false identification. Felon showed the new gun to Bud and Lou, friends of his. Bud asked to handle the gun. Felon carefully engaged the safety on the gun, which is supposed to prevent the gun from firing accidentally. In handing the gun to Bud, however, it slipped out of his hands and fell to the floor. The gun went off, wounding Lou in the leg. Investigation reveals that the type of safety used on the gun is ineffective when the gun receives a sharp impact, as in being dropped. If Lou sues Dudley in strict products liability, what type of product defect will he attempt to establish?

    A. Manufacturing Defect.

B.   Marketing Defect.

C.   Design Defect.

D.   Failure to Inspect.

11.   Use the same facts as Question 10. If Lou sues Dudley in strict products liability, who will prevail?

A.   Dudley will prevail because Lou was neither a user nor consumer.

B.   Dudley will prevail because dropping the gun constitutes misuse.

C.   Lou will prevail because Dudley is vicariously liable for Gunshop's conduct in selling the handgun to Felon.

D.   Lou will prevail because he is a foreseeable victim.

12.   Use the same facts as Question 10. If Lou sues Gunshop in strict products liability, who will prevail?

A.   Gunshop will prevail because Lou is not in privity of contract.

B.   Gunshop will prevail because the test for a design defect is basically a negligence standard, and Gunshop committed no negligence with regard to the design.

C.   Lou will prevail because Gunshop sold the product to Felon.

D.   Lou will prevail on the theory of respondeat superior.

13.   Use the same facts as Question 10. If Lou sues Felon, who will prevail?

A.   Lou can prevail on both negligence and strict products liability theories.

B.   Lou can only prevail on a negligence theory.

C.   Lou can only prevail on a strict products liability theory.

D.   Lou will have no claim on either a negligence or a strict products liability theory.

14.   Plaintiff, a consumer, sues Defendant in breach of warranty for personal injuries suffered because ordinary consumer goods sold to Plaintiff by Defendant were unmerchantable. Defendant argues

that under the Uniform Commercial Code, the contract of sale limited Plaintiff's remedy to replacement of the goods, and excluded liability for consequential damages for personal injury.

    A.   Under the U.C.C., limits on damages for personal injury are prima facie unconscionable.

    B.   Under the U.C.C., such limits on remedies are never enforced.

    C.   Under the U.C.C., such limits on remedies are strictly upheld.

    D.   Under the U.C.C., limits on damages for personal injury are prima facie commercially reasonable.

15.   Which of the following is a type of damage that can be recovered in breach of warranty but usually not in strict products liability?

    A.   Medical expenses

    B.   Property damage

    C.   Lost wages

    D.   Pure economic loss.

16.   Use the following facts for Questions 16 and 17. "Legal Moonshine" is, as the name suggests, distilled by a properly licensed and taxed distillery. The product claims to be just like real "moonshine" whiskey: grain alcohol highly distilled and bottled without aging or filtering. The product is bottled at 160 proof, which means that it is 80% pure grain alcohol, or twice as strong as ordinary whiskeys. Peter drank a pint bottle of Legal Moonshine and died of acute alcohol poisoning. The label contains no warning of this danger. Peter's wife wishes to bring a wrongful death claim against the manufacturer of Legal Moonshine based on failure to warn. Which of the following is the strongest argument for imposing a duty to warn of this danger?

    A.   Peter did not in fact realize the danger of acute alcohol poisoning.

    B.   Peter did not know any of the dangers of drinking alcoholic beverages.

    C.   Legal Moonshine poses unusually severe risks of alcohol poisoning because of its unusual strength.

D. Legal Moonshine's manufacturers were aware of the risk.

17. Use the same facts as Question 16. In a wrongful death action by Peter's wife against the manufacturer of Legal Moonshine based on failure to warn, what is the strongest argument **against** imposing liability for failure to warn?

A. Alcohol by definition is not unreasonably dangerous.

B. The dangers of alcoholic beverages are well known to ordinary members of the community.

C. Liability will increase the price of alcoholic beverages.

D. No one actually reads warning labels.

18. Use the following facts for Questions 18 through 23. Resale, Inc. is a dealer in used and rebuilt equipment. Resale obtained a used crane originally manufactured by the Crane Co. The crane was designed for heavy lifting. Resale installed a new engine and a new lifting cable on the crane. The cable was manufactured by Cable Co. Resale then sold the crane "as is" to Contractor, in a contract of sale which disclaimed all express and implied warranties. Contractor then used the crane in construction work. While using the crane on the job six months later, an accident occurred. Employee, who was operating the crane at the time, was severely injured, and the construction job was delayed for a week while a replacement crane and operator were obtained. This accident occurred when the lifting cable proved to be defective and snapped, causing the steel beam that was being lifted to fall on the crane and injure Employee. If Employee sues **Crane Co.** based on strict products liability, who will prevail?

A. Crane Co. will prevail because there is no privity of contract between Crane and Employee.

B. Crane Co. will prevail because the defect was not present when the crane was manufactured.

C. Employee will prevail because Crane Co. placed the Crane in the stream of commerce.

D. Employee will prevail because the mere passage of time will not relieve Crane of responsibility for a defective product.

19. Use the same facts as Question 18. If Employee sues **Resale** based on strict products liability, Employee's best argument for prevailing on this theory would be the following:

A. Resale put the crane into the stream of commerce and should be responsible for any defects it contains.

B. Resale must be held to a duty of due care when it resells.

C. Resale must be held to a duty of due care when it refurbishes equipment.

D. Resale did more than simply resell and therefore is more like a manufacturer.

20. Use the same facts as Question 18. If Employee sues **Cable Co.** based on strict products liability, who will prevail?

A. Employee will prevail only if Cable Co. failed to inspect the cable properly.

B. Employee will prevail as long as the cable was defective when Resale sold the crane to Contractor.

C. Cable Co. will prevail unless Employee can prove that the defect was present when the cable was manufactured.

D. Cable Co. will prevail because there is no privity of contract between Cable and Employee.

21. Use the same facts as Question 18. If Employee successfully sues Resale in strict liability for the injury, would Resale have any claim for contribution or indemnity from any other party?

A. An indemnity claim against Cable Co., assuming Resale was not itself negligent in inspecting the cable.

B. A contribution claim against Crane Co. based on the manufacturing defect.

C. An indemnity claim against Crane Co. based on the manufacturing defect.

D. A contribution claim against Contractor, as the employer.

22. Use the same facts as Question 18. If Contractor sues Resale based on breach of warranty for damages caused by the delay in the construction project, who will prevail?

A. Contractor should prevail because contract disclaimers are ineffective in tort law.

B. Contractor should prevail because the Crane was defective.

C. Resale should prevail because the Crane was sold "as is."

    D. Resale should prevail because economic loss is not recoverable in breach of warranty.

23. Use the same facts as Question 18, but modify them as follows: Suppose Contractor attached a wrecking ball to the crane and used it to knock down an old building on the construction site by swinging the wrecking ball from side to side. If the accident occurred when the crane tipped over while being used in this fashion, and Employee brings a strict products liability claim against Crane Co. alleging a design defect, who will prevail?

    A. Crane Co. would prevail if it shows that the Crane was not designed to be used in this fashion.

    B. Crane Co. would prevail if it shows that such use was an unforeseeable misuse of the crane.

    C. Employee would prevail because the Crane tipped over.

    D. Employee would prevail if a design change would have prevented the accident.

24. Use the following facts for Questions 24 and 25. Drugco introduced a new prescription drug that provided great benefits to most people but caused serious side effects in a few individuals. Patient took the drug and suffered injuries from the side effects. Assume that the risk was not known until Patient's illness. If Patient sues Drugco based on strict products liability, what theory of defect, if recognized by the court, will give Patient the best chance of success?

    A. Failure to warn.

    B. Defect based on the risk-utility balance.

    C. Defect based on the consumer expectation test.

    D. Manufacturing defects.

25. Use the same facts as Question 24, only for the purposes of this question assume that the risks were known in advance to Drugco but were not disclosed to Patient on the packaging for the drug, Drugco would probably defend a failure to warn case by relying on the following doctrine:

    A. Imputed negligence

    B. Risks known to the ordinary consumer

    C. Learned Intermediary

    D.   Unforeseeable misuse

26.   Pharmo Drug Company manufactures an antibiotic drug called Killum, which is often effective against bacteria that are resistant to other antibiotics. Unfortunately, it has a side effect of causing numbness and loss of coordination of the hands. For this reason, Killum is not usually prescribed unless it is clear that conventional antibiotics are not working. It is also not prescribed, because of its toxicity, to women who are pregnant, may become pregnant, or are nursing; nor to children under age 18 and adults over 60; nor to anyone with glaucoma, liver or kidney problems, stomach ulcers, or irritable bowel syndrome. If a patient injured by one of the side effects of the drug brings suit on a design defect theory, who will prevail if the court uses the test adopted by the Third Restatement of Torts, Products Liability?

    A.   Pharmo will prevail as long as the benefits outweigh the risks for some class of patients, and adequate warnings are given.

    B.   Pharmo will prevail because there is no such thing as a defectively designed drug.

    C.   The patient will prevail because so many risks show that the drug is unreasonably dangerous

    D.   The patient will prevail because the existence of other antibiotics shows that an alternative design exists.

27.   Peggo manufactures toy building sets containing many small, interlocking bricks. Parents purchase a set for their twelve year old son, Bobby. The box contained a prominent warning that the building set is not safe for children under three years of age because of the danger that a young child might swallow one of the bricks and choke to death. Unfortunately Bobby's little brother, Tim, who was two years old, got into Bobby's room, swallowed one of the bricks, and suffered a severe injury from choking. In an action brought on behalf of Tim against Peggo based on strict liability for a design defect,

    A.   Tim would prevail because a different design would have prevented the accident.

    B.   Tim will prevail because the building set was more dangerous than the ordinary three year old would expect.

    C.   Peggo will prevail because Tim assumed the risk.

D. Peggo will prevail because making the bricks too large for a two-year-old to swallow would destroy its utility for older children.

28. Plaintiff's hand was crushed while using a punch-press machine at work one day. The machine was manufactured by Presto Pressco. Presto offered the machine either in a basic configuration without safety devices or with a variety of optional safety features including interlocks and guards. Presto's catalogue recommends the model without safety devices "for automated operations only." Plaintiff's employer, Speedy Tool & Die, purchased the basic model even though it would be fed by hand, because the machine was more productive if operated without the safety devices. Plaintiff sued Presto based on strict products liability for a design defect because of the lack of safety features, and Presto defends by asserting that Plaintiff's failure to use due care for his own safety is a complete bar to recovery:

A. The defense will succeed because contributory negligence represents misuse by the Plaintiff.

B. The defense will succeed because contributory negligence negates the existence of a design defect.

C. The defense will be rejected because the whole purpose of safety features is to protect against Plaintiff's carelessness.

D. The defense will be rejected because the Plaintiff's conduct is irrelevant in strict liability actions.

29. Tolbert lost his leg in an industrial accident. Ortho Hospital treated the original injury, and then provided and fitted a prosthetic leg. Ortho also trained Tolbert in the use of the prosthesis. After his release from Ortho, Tolbert was injured while out walking because his prosthesis broke due to a defect in the materials. Tolbert fell and suffered injuries. Tolbert now sues Ortho Hospital in strict products liability for selling him a defective prosthetic leg. Who will prevail?

A. Tolbert will prevail because Ortho sold him the defective prosthesis.

B. Tolbert will prevail because strict liability is applied to the provision of hospital services.

C. Ortho will prevail only if it sold the prosthesis "as is."

D. Ortho will prevail because this situation represents the provision of services rather than the sale of a product.

30.   Pittman took his car to Mega Lube for an oil and filter change. Mega Lube installed a defective new oil filter. The filter leaked oil, resulting in significant damage to the engine of Pittman's car. Pittman sues Mega Lube in strict products liability for selling him a defective filter. Who will prevail?

   A.   Pittman will prevail because Mega Lube sold him the defective oil filter.

   B.   Pittman will prevail only if reasonable inspection would have found the defect.

   C.   Mega Lube will prevail only if it sold the filter "as is."

   D.   Mega Lube will prevail because this situation represents the provision of services rather than the sale of a product.

31.   Homer was repainting his basement. He needed to open a can of paint, but found that he did not have any sort of tool handy with which to pry off the lid of the paint can. Fortunately, his fishing tackle box was stored in the basement, so Homer looked in there to find a likely implement. The only thing he could find, however, was his filleting knife, which has a thin flexible blade used for filleting fish. He tried to pry the lid off with the filleting knife, but the blade snapped and a piece struck him in the eye. Homer then sued Bladz, Inc., the manufacturer of the knife, in strict products liability, claiming that the blade of the knife was defective because it snapped. The trial court granted Bladz's motion for summary judgment. Which of the following is the best explanation for why the trial court's decision was correct?

   A.   Homer was contributorily negligent in his use of the defective product.

   B.   Homer's misuse of the defective product is a superseding cause of the harm.

   C.   The knife was not defective.

   D.   Homer assumed the risk.

ANSWERS:

1.   The answer is A. In responding to questions regarding products liability it is crucial to pay close attention to the particular parties and theories of recovery referred to. In this case, the question asks about claims by Pat against Motorco in strict products liability. Under that theory, the defect in the bolt was a manufacturing defect: the bolt did not turn out the way it should have. This rules out design defect. Since Pat was wearing a seat belt, no issue of failure to warn about the importance of wearing the belt arises.

2.   The answer is D. This answer most accurately states the prima facie case of strict products liability. A defect by itself is not sufficient; the plaintiff must show that the defect was a cause of the harm. On the other hand, this is strict liability, so the reasonableness of the inspections performed and the failure of those inspections to discover the defect are not relevant. The important fact is that the defect in fact existed in the product and contributed to causing Pat's injuries.

3.   The answer is C. Again, it is important to note that the question specifically asks about defenses to strict products liability. Under this theory, the amount of care expended by the defendant in inspecting the bolts does not matter. Even if the defect was not detectable, the defendant would still be liable; that is what strict liability for manufacturing defects means. Furthermore, the case involves a manufacturing defect, so proper design of the offending bolt would not defeat liability either. What would defeat liability is proof that the defect did not exist in the product when the defendant sold it. In other words, the product must be defective when it leaves the factory in order for the manufacturer to be liable. Defects introduced after the product is sold by the manufacturer are not that party's responsibility. For that reason, if the bolt was installed later as a replacement, the manufacturer would not be liable.

4.   The answer is A. Note that this question specifies that Pat is pursuing a negligence action against Motorco. For that reason, a different set of defenses are possible. Of those set out as choices, the best would be the one that suggests that Motorco was not negligent, because it met the standard of exercising due care by inspecting the bolts itself, rather than relying on someone else. Not so good is trying to defend by asserting that another party, namely Driver, is also liable. In this case, that might lead to a claim of contribution against Driver, but that is not as effective as a defense that could totally eliminate liability. Finally, the good design is not a defense, because the problem lay in the manufacture of the bolt.

5.   The answer is C. That another party also committed a tort and could be liable is not a complete defense; rather, it creates a joint tortfeasor situation. In situations like this, it does not matter that one party is liable on the basis of negligence and the other on the basis of strict liability, because most jurisdictions have rules of joint responsibility that will allow both to be held liable to the plaintiff. On the other hand, Motorco would not be entitled to indemnity because it is not a purely passive defendant. Motorco's defective bolt contributed to the injuries, and so it would be entitled in most jurisdictions to some form of contribution from Driver if both are held jointly and severally liable.

6.   The answer is C. Because a warning was given, plaintiff will have to show that it was somehow insufficient. For example, the plaintiff could argue that it was not prominent enough, not worded properly, or not urgent enough given the significance of the risk involved. It will not be enough for Driver to say he never saw the warning if it was, in fact, sufficiently prominent that he should have seen it. On the other hand, the mere existence of the warning is not automatically dispositive if the warning was not sufficiently clear or prominent.

7.   The answer is A. Under the Third Restatement approach, the plaintiff must show that a reasonable alternative design, which would have eliminated or reduced the harm, was available, and that the failure to use the alternative design made the product not reasonably safe. The formula "not reasonably safe" invokes the risk-utility test for design defect developed under section 402A of the Second Restatement. The plaintiff has the burden of establishing both parts of this test, although not necessarily to prove all the risks and benefits of the product. Answer B reflects the approach of the California Supreme Court in *Barker v. Lull Engineering Co., Inc.*, 573 P.2d 443 (Cal. 1978). It is not the approach adopted by the new Third Restatement. Finally, the plaintiff does not have to show that the alternative design is actually in use anywhere, much less that the use of the alternative design is customary. It is sufficient that the alternative was feasible.

8.   The answer is D. Because the design defect is judged on a risk utility standard, merely showing that an alternative safer design was feasible is not enough. Many other factors come into play in determining the question of safer design, including the relative advantages and disadvantages of the actual design and the proposed safer design. In this problem, it may be of significance that the car was designed to be a basic and inexpensive vehicle. The jury would have to consider whether the increased cost of the side curtain air bags would in fact by offset by the gains in safety from the air bags.

In any event, it is certainly not the case that a particular product must include every possible safety feature in order to be "reasonably safe."

9. The answer is C. Component part manufacturers can be liable to injured consumers if the component part itself was defective when manufactured, and the defect was a cause of the plaintiff's harm. In this situation, the relevant sale is the sale of the component to the company that assembled the final product. This claim does not, however, rule out the possibility of also suing the manufacturer of the car.

10. The answer is C. The problem with the gun is not that it was put together improperly, but that the safety mechanism does not work properly. Because this problem would be shared by all examples of this particular type of handgun, the problem is one of design.

11. The answer is D. Although the Second Restatement originally took no position on the ability of bystanders like Lou to recover for defective products, the courts soon extended the right to recover. And while it might be considered "misuse" to drop the gun, it is the sort of foreseeable mistake that a gun designer should anticipate and do something about, such as designing a safety mechanism that will prevent the gun from firing even if dropped. That is, after all, part of the point of having a safety mechanism on a gun. Lou can recover because he is exactly the sort of potential victim a properly designed safety would protect.

12. The answer is C. The retailer, as a seller of the product, is strictly liable if the product proves to have a defect that injures a person. This is true even where the retailer has no responsibility for causing the product to be defective, as in this scenario in which the problem lies in the manufacturer's design of the safety mechanism of the gun. The retailer probably had no ability to control the design of the gun, but is liable for putting the defective product in the hands of consumers. The lack of privity of contract is no barrier to this tort claim, so Lou will be able to recover from the seller even though the seller committed no negligence (if that be the case). If the retailer is truly innocent here, the retailer can obtain indemnity from the manufacturer.

13. The answer is B. Strict products liability is not a viable theory because Felon is not a seller of the gun.

14. The answer is A. Pursuant to U.C.C. 2–719(3), limitations on the recovery of consequential damages for injuries resulting from consumer goods are "prima facie unconscionable."

15.   The answer is D. Pure economic loss in product liability usually represents loss resulting from the disappointing performance of the product. It is distinguished from damages, including economic damages, stemming from personal injury or damage to other property. The latter damages are of course recoverable in an action based on the tort theory of strict products liability. For pure economic loss, however, a party usually has to resort to the remedies available under commercial law, which is designed to deal with private allocation of risks.

16.   The answer is C. The problem here is that it is not necessary to warn against dangers that are generally known and recognized, as comment *j* to section 402A states, giving the dangers of overconsumption of alcoholic beverages as an example. For this reason, the distillers in this question would not be required to warn against the ordinary dangers of excessive drinking. What could trigger a duty to warn, however, would be a danger that the ordinary consumer would not expect to encounter. In this case, the whisky is twice as strong as usual, and a consumer who knew the general dangers of over consumption might not be aware of how quickly a beverage like that could lead not only to intoxication, but also to acute alcohol poisoning. The fact that Peter did not in fact know of the danger is not the strongest argument for a warning because the test is whether the danger is generally known. Also, awareness of the risk by itself does not require a warning, unless the risk is one that the ordinary consumer would not also know.

17.   The answer is B. As noted in the explanation to Question 16, a manufacturer is not required to warn against dangers that are already known to ordinary consumers. The defendants could argue that the dangers of alcohol, including the dangers of alcohol poisoning, are generally known. While alcohol poisoning is certainly not the most common danger of drinking, in fact enough unfortunate examples from initiations and such are publicized that the danger is probably known. Furthermore, the strength of the alcoholic beverage in this case would be printed on the label, so the fact that it was so strong was not hidden from the consumer. This is therefore the best of the available choices.

18.   The answer is B. The facts state that Resale replaced the cable, so the cable was not original equipment on the crane. In order for a product seller to be liable in strict product liability, the product must be defective when sold. Here the defective component, the cable, was introduced later when the crane was refurbished. Therefore the manufacturer will not be liable in strict products liability.

19.   The answer is D. The general rule is that sellers of used products are not strictly liable in tort if the product proves to be

defective. The rationale seems to be that such sellers are not in a good position to spread losses that result from product defects, and that consumers do not have the same expectations of quality with respect to many types of used goods. The exceptions to this rule are phrased in various ways. First, the seller must use due care or be liable in negligence. However, this question specifies a claim based on strict products liability. The Third Restatement of Torts, Products Liability, would also make the reseller liable if the product is marketed as being as good as new. (See section 8(b).) Finally, many jurisdictions as well as the Third Restatement will hold the reseller liable if the reseller remanufactures or refurbishes the product. The argument would particularly strong in this case, because it is the very part that Reseller replaced (the lifting cable) that proved to be defective and caused the accident.

20.   The answer is C. As above, the answers regarding a failure to use due care are a distraction here, since once again the question specifies strict liability. The crucial requirement for the plaintiff will be to prove that the cable was defective when this defendant, the Cable manufacturer, sold the product. If the defect was introduced later, perhaps as a result of mishandling by Resale, Crane Co. would not be liable.

21.   The answer is A. Because the crane did not have the defect when it was sold by Crane Co., Resale would have neither a contribution nor an indemnity claim against it. Similarly, Contractor would have no liability under a strict liability theory. However, since the defect occurred in the lifting cable, the manufacturer of the cable could be liable for contribution or indemnity. If Resale was itself responsible in some way, such as negligent failure to inspect the cable, Resale would still be entitled to contribution. If, however, Resale is strictly liable and had no actively tortious role in causing the injury, Resale would be entitled to indemnity from the manufacturer, Cable Co.

22.   The answer is C. This is a claim for the economic loss caused by the failure of the crane to perform as the contractor desired. As such, these are the sort of pure economic loss typically not recoverable under strict products liability or negligence. Losses of this type are more properly sought in a suit for breach of warranty. However, warranty claims are subject to the limitations of commercial law, including the ability to limit or disclaim warranties and to limit remedies. In this case, the crane was sold "as is" and with disclaimers of all warranties. Although courts often scrutinize such clauses in consumer transactions, it would seem unlikely that the courts would find any unfairness in such clauses in a contract for the sale of used construction equipment between a reseller of used products and a contractor.

23. The answer is B. Even if the crane was not specifically designed to be used in this way, it may be that such a use is in fact common and foreseeable enough that the crane should be designed so that it can be used safely for this purpose. On the other hand, a lot of machines are sufficiently specialized that they would never be used for any but their designed purpose. Accordingly, whether Crane Co. should have designed the crane to be safe for use with a wrecking ball will depend on what sorts of uses Crane Co. ought to have anticipated. It will not be sufficient to simply claim that the crane was not intended for this use if such use is foreseeable. On the other hand, Crane Co. would not be liable simply because the crane tipped over or because some design change could have prevented the accident, if Crane Co. was not obligated to anticipate such uses.

24. The answer is C. To be clear, most jurisdictions would not adopt a pure consumer expectations test for a drug side effect tort like this. Nevertheless, it is the only one of the named theories that would give the plaintiff the slightest chance of success. Failure to warn will not work because the side effect was not known before Patient took the drug, and most courts do not require drug companies to warn about risks of which they are unaware. The risk utility balance would not help the plaintiff, because on the facts it appears that the drug's benefits outweigh the risks of harm. Finally, nothing in the facts indicate that the drug was improperly manufactured. What has occurred is that the drug proved to be more dangerous than Patient expected, which is basically the consumer expectation test.

25. The answer is C. For most prescription drugs, the duty of the manufacturer is to provide full warnings to the learned intermediary, usually the doctor. It is then up to the doctor to provide appropriate warning to the patient. For this reason, the absence of warnings on the package is not decisive here, as long as proper warnings were provided to the physician.

26. The answer is A. The Third Restatement treats most cases involving prescription drugs under a failure to warn theory. If the patient is informed of the risks of the drug treatment, the manufacturer is not responsible simply because unavoidable and dangerous side effects are possible. The Third Restatement does recognize liability for prescription drugs under a design defect theory, but only in a limited circumstance. The risks must outweigh the benefits for all possible classes of patients. If some class of patients exists for whom a reasonable medical practitioner would prescribe the drug (because for that class, the benefits outweigh the risks) then drug is not defectively designed. At that point, the plaintiff would have to show that adequate warnings were not given. Under this approach, a drug that has severe risks for many classes of patient would not

automatically be considered defective in design. As long as some class of patients would benefit, the design is not considered defective. This is true even if alternatives are available.

27. The answer is D. Toys that are intended for infants and toddlers certainly need to take into account the dangers of choking, but to enforce such a rule on toys intended for older children would render them useless. Part of the interest for the older child would lie in the construction of intricate designs using the smaller and more versatile bricks. Requiring toys intended for older children to be safe even for the youngest child would probably also rule out such common items as chemistry sets and electronics. A warning, if prominent and clear, is probably the best that can be done in this situation.

28. The answer is C. The reason why machines need safety mechanisms is that we recognize that a moment of inattention can result in serious injury. Such moments of inattention do not represent misuse of the machine, nor do they negate the possibility of defect. To put it another way, it would be pointless to argue that the absence of a safety feature is a design defect, if the plaintiff's foreseeable carelessness, which makes the safety feature necessary in the first place, could at the same time defeat any cause of action. On the other hand, the plaintiff's conduct is not irrelevant, although courts have disagreed on what kind of conduct by the plaintiff can in fact bar or reduce recovery.

29. The answer is D. This is an example of professional services, which are judged under a professional negligence standard rather than a strict liability standard, even if products are supplied in the course of providing the services.

30. The answer is A. The services rule only applies to "professional" services. In this situation Mega Lube would be regarded as a seller of the oil filter, and so would be strictly liable.

31. The answer is C. The issue of misuse of the product can affect the analysis of several of the elements of the strict product liability case. It could indicate contributory negligence or assumption of risk. It can also act as a superseding cause. In this case, however, the best analysis would be that the knife was not defective at all. As the facts make clear, the knife was thin and flexible so it would serve to fillet fish. Such an implement is clearly not intended for use as a pry bar. The fact that a thin bladed knife snapped when used in this fashion is therefore no indication of defect. So the most accurate analysis of this scenario is that the knife was not defective at all.

CHAPTER 9
DEFAMATION

QUESTIONS:

1. Use the following facts for Questions 1 through 6. Bill and Sam were both salesmen. They were both trying to make a big sale to XYZ Corporation. Sam got the sale, and Bill got very angry. Bill called the employee of XYZ Corporation that was responsible for making the order and said several things about Sam. Bill said, "Sam is a liar and a cheat. Those goods he sold you are of low quality and will not hold up. Sam has cheated other companies, so you better watch him closely." All of the statements were false. Although the sale should have been final, XYZ Corporation cancelled the order with Sam. Sam found out what Bill had said, and wants to sue Bill. If Sam sues Bill for defamation, is the statement sufficiently defamatory to be actionable?

   A. Yes. It holds Sam up to ridicule, hatred, and/or loss of reputation.

   B. Yes. All false statements are defamatory.

   C. No. Only written statements can be defamatory.

   D. No. The statement may be a misrepresentation, but it is not defamatory.

2. Use the same facts as Question 1. If Sam sues Bill for defamation, the action will be based on which of the following?

   A. Libel, since it harms Sam's reputation.

   B. Libel, since it is spoken.

   C. Slander, since it harms Sam's reputation.

   D. Slander, since it is spoken.

3. Use the same facts as Question 1. If Sam does sue for defamation, which of the following is most accurate?

191

A. Sam will have to prove special damages since the action is slander.

B. Sam will not have to prove special damages since the action is libel.

C. Sam will have to prove special damages since the action is libel.

D. Sam will not have to prove special damages since the action is slander per se.

4. Use the same facts as Question 1. If Sam wants to claim that the action is for slander per se, what will he need to show?

A. The statements affect Sam's trade or business.

B. The statements are false.

C. The statements were written or read from a script.

D. The statements attack the good moral character of Sam.

5. Use the same facts as Question 1. If Sam is unable to prove that the statements are slander per se, will he be able to prove special damages?

A. No. Special damages are for pain and suffering.

B. No. Special damages are for disfigurement.

C. Yes. Special damages are some economic loss.

D. Yes. Special damages are harm to reputation.

6. Use the same facts as Question 1. Assume that the story of Bill and Sam's problem gets picked up and written about in the newspaper. Publication in a newspaper is:

A. Libel per quod.

B. Libel.

C. Slander

D. Slander per se.

7. The Daily News, a local newspaper, wrote an editorial. It seems that the author of the editorial had been doing some checking and found out that there were several ethical violations against several lawyers in the state. In a state of 5000 lawyers, 100 lawyers had

been found guilty of ethical violations during a 10 year period. The violations ranged from not completing the required number of CLE credits to actually stealing a client's money. The editorial said, "The situation in this state is serious. All of the lawyers in this state are crooks. They are all engaging in ethical violations. The problem is, not all of them have been caught." Susan Doe, a lawyer in that state, sued the newspaper for defamation. Ms. Doe had never been found guilty of an ethical violation. The best answer concerning this action is:

    A.   She will win since she is a member of the class that was defamed.

    B.   She will lose since the defamation concerns all members of a large class, even though she is a member of that class.

    C.   She will win since the statement is defamatory and false. Not all of the lawyers had committed ethical violations.

    D.   She will lose since it is impossible to prove she has not committed some type of ethical violation over the whole course of her career.

8.   Use the following facts for Questions 8 through 13. Jane Jones is a very good trial attorney. She is representing a man who is accused of murder. The local newspaper ran an article that said, "Attorney Jane Jones is a dishonest crook. She knows that her client committed murder and yet she is trying to get him acquitted. Jane Jones is actually a member of organized crime and is representing this murderer as part of her job for the crime family." The story was false. Jane Jones is an honest, hard working lawyer. She handles criminal cases on a regular basis. She is not part of organized crime. If Ms. Jones decides to sue the newspaper, she will have to face the issue of whether she is a public or private figure. Which of the follow is the best answer?

    A.   She is a private figure.

    B.   She is a public figure since, as a lawyer, she is an "officer of the court."

    C.   She is a public figure since the murder trial was important enough for the newspaper to write about.

    D.   She is a public figure since she handles criminal cases.

9.   Use the facts from Question 8. If, during the trial, Ms. Jones was also running for mayor, would she be a public or private figure?

    A.   She would be a private figure.

B.   She would be a public figure since she ran for office.

C.   She would be a public figure since the newspaper always writes about mayor's races.

D.   She would be a public figure since she thrust herself into the public eye to have an impact on decisions.

10.   Use the facts from Question 8. Assume that Ms. Jones is not running for mayor, but had some reputation before trying this case. In attending the university in this city, she was the star center on the University women's basketball team. Before law school, she played for 5 years on a well known professional women's basketball team. During those years, she became known as the spokesperson for several athletic apparel companies and several charitable organizations. While attending law school, she kept her name before the public by advertising for the athletic apparel companies and the charitable organizations. Her name constantly appears in Sports Magazines as one who comments on women's basketball. For purposes of her career as a lawyer, would she be a public or private figure?

A.   She would be a private figure.

B.   She would be a public figure since the newspaper wrote about her.

C.   She would be a public figure since she gained general notoriety.

D.   She would be a public figure since she is a lawyer.

11.   Use the facts from Question 8. Assume that the story that the newspaper reported is not true. If Ms. Jones is a private figure, she will have to prove which of the following?

A.   The story is false.

B.   The story is false and the newspaper knew it was false.

C.   The story is false and the newspaper had no belief in its true.

D.   The story is false and the newspaper failed to use reasonable care to determine whether it was true or false.

12.   Use the facts from Question 8. If Ms. Jones is a public figure, she will have to prove which of the following?

A.   The story is false.

    B.   The story is false and the newspaper acted with "actual malice."

    C.   The story is false and the newspaper wrote the story because they hated Ms. Jones.

    D.   The story is false and the newspaper failed to use reasonable care to determine whether the story was true or false.

13.   Use the facts from Question 8. Ms. Jones is somewhat amazed at the reaction of the public after the article runs. Although some of her friends try to avoid her and many members of the public are afraid that she is a member of organized crime, her legal business increased. It seemed that criminals wanted her to represent them. In short, she has lost some friends and her reputation, but she is making a lot more money. If she sues from defamation, what can she recover?

    A.   Damages for her lost friends and reputation, but no loss of business.

    B.   Nothing since she must prove "special damages" in order to recover any damages.

    C.   Nothing since loss of friends and reputation is not sufficient to meet the "actual damages" requirement.

    D.   Nothing since loss of reputation cannot be measured.

14.   Use the following facts for Questions 14 through 18. John Jones was running for governor of his state. For a two day period, just before the election, Mr. Jones seemed to have disappeared. No one knew where he was. The local newspaper wrote the following article. "We have just been informed that Mr. John Jones, candidate for governor, spent two days having a romantic weekend with his girlfriend. We understand that Mr. Jones' wife is extremely upset, but is denying that her husband has a girlfriend." Although John Jones had been leading in the polls, his numbers fell dramatically. The election came so suddenly after the story appeared in the newspaper, Mr. Jones did not really have time to refute it. It turns out that the story was false. Mr. Jones was, in fact, checking on his elderly mother who lived in a different state. His mother had several health problems and needed some attention. If Mr. Jones sues the newspaper, which of the following is true?

    A.   He is a private figure.

    B.   He is a public figure since he is running for office.

C. He is a public figure if he had been of general notoriety before the election.

D. He is a public figure since romantic affairs by married men are always public information.

15. Use the facts from Question 14. If Mr. Jones brings an action against the newspaper, it will be one in:

A. Slander per se since it alleges a lack of chastity.

B. Slander per se since it affects his trade or business.

C. Libel since it was written.

D. Slander since it was written.

16. Use the facts from Question 14. If Mr. Jones is able to prove that, in addition to the facts appearing above, the newspaper had also endorsed the opposing candidate for governor, what impact will that have on the case?

A. It will prove "actual malice" since it is evidence that the newspaper wanted to opposing candidate to win.

B. It will show common law malice which is necessary for a public figure to win a defamation action.

C. It will show that the newspaper failed to use reasonable care to determine the truth of the story which is necessary for a public figure to win an action for defamation.

D. The evidence will have very little impact on the case.

17. Use the facts from Question 14. The newspaper had gotten the story from a source within the opposing candidate's party. The source promised the story was true. The newspaper then contacted Mr. Jones' party and asked where he was. Mr. Jones' party just said, "No comment." The newspaper called Mr. Jones' wife and asked the same question. She knew where her husband was, but did not want him bothered. Mrs. Jones said, "I'm not sure where he is." Since the election was coming up quickly, the newspaper wrote the story on that basis. Which of the following is the best answer?

A. Mr. Jones will probably win the lawsuit since the newspaper failed to sure reasonable care to determine whether the story was true.

B. Mr. Jones will probably lose the lawsuit since the newspaper did not know the story was false.

    C.   Mr. Jones will probably win the lawsuit since the story was false.

    D.   Mr. Jones will probably lose the lawsuit since his own party failed to confirm or deny the truth.

ANSWERS:

1.   The answer is A. A defamatory statement is one that harms the reputation of another. It may also need to be false in order to bring the action, but harm to reputation is the definition of defamatory.

2.   The answer is D. Oral or spoken defamation is slander.

3.   The answer is D. Special damages are, ordinarily, required for slander actions. Special damages are not necessary where the action is for slander per se. This claim would be one for slander per se.

4.   The answer is A. In order to prove that the statements are slander per se, Sam would have to show that they affected his trade or business. It does appear that they would. The other types of slander per se are statements that allege that the plaintiff has a loathsome disease, committed a serious crime, or lacks chastity.

5.   The answer is C. Special damages are some form of economic loss. In this example, Sam lost the sales contract. The other suggested answers would be different forms of general damages.

6.   The answer is B. Written defamation is libel.

7.   The answer is B. When a defendant defames a large group and includes all or most of the members of that group, no one member of that group can sue.

8.   The answer is A. Lawyers are not public figures just because they are "officers of the court." The rules that determine whether a person is a public figure also assume that unwilling public figures are rare. Being written about in the newspaper does not make one a public figure.

9.   The best answer is B. Running for public office would make someone a public figure. Answer D is one that could also be considered. Someone who thrust themselves into the public eye to have an impact on decisions is also a public figure. In this case, the fact that Ms. Jones is running for public office is probably enough to make her a public figure.

10.   The answer is C. This question is a little harder. A person who gains general notoriety is considered a public figure. It is easy to imagine that sports starts, entertainment celebrities, and other such well known people are public figures. Whether Ms. Jones should be a public figure in her law practice because of her previous general notoriety is a little more difficult.

11.   The answer is D. When a plaintiff is a private figure, the courts may use any basis of liability as long as it is not strict liability. In this case, the answer D suggests that negligence would be an adequate basis of liability. Merely proving falsity of the statement alone would not be enough.

12.   The answer is B. If the plaintiff is a public figure, the plaintiff must prove "actual malice." Answer C may have confused some students. "Actual malice" means that the defendant knew the statement was false or acted in reckless disregard of the truth. Answer C is more in the nature of old common law malice. That would not be adequate to form the basis of a defamation claim against a public figure.

13.   The answer is A. The modern constitutional decisions require that a plaintiff suffer "actual damages" before being allowed to recovery any damages. A plaintiff cannot recover "presumed damages." Loss of reputation, however, is sufficient for "actual damages."

14.   The answer is A. Running for public office, especially that of governor, is sufficient to make one a public figure.

15.   The answer is C. Written defamation is libel. The slander per se issues are irrelevant.

16.   The best answer is D. For a public figure to win a defamation action against a news media, that plaintiff must prove "actual malice." Actual malice means that the defendant knew the statement was false or acted in reckless disregard of the truth. The mere fact that the newspaper was supporting the other candidate does not show that they knew the statement was false.

17.   The best answer is B. Since Mr. Jones is a public figure, he will have to prove "actual malice." "Actual malice" means that the defendant knew the statement was false or acted in reckless disregard of the truth. The standard of care is fairly strict. From these facts, it does not appear that the newspaper knew the statements were false. They got the statements from a fairly reliable source and they tried to check the facts from Mr. Jones' own party and family. With the election coming quickly, it appears they could write the story.

CHAPTER 10
PRIVACY

QUESTIONS:

1. Use the following facts for Questions 1 and 2. Joan was a hardworking law student. She was in a second year and near the top of the class. Several students were teasing with her one day, and said they were amazed she was now doing advertisements for one of the law book publishing companies. When she said she didn't know what they were talking about, they showed her an advertisement they had received in the mail. Sure enough, the ad showed Joan, sitting in the library, reading a book published by they law book publisher. The picture was one a friend of hers had taken and posted on one of the social network pages on the internet. If Joan sues the law book publisher, what is the likely result?

    A.   She will lose since the photo was taken in a public place.

    B.   She will lose since the photo was found on a public social network internet cite.

    C.   She will win since the photo intrudes upon her seclusion of study.

    D.   She will win since the law book publisher used the photo for commercial purposes.

2. Use the facts from Question 1. If Joan sues and wins the lawsuit, what would be the measure of her damages?

    A.   The value of her name or likeness.

    B.   The humiliation and suffering.

    C.   The profits realized from the advertising campaign.

    D.   The economic loss that Joan suffered.

3. A law book publisher finds a picture of one of the Supreme Court justices reading one of the publisher's books. The picture was

obviously taken inside of the justice's office. If the law book publisher uses that photo in an advertising campaign, and the justice
decides to sue, what is the likely result?

    A.   The publisher would win since Supreme Court Justices are
          public figures.

    B.   The publisher would win since a Supreme Court Justice's
          office is a public place.

    C.   The Justice would win since the publisher used his/her
          likeness for commercial purposes.

    D.   The Justice would win since public figures are barred from
          making advertisements.

4.   Use these facts for Questions 4 and 5. Susan Songbird is a
famous pop singer. She has won numerous awards, multiple gold
records, and her songs are the number one downloads on several
different web sites. Billy Bob, a used car lot owner, decided he would
really like a celebrity to advertise his car lot. He called Susan
Songbird's agent and asked if she was interested. The agent said no.
Billy Bob was not to be deterred. He downloaded a couple of Susan
Songbird's songs, put together a good television ad, and put her song
with it. The ad was only aired once, when Susan sued Billy Bob.
What is the likely outcome of the litigation?

    A.   Susan would lose since her songs were generally available
          on the internet.

    B.   Susan would win since Billy Bob used her name or likeness
          for commercial reasons.

    C.   Susan would lose since she is a public figure.

    D.   Susan would win since Billy Bob made a public disclosure
          of Susan's songs.

5.   Use the facts from Question 4. Rather than downloading Susan's
songs, Billy Bob finds a singer that sounds exactly like Susan. Billy
Bob has this other singer sing the songs for the ad. If Susan
Songbird should sue in this example, what is the likely result?

    A.   Susan will lose since she is not being used for commercial
          purposes.

    B.   Susan will win since her singing style is being used for
          commercial purposes.

    C.   Susan will lose since her style is open to interpretation by
          the public.

    D.   Susan will win since Billy Bob has intruded into her seclusion.

6.   John believed that his neighbor Jim had written the manuscript for a best selling novel. While Jim was out of his house, John broke in, and searched the house. John was unable to find the manuscript and left without doing any damage or taking anything. Jim later found out about the break in and sued. What is the likely result of that action?

    A.   Jim will win in an action for intrusion.

    B.   Jim will lose an action for intrusion since John was not a police officer.

    C.   Jim will lose an action for intrusion since nothing was damaged.

    D.   Jim will lose an action for intrusion since nothing was taken.

7.   Officer Smith is a member of the local police force. He saw Fred walking down the street and thought he would harass Fred a bit. Officer Smith stopped Fred on the street, made Fred empty all of this pockets, and then searched Fred. If Fred sues Officer Smith for this conduct, will it be appropriate to add a claim of intrusion into seclusion?

    A.   No. The claim should only be for the federal constitutional claims.

    B.   No. The claim should only be for the constitutional/42USC1983 claims.

    C.   No. Police offers are exempt from intrusion claims.

    D.   Yes. The state claim for intrusion can be joined with the federal claims.

8.   The governor of the state was a married man. Unknown to his wife, the governor was having an affair with a woman that lived in another state. The local newspaper found out about the affair and investigated it. The newspaper was able to get the full story and a couple of pictures of the governor and his girlfriend in a small restaurant. The newspaper ran the story with the pictures. If the governor sues for public disclosure of private facts, can he win?

    A.   No. The facts are true and as a public figure those facts are not private.

B.   No. The facts are true.

C.   Yes. Although the facts are true, he is entitled to some privacy for his affairs.

D.   Yes. This is the public disclosure of private facts.

9.   Mr. Smith was named as the principal of the major local high school. After that announcement, the newspaper discovered that when Mr. Smith was a young man of 20, he had been arrested and convicted of being drunk and disorderly. That information came out of the local court records. The newspaper wrote a story that reported that. If Mr. Smith sues the newspaper for pubic disclosure, he will:

A.   Win, since the paper make private facts public.

B.   Lose, since the court report was public record.

C.   Win, since the report casts Mr. Smith in a false light.

D.   Lose, since Mr. Smith is a public figure.

10.   Jane went to her doctor for a regular examination. The doctor performed the examination and discovered that Jane had several minor health problems. It would be necessary for Jane to take a little time off from her job, but recovery should be complete. Jane did not want the doctor to tell anyone about her health issues until she had a chance to discuss it with her employer. The doctor, however, wrote a letter to Jane's employer to explain her condition. The doctor claims that the employer would be entitled to know of Jane's condition and upcoming treatment. If Jane sues the doctor what is the likely result?

A.   Jane will lose since the intrusion into her solitude during the examination was with her consent.

B.   Jane will lose since the statements made by the doctor were true.

C.   Jane will win since the doctor made a public disclosure of private facts.

D.   Jane will win unless the doctor was paid through a group health plan for which the employer paid part of the premium.

11.   Doctor Smith told one of his friends that Bill Jones had come to his office for a check up. Doctor Smith had determined that Bill Jones had an incurable and fatal disease. Doctor Smith told his

friends that Bill Jones would be dead in 6 months. Some of the people that had heard the story also knew Bill Jones. They were very nice to Bill and tried to do things for him. After several weeks, Bill discovered what the doctor had said. Upon confronting Doctor Smith, the doctor rechecked the tests and discovered he had been wrong. Bill Jones was fine. If Bill Jones wishes to sue Doctor Smith, what would be the best claim for relief?

A.   Slander

B.   Public Disclosure

C.   Libel

D.   False Light

12.   Jane James is a famous movie star. She was filming a movie on location in Africa, when a story was published by a newspaper in the United States that she had been killed. The out cry was immediate. People lined the street near Ms. James' Hollywood home. The 24 hour news channels talked of nothing but what a great film personality she had been. The 24 hour movie channels began to show nothing but her movies. The story, however, wasn't true. Ms. James was alive and well. Being so far away from home, it took about two days for the story to reach the film crew in Africa and get some news back to the United States that Ms. James was still alive. For about another day, one of the 24 hour news channels continue to say she was dead and argue about the propriety of claiming she was alive. If Ms. James wants to win an action for false light against some of those media outlets, she would have to prove which of he following:

A.   The statement was false and the news outlet knew it was false.

B.   The statement was false.

C.   The statement was false and defamatory.

D.   The statement was concerning a private fact.

ANSWERS:

1.   The best answer is D. Commercial appropriation is one of the claims for relief for invasion of privacy. Since the publisher took her likeness and used it for commercial purposes, they would be liable for commercial appropriation.

2.   The answer is A. The damages for commercial appropriation are the value of the person's name or likeness.

3.   The answer is C. Although a Supreme Court Justice is a public figure that does not mean that their names or likenesses can be used for commercial purposes.

4.   The answer is B. Even though Susan is a public figure, taking her songs for commercial purposes is actionable. Susan makes her living singing and charging people for her songs. Billy Bob took the song without paying for the advertising value.

5.   The answer is B. This type of case is more in the nature of a right of publicity. Although it wasn't actually Susan singing the songs, Billy Bob was trying to cause confusion in the market place and make people think Susan was singing the songs. That is adequate for an action in commercial appropriation.

6.   The answer is A. The intrusion into the seclusion of Jim, in a manner that is highly offensive is actionable.

7.   The best answer is D. There is no doubt that several federal claims would be a part of the litigation. The state claim for intrusion, however, could be joined to those federal claims.

8.   The best answer is A. The tort of pubic disclosure is a difficult one. Modern defamation cases require that a statement be false and that the plaintiff prove that it is false. A claim for public disclosure would allow a claim for the public disclosure of true facts. It would seem odd that a defamatory statement would only be actionable when false, but a non-defamatory statement could be actionable when true. Because of this issue, recovery for public disclosure would be difficult. In this set of facts, the plaintiff is a public figure/elected official. There is very little, if anything, about his life that is private. There would be no action here.

9.   The best answer is B. This question is a little difficult. Just because Mr. Smith is a school principal, it is unlikely that he is a public figure. The court records are "public records." As such, the newspaper published matters that were already public. Although most of the public did not know the information, it was public.

10. The answer is C. This is one of the examples where public disclosure would still be appropriate. There are still some areas of information where private figures have the right to keep private information out of the hands of others. Even though the information that was provided was true, passing that information on to the employer would be actionable.

11. The answer is D. The defamation claims would require proof that the statements harmed Bill's reputation. It is unlikely that people had begun to hate or shun Bill. More than likely, they would be sorry for him. Slander and libel would be inappropriate. Public disclosure is the making public of true, private facts. The best claim would be false light. That is the revealing of false information to the public.

12. The best answer is A. The statement is probably not defamatory. The report of her death would not have defamed her character. In order to recover for false light, public figures must prove the same type of "actual malice" that is necessary for defamation. For a false light claim, therefore, it would be necessary to prove that the statement was false and that the news media knew it was false.

CHAPTER 11
MISREPRESENTATION TORTS

QUESTIONS:

1. Use the following facts for Questions 1 and 2. Dan, the owner of Dan's Diner, decided to change the brand of hot dogs served in his establishment. Dan advertised widely that he now served only Doggie Dogs. Dan made the change on the basis of the statement by Sales, an employee of the Doggie Dog Co., that Doggie Dogs are 100% pure American Beef. In fact Doggie Dogs are made with no beef at all, and what they are in fact made of is so revolting it cannot be repeated here. When the U.S. Department of Agriculture shuts down Doggie Dogs and reveals what Doggie Dogs are really made of, Dan loses almost all his customers, and soon goes out of business. If Sales was aware that Doggie Dogs contained no beef, Dan would have a cause of action for:

   A. Fraud, but only if Dan had used due care in checking out the truth of Sales's statements

   B. Negligent misrepresentation, but only if Dan would foreseeably rely on the truth of the representation.

   C. Negligent misrepresentation.

   D. Fraud, if the statements were intended to persuade Dan to switch to Doggie Dogs.

2. Use the same facts as Question 1. If Sales was aware that Doggie Dogs contained no beef, Dan could recover as damages:

   A. The difference between what he paid and what the hot dogs were worth, plus consequential damages for the loss of the business.

   B. Punitive damages only, if he paid the normal market price for Doggie Dogs.

    C.   Only the difference between what he paid and what the hot dogs were worth.

    D.   Damages based on his expectancy of future profits from the sale of the hot dogs.

3.   This question is also set in Dan's Diner. Suppose that instead of relying on Sales, Dan switched to Doggie Dogs on the basis of the statement by Joey, one of Dan's regular customers, that he (Joey) had tried Doggie Dogs and that they had a real beefy taste because they were all beef. Joey said he had read that Doggie Dogs were made with the highest quality beef. In fact, Joey had eaten and read about Diggety Dogs, which were indeed all beef, but Joey carelessly got the name wrong. As above, Doggie Dogs is shut down, consumers are revolted by the disclosures, and Dan goes out of business. If Dan sues Joey for the misrepresentation,

    A.   Dan will prevail because Joey had a duty to speak accurately if he spoke at all.

    B.   Dan will prevail because Joey's relationship as a customer gives Joey a pecuniary interest sufficient to support a duty of care.

    C.   Joey will prevail because he had no interest in the transaction.

    D.   Joey will prevail because his statements were mere "puffing."

4.   Use the following facts for Questions 4 through 7. Barbara, owner of Barbara's Burger Barn, decided to buy a new deep fat fryer. She was determined to buy one made in America, because she believed strongly in the Buy American campaign. At Appliance Store she found a fryer that seemed to meet her needs, and asked Hawker, the salesperson, if it was American made. Not knowing, but believing that it was because of the brand name, Hawker told Barbara that it was made in America. Barbara bought the fryer and installed it in her restaurant, where it performed most satisfactorily. One year later, while performing routine cleaning on the fryer, Barbara found a plate indicating that a foreign company manufactured the fryer. If Barbara sues Appliance Store for misrepresentation, what type of misrepresentation could she establish given the facts above?

    A.   Deceit.

    B.   Negligent misrepresentation.

    C.   Innocent misrepresentation.

D. Non-actionable opinion.

5. Use the same facts as Question 4, with the following modification: If Hawker, in response to Barbara's question, had said, "I have myself checked the manufacturing plate, and this fryer is American made," when in fact Hawker had not checked and did not know whether the machine was American made, what type of misrepresentation could she establish?

A. Deceit

B. Negligent Misrepresentation

C. Innocent Misrepresentation

D. Mutual Mistake

6. Use the same facts as Question 4. If Barbara sues Appliance Store for damages for misrepresentation, what is Store's best defensive argument?

A. That Barbara did not in fact rely on Hawker's representation.

B. That Barbara had an obligation to check the manufacturer herself.

C. That Barbara has suffered no damages.

D. That Hawker's representation was mere "puffing."

7. Use the same facts as Question 4. If Barbara sues Appliance Store for rescission of the sale, what is Store's best defensive argument?

A. That Barbara has suffered no damages.

B. That Barbara has delayed too long in seeking a remedy.

C. That Barbara had an obligation to check the manufacturer herself.

D. That Hawker was merely negligent.

8. Breyer was interested in buying some vacant land well outside the city center to use for development. He examined some acreage belonging to Duff which might suit his needs. In the course of negotiations, Duff said, "I sure hate to sell this land. The city council is considering running a light rail line out here, and when they do the price of land will skyrocket. I just need the money now." Breyer

was excited to hear that a rail line was planned and quickly closed the deal to buy the land. In fact, as Duff well knew, the city council had rejected the proposal to build a light rail system, and in particular had refused to run a line out to the area in question because it was so sparsely populated. If Breyer sues Duff for misrepresentation, who will prevail?

    A. Duff will prevail because this was a non-actionable prediction of future events.

    B. Duff will prevail because this was a non-actionable expression of opinion.

    C. Breyer will prevail because predictions and opinions are just as actionable as statements of fact.

    D. Breyer will prevail because Duff knew that the light rail line had in fact been rejected by the city council.

9. Use the following facts for Questions 9 through 11. Counter, a certified public accountant, regularly kept the account books for the restaurant operated by her friend, Phoney. For the most part, this involved merely copying the figures that Phoney provided and making sure they added up and the books balanced. One day Phoney asked Counter to prepare a balance sheet for the restaurant, explaining that he wanted to get a loan to purchase a new pizza oven. Counter compiled a statement from the account books she kept without doing any further investigation, but noted on the front that the statement was not audited. Counter sent the statement to Phoney, and at Phoney's request also sent a copy to Loanco, with a note stating that it was in regard to Phoney's loan. Phoney succeeded in getting the loan by assuring them that Counter would issue a certificate stating that she had audited the statement. Phoney then absconded with the loan funds, and it was discovered that the restaurant was insolvent because Phoney had not in fact made the bank deposits he had told Counter about. Loanco now sues Counter for deceit; who will prevail?

    A. Counter will prevail because her duty not to misrepresent the financial condition of the restaurant ran only to Phoney.

    B. Counter will prevail because she neither knew the statement was false nor represented it as true of her own knowledge.

    C. Loanco will prevail because Loanco was a foreseeable victim.

D. Loanco will prevail because Counter is vicariously liable for the misrepresentation of Phoney.

10. Use the same facts as Question 9. If Loanco sues Counter for negligent misrepresentation, who will prevail?

A. Counter will prevail because on these facts her duty not to misrepresent the financial condition of the restaurant ran only to Phoney.

B. Counter will prevail because she neither knew the statement was false nor represented it as true of her own knowledge.

C. Loanco will prevail because Loanco was a foreseeable victim involved in a known transaction.

D. Loanco will prevail because Counter is vicariously liable for the misrepresentation of Phoney.

11. Use the same facts as Question 9. If Loanco sues Phoney for deceit, who will prevail?

A. Loanco will prevail only if the financial statement was audited.

B. Loanco will prevail provided it relied on the misrepresentations.

C. Phoney will prevail since Counter actually was responsible for preparing the financial statement.

D. Phoney will prevail because Loanco was contributorily negligent in relying on the statement.

12. Hunter was searching through Cindy's Antique Boutique when he found a badly tarnished Victorian silver picture frame. What interested Hunter was the picture inside the frame, however, which appeared to be an early photograph of President Buchanan. Convinced that the picture was much more valuable than the twenty dollars that Cindy was asking for the frame, Hunter bought it without disclosing any of his speculation to Cindy. He later authenticated the picture and sold it for ten thousand dollars. Cindy sued Hunter for deceit by non-disclosure for buying the frame and photograph without informing her of what it was. Who will prevail?

A. Cindy will prevail because a party to a transaction owes a duty to disclose all pertinent information about the subject of the transaction.

B. Cindy will prevail because Hunter had a duty to correct the information about the value of the frame

C. Hunter will prevail because he owed no duty to disclose in an arm's length transaction.

D. Hunter will prevail because Cindy misrepresented the value of the picture and frame.

13. Mellings sold her used car to Plum. Plum asked for a vehicle history report on the car, which Mellings provided as requested. Mellings knew that the vehicle history report did not disclose the fact that the car had been involved in a flood, which caused hidden rust damage to the frame of the car. These defects were not apparent upon an ordinary inspection, and significantly lowered the market value of the car. Mellings simply turned the vehicle history report over to Plum without comment. Plum later discovered the flood damage and now sues Mellings for fraud. Who will prevail?

A. Plum will prevail because Mellings had a duty to disclose all pertinent information about the transaction.

B. Plum will prevail because Mellings knew that the vehicle history report was incomplete and misleading.

C. Mellings will prevail because she owed no duty to disclose in an arm's length transaction.

D. Mellings will prevail because Plum was negligent in not discovering the damage.

14. Use the following facts for Questions 14 and 15. Billings sold Pym a used car by forging a vehicle history report showing that the car had never been in an accident. In fact, the car had been involved in a serious collision, which significantly bent the frame of the car. If the car had not been in an accident, its fair market value as a used car would have been $10,000. As a damaged car, the fair market value was only $3,000. Pym paid Billings $6,000 for the car. Pym later discovered that the car was damaged and sues Billings for fraud. If the court employs the out of pocket method of calculating damages, how much will Pym's damages be?

A. $3,000

B. $4,000

C. $7,000

D. $10,000

15.   Use the same facts as Question 14. What will Pym's damages be if the court employs the benefit of bargain measure of damages?

A. $3,000

B. $4,000

C. $7,000

D. $10,000

16.   Tam took a painting she had inherited to Mort, an art appraiser. Mort immediately recognized the painting as the work of an early 20th Century painter named Singer, whose work had increased in value enormously in recent years. Mort told Tam that the painting was by an undistinguished nobody and offered to buy it for $500. "Twice what it is really worth," Mort said. Tam agreed and sold the painting to Mort. Mort resold the painting for $20,000. Tam now sues Mort for fraud. What is the proper measure and amount of damages.

A.   The benefit of the bargain measure must be used, under which Tam gets nothing, since she was paid more than she was told the painting was worth.

B.   The benefit of the bargain measure should be used, under which Tam will recover $19,500.

C.   The out of pocket measure should be used, under which Tam will recover the painting's value, $20,000.

D.   The out of pocket measure should be used, under which Tam will recover $19,500.

ANSWERS:

1.   The answer is D. This question involves the mental state of the defendant who has made the misrepresentation. Here the facts state that Sales knew that the hot dogs contained no beef, while the misrepresentation claimed that they did. Sales therefore knew the representation was false, so the statement constitutes fraud, also known as deceit. Either name connotes knowing misrepresentation. Answer D also includes the necessary element of intent to induce reliance, so it is the better of the two choices involving fraud. Answer A is wrong because the recipient of a fraudulent misrepresentation is not required to investigate, and is justified in relying unless the falsity of the statement is known or obvious.

2.   The answer is A. For fraudulent misrepresentation, the plaintiff is entitled to recover damages from the transaction itself, of course. In this case that measure could be the difference between what the hot were worth and what was paid for them, also called the out of pocket measure of damages. However, the victim of fraud can also recover consequential damages: Consequential damages are those caused by the reliance of the plaintiff on the misrepresentation. In this case, Dan relied on the representation and not only purchased Doggie Dogs, but advertised that he was doing so, in the belief that he was selling an attractive product: all beef hot dogs. The disclosure that the hot dogs were not all beef and were in fact disgusting had the result of inflicting severe harm on his business. These losses are the consequence of the misrepresentation, and are recoverable in cases of fraud. The only limit is that the fraud be the legal cause of the consequential harm.

3.   The answer is C. The facts make it clear that Joey made a mistake in naming Doggie Dogs as the all beef hot dogs he liked. We are therefore in the realm of negligence rather than intentional deceit. Once this analytical step is made, it is necessary to consider the elements of negligent misrepresentation in order to determine if Dan would have a case. The problem for Dan is that Joey under these circumstances would not have had a duty of care to speak accurately. The elements of negligent misrepresentation require that the false statement be made as part of the defendant's business, profession, or employment, or in the course of a transaction in which the defendant has a pecuniary interest. In this case, Joey has no pecuniary interest in the transaction between Dan and Doggie Dogs; Joey is simply making a comment about a product he had once tried. Joey will gain no pecuniary advantage if Dan should decide to buy one brand of hot dog rather than another. For these reasons, Dan's claim against Joey will fail.

4. The answer is B. The facts indicate that Hawker failed to use care before telling Barbara who manufactured the product. Instead of checking, he stated his belief that it was an American made product. The facts therefore seem to rule out fraud as a possibility here. Hawker did not know his statement was false, and he seems to have actually believed that what he was saying was correct. On the other hand, having been asked a direct question he failed to use care to be sure his answer was correct. Many companies with American names sell products manufactured in foreign countries, so relying simply on the nameplate was probably unreasonable. Thus the facts here establish negligent misrepresentation.

5. The answer is A. What has changed from the previous question is that Hawker has misrepresented the state of his own knowledge. The misrepresentation is that Hawker has checked manufacturer, when in fact Hawker did not do so. This would be a knowing misrepresentation, because Hawker knows whether he checked the manufacturing plate or not. The assurance that he has done so lends weight to the claim that the fryer is American made. It makes it more likely, therefore, that Barbara will rely on it and purchase the fryer. This is deceit.

6. The answer is C. It is hard to find the pecuniary harm to Barbara in this fact situation. The fryer works perfectly well. Barbara has not been able to fulfill her desire to purchase an American made product, but in terms of economic loss, there is none.

7. The answer is B. Rescission is an alternative remedy sometimes employed to remedy misrepresentation. Rescission involves the unwinding of the transaction in an attempt to put the parties back in their respective positions before the transaction occurred (often referred to as the "status quo ante"). Under this approach, if both sides return the consideration that each received in the transaction there will be no harm to either party. This remedy is available whether or not the misrepresentation was deliberate. The problem here, however, is that the delay in seeking a remedy means that the status quo ante cannot easily be restored. Barbara has had the use of the fryer for a year. It is no longer possible to return a pristine, unused fryer to Appliance Store. Some adjustment could be made for the rental value of the machine, but given the lack of pecuniary harm courts would be reluctant to overturn this transaction after such a long passage of time.

8. The answer is D. It is true that expressions of opinion or judgment that are simply the belief of the speaker, without indicating any kind of certainty or factual basis, are not actionable. Similarly, predictions of the future are not actionable because the

future is inherently uncertain. These rules reflect the concern that these sorts of statements are not worthy of serious reliance. In this situation, however, the defendant has done more than simply express a guess about the future course of events. The defendant here has misrepresented a fact, namely that the city council is presently considering running a light rail line out to the area. The fact known to Duff is that no such consideration is presently going on because the council has in fact already rejected the idea. The prediction, in other words, falsely implies a state of facts regarding the status of the light rail project, which Breyer relied on in purchasing the land.

9. The answer is B. Under these facts, Counter may have been negligent in not checking, but it does not appear that Counter knew that the financial statement was fraudulent. Counter did not do an audit to determine whether the numbers in the statement were backed up by real deposits, but on the other hand she noted that fact on the front of the document. Therefore, Counter did not falsely suggest that she had checked the numbers herself. For these reasons, Counter lacked scienter, or the state of mind of knowing falsehood. Loanco cannot therefore succeed in an action for deceit. It is worth noting that answer B is wrong because responsibility toward third parties is greater in the case of deceit than it is for negligent misrepresentations.

10. The answer is C. Counter would owe a duty of care to Loanco under these circumstances, under the standards of the Second Restatement of Torts section 552(2). Counter knew that Phoney was going to try to use the statement to get a loan from Loanco. To underline this point, Counter even sent a copy to Loanco. Counter therefore knew the party who would rely, and knew about the transaction that the statement was intended to influence. Under these circumstances the Restatement would impose a duty to use reasonable care in communicating the information about the financial condition of the restaurant.

11. The answer is B. Phoney knowingly misled Loanco about the true financial condition of the restaurant, by supplying false information about bank deposits to Counter. It appears that Loanco in fact relied on the statement in making the loan, resulting in loss when Phoney absconds with the funds. This meets all the elements of a cause of action for deceit. The mere failure of Loanco to investigate further would not bar this claim. Loanco would have to either know the statement was inaccurate, or else the inaccuracy would have to be obvious, before reliance would be unjustifiable.

12. The answer is C. In order for non-disclosure to amount to deceit, the defendant must have a duty to disclose. The circum-

stances under which such a duty exists are limited and would not apply in an arm's length transaction such as this. Hunter owed no fiduciary duty to Cindy. Hunter did not mislead Cindy about the nature or value of the item, nor did Hunter cause Cindy to underestimate the value of the frame. Hunter therefore would owe Cindy no duty to correct an earlier mistaken impression. Finally, this is not a case in which a prior relationship or custom of the trade or business would call for disclosure. Antique buyers are notoriously on the lookout for hidden value that others have missed, and for that reason the custom of the trade seems to be that one is allowed to profit from one's superior knowledge and powers of observation. Hunter would not be liable for the non-disclosure in this case.

13. The answer is B. This is an example of a representation that is false because it is incomplete. The vehicle in this case has a latent defect known to the seller but not to the buyer, and one not easily discoverable by the buyer on inspection. The seller also knows that the vehicle history report is incomplete, lacking information that might alert the buyer to the potential for problems. By turning over the vehicle history report without further comment in these circumstances, Mellings is effectively making a misrepresentation because she knows that the report will be misleading. This could also be viewed as a form of non-disclosure. Mellings would have a duty to disclose the flood damage in order to prevent the vehicle history report from being misleading because incomplete.

14. The answer is A. The out of pocket measure of damages is the value given by the plaintiff less the value of the thing received. By awarding the difference between these two figures, the plaintiff is compensated in the sense that the plaintiff incurs no net monetary loss. In this case, Pym paid into the transaction the purchase price of $6,000. In exchange, Pym received a damaged used car with a fair market value of $3,000. Thus, the formula would take the difference between these two figures and award $3,000. Plaintiff now is in the same economic condition as before the transaction, holding assets worth $6,000.

15. The answer is C. The benefit of the bargain measure of damages operates to give the plaintiff the value that would have been realized if the object of the transaction had been worth what the defendant promised. The formula takes the difference between what the plaintiff was promised and what the plaintiff actually received from the defendant. In this case, Billings used the forged vehicle history report to represent that the car was undamaged, and therefore having a fair market value of $10,000. What Pym actually got was a damaged car with a market value of only $3,000. The difference between these two values is $7,000. Pym is now in the

position he would have been in if the representations made by
Billings had been true: in possession of assets worth $10,000.

16. The answer is D. The peculiar aspect of this problem is that,
reversing the usual situation, the buyer is defrauding the seller.
(Compare Questions 14 and 15, above.) When the buyer defrauds
the seller, the benefit of the bargain measure of damages simply
does not work. This is because, unlike the fraudulent seller, the
defrauding buyer wants to minimize the value of the object of
exchange. The seller then gets exactly what was promised, which is
far less than the actual value of the object. In this example, the
plaintiff was promised $500 and in fact got $500. If we used the
value that Mort represented the painting to have, we would con-
clude that Tam got more than the represented value. By contrast,
the out of pocket measure of damages works perfectly well. The
value given by Tam is a painting worth $20,000. The value received
is $500 cash. The difference is $19,500, and this amount will make
the plaintiff whole, with economic assets of $20,000, only now in the
form of cash.

CHAPTER 12
DAMAGES

QUESTIONS:

1. Biff was injured while driving when a vehicle driven by Dorf ran a red light and broadsided Biff's car. The car was badly damaged and Biff suffered a concussion and injuries to his back. The back injury left Biff in constant pain. The concussion has affected his balance. Biff now can walk only with the assistance of a cane. As a result, Biff can no longer work at his previous job as a construction worker on skyscraper projects. Under the above facts, which of the following constitutes "general damages?"

    A.   The damage to Biff's automobile.

    B.   Biff's lost earnings from his job up to the time of trial.

    C.   Biff's pain and suffering.

    D.   Biff's expenses for doctors and hospitals.

2. Use the same facts as Question 1. If Biff in fact gets a full time office job and begins to earn a regular wage again, which of the following statements is most correct?

    A.   The amount actually earned will be credited, dollar for dollar, against his claim for lost wages.

    B.   These amounts would not reduce his claims because these earnings are from a collateral source.

    C.   These earnings are irrelevant because the entire claim would be barred by workers compensation.

    D.   Evidence of these amounts should be excluded as likely to confuse the jury, since his future ability to work is inherently speculative.

3. Use the same facts as Question 1. Biff has medical insurance provided by his employer which paid a portion of the medical bills

Biff incurred for treatment of his injuries. Under the traditional collateral source rule, which of the following statements is most correct?

    A.   The amounts received would be deducted dollar for dollar by the trial judge from the jury's award to prevent a windfall for Biff.

    B.   The amounts received would be deducted dollar for dollar by the jury, provided that Dorf's attorney made a proper proof of the amounts at trial.

    C.   Proof of the amounts received would be inadmissible at trial because these payments would not affect the amount of damages that Biff could recover.

    D.   These amounts would be paid directly to Biff's medical insurer by the defendant upon the medical insurer's motion to intervene.

4.   Lorenzo suffered an injury to his back in a slip and fall accident at Monster Mart. Lorenzo incurred medical bills and was unable to work for six months. He brought an action for his injuries against Monster Mart. By the time of trial, Lorenzo had recovered from his back injury and had returned to full time employment at his old job. His proof of damages included $100,000 for medical and hospital bills, plus $40,000 in lost earnings. His calculation of lost earnings included a merit pay increase which his attorney showed he would have earned if not for the accident. At the time of trial the rate of interest on one year Certificates of Deposit was two percent, and inflation was at one percent. The suit was heard in federal court. What would be a proper discount rate for the proved $140,000 in damages?

    A.   These damages should not be discounted.

    B.   The court should use the "real rate of interest" approach.

    C.   The discount rate should be based on the current rate for Certificates of Deposit.

    D.   The discount rate should be based on the rate of inflation.

5.   Barkly suffered a knee injury due to the negligence of Fister. The injury prevented him from working at his profession as a long distance truck driver. As a result, Barkly's income was greatly reduced. A simple arthroscopic surgical procedure, using local anesthetic, has a high probability of repairing the knee injury and restoring Barkly's leg to full function, enabling him to return to his

profession. Barkly, however, has refused to undergo the operation, claiming that he distrusts surgeons. Fister's attorneys will argue that Barkly's refusal to undergo the operation should prevent Barkly from recovering future lost earnings. Fister's attorneys will cite which doctrine?

A. The thin-skulled plaintiff rule.

B. The avoidable consequences rule.

C. The credit for benefit rule.

D. The last clear chance rule.

6. Use the same facts as Question 5. Barkly's duty to undergo the surgical procedure would be determined on what basis?

A. On Barkly's own personal assessment of the risks and benefits of the surgery.

B. On whether Fister offered to pay for the surgery.

C. On whether a reasonable person under the same circumstances would agree to undergo the surgery.

D. No such duty exists out of respect for the personal autonomy of the plaintiff.

7. Filbert was injured in an automobile accident. He suffered an injury to his foot which resulted in an abscess that did not heal properly. This problem was worsened because Filbert suffered from diabetes and had poor blood circulation in his feet. At the time of trial Filbert had returned to full-time employment as an accountant, but was still suffering from problems with the sore on his foot. Doctors at the trial testified for Filbert that future operations would be necessary to try to heal this wound, explaining the likely type of procedure and when it would be needed. In the meantime, Filbert would continue to suffer pain and be limited in his ability to walk. Attorneys for the defendant object to evidence of the need for future operations on the ground that the need for these procedures was speculative and was caused by Filbert's pre-existing diabetes rather than the accident. How should the court rule on this objection?

A. The court should overrule the objection based on the thin-skulled plaintiff rule and sufficient evidence of the need for the operation.

B. The court should overrule the objection because questions of the amount of damages are for the jury.

C. The court should grant the motion because the plaintiff cannot recover speculative damages.

D. The court should grant the motion because of the plaintiff's pre-existing medical condition.

8.   Use the same facts as Question 7. Which of the following items of damage would most properly be discounted to present value?

A. Medical expenses up to the time of trial.

B. Future pain and suffering.

C. Lost wages.

D. Future medical expenses for treatment of his foot.

9.   Marta, who was right handed, injured her left hand as the result of an accident caused by a defective glass coffee pot, which shattered and severed the nerves and tendons in her left wrist. At the time of trial the wound had healed and she was pain-free, but the injury substantially disabled the use of her left hand. As a result, Marta could no longer play the violin. Marta was not a professional, but she was a member of the local amateur symphony orchestra and several local chamber music groups. At trial, Marta asserts a claim for pain and suffering and hedonic damages for the loss of enjoyment of life as the result of the accident. Which of the following statements is most correct?

A. Since Marta is no longer in pain, Marta cannot recover any future hedonic damages.

B. Marta can recover damages for the pain of the injury and for loss of enjoyment of life.

C. Marta cannot recover hedonic damages because these are disfavored by the courts as a separate element of recovery.

D. Marta must develop new interests in order to mitigate her damages.

10.   Barta suffered from terminal lung cancer. Doctors reliably estimated that he had about six months to live. The day after this diagnosis, a drunk driver ran down Barta and killed her. In a wrongful death action against the drunk driver, the defendant argued that future lost wages should be based on a six month working life expectancy, at most. The plaintiffs oppose this suggestion, claiming that it would violate the thin skulled plaintiff rule, in which you must take the victim as you find her. Which of the following statements is most correct?

A. By virtue of the thin skulled plaintiff rule, the damages for future lost wages should be based on a normal working life expectancy for someone of Barta's age.

B. By virtue of the thin skulled plaintiff rule, the damages for future lost wages should be based on a normal working life expectancy for someone of Barta's age, but should be discounted using current market rates of interest.

C. Damages for future lost wages should be based on the plaintiff's actual working life expectancy, if it can reliably be shown that this would be shorter than normal

D. Damages for future lost wages are not recoverable in wrongful death actions.

11. Pearson, a state prison guard, brought his pet rattlesnake, Fang, to work one day. Although Pearson honestly believed the snake would not bite, his supervisor objected to the idea that the snake should be allowed to just slither around all day. To satisfy the supervisor's concerns, Pearson decided to put Fang into a cell. After some searching, Pearson found a cell with only one occupant, a man named Crookshank who had been convicted of forgery. Assuring Crookshank that Fang never bit anyone, Pearson put Fang into the cell with Crookshank and departed. At the end of his shift he noticed a commotion around the cell, and discovered that Fang, against all his expectations, had in fact bitten Crookshank. Crookshank sued Pearson, seeking both compensatory and punitive damages. Pearson moves to strike the claim for punitive damages. What is the proper ruling on this motion?

A. The motion should be denied because Pearson's actions created an unreasonable risk of harm.

B. The motion should be denied because Pearson acted with reckless disregard of the safety of the prisoner.

C. The motion should be granted because under federal law state prison guards are immune from awards of punitive damages.

D. The motion should be granted because punitive damages are awarded only upon a showing of actual malice, which requires a subjective intent to cause harm, which Pearson lacked.

12. Hallie was the owner and operator of a small hotel in a rural community. In the fall, many deer hunters stayed at her establish-

ment. One of these deer hunters actually brought the carcass of a deer into the hotel room, which angered Hallie very much. Hallie discovered that the room was now infested with deer ticks, which can transmit a serious illness called Lyme disease. In spite of this discovery she rented the room out to another party the next day, because it was her busy season and she wanted to make the most of it. The next morning, one of the guests who had stayed in this room discovered a tick attached to his arm. He also discovered other ticks on the furniture and carpet. Further inquiry disclosed the facts about how the room came to be infested. The guest had to seek medical treatment after he contracted Lyme disease as the result of the bite. (The treatment for Lyme disease is a three week course of antibiotics.) The guest sued Hallie seeking compensatory and punitive damages. The compensatory damages consisted of $1,000 for doctor and pharmacy bills. The jury also awarded $15,000 in punitive damages. Hallie moved to strike the punitive damage award as a violation of due process under the standards set forth in recent decisions of the United States Supreme Court., because the ratio of punitive damages to compensatory damages exceeded ten to one. Which of the following would be the best argument in support of the award of punitive damages?

A. The ratio of punitive damages to compensatory damages is irrelevant to due process analysis of the propriety of a punitive award.

B. The due process clause only requires understandable jury instructions, which the jurisdiction in fact has.

C. Punitive damages should be higher because the jurisdiction in question has only minor civil penalties for such conduct by innkeepers.

D. Hallie's conduct was particularly reprehensible, because it involved knowingly exposing others to a risk of serious illness.

ANSWERS:

1. The answer is C. General damages are usually defined as those that follow inherently and necessarily from the wrong. In personal injury cases, this definition would include damages for pain and suffering. All the other losses named in this question would be examples of special damages, sometimes referred to as consequential damages. Special damages are the pecuniary losses that follow as the result of the injury. In many jurisdictions this distinction would be significant because more stringent pleading requirements are often put on claims for special damages

2. The answer is A. If the plaintiff actually earns money from a substitute job, these funds will reduce the amounts owing for past lost wages. This can be viewed as a form of avoidable consequences, or as a conclusion that the lost wages should include only the amount not actually earned. It is not regarded as a form of collateral source. Also, workers compensation has nothing to do with this claim; nothing in the facts would suggest that Dorf is Biff's employer, or connected with Biff's employer. Finally, while calculations of future damages are always somewhat speculative, there would be nothing speculative about the formulation contained in answer A. If Biff actually earned the money it is clear that this would be a non-speculative deduction from the lost earnings claim. In fact, however, courts often will make a similar adjustment for future lost earnings as well.

3. The answer is C. The collateral source rule says that amounts received by the plaintiff from medical or disability insurers and the like do not reduce the amount of damages for which the defendant is liable. This rule has been changed by statute in a number of states, in part because of arguments about the rule creating a windfall for plaintiffs. In fact, in many cases the insurer will have rights of subrogation or reimbursement which allow them to recoup their payments to the plaintiff out of the tort recovery. When this occurs no windfall recovery occurs.

4. The answer is A. According to the facts of the problem, all the damages were incurred before trial. Lorenzo has recovered from the injury, so presumably the medical expenses have ceased, and he is back at work, so there are no future lost earnings. Accordingly, no discount should be applied. The discounting of damages to present value is only appropriate for awards of future economic losses, in cases in which the plaintiff will have ongoing medical expenses and is unable to work.

5.   The answer is B. This rule is sometimes called "mitigation of damages," but the more correct term is "avoidable consequences." This is a general rule of damages that requires the plaintiff to make reasonable efforts to limit the extent of any injury received as the result of the defendant's conduct. It applies to both situations of economic loss as well as to cases of personal injury. In personal injury cases, the rule may require the plaintiff to obtain medical treatment of injuries so that they do not become disabling or require more expensive treatment later.

6.   The answer is C. The duty here is essentially one of reasonable conduct. Although personal autonomy is an important value, the rule does not allow the plaintiff to decline medical treatment on purely personal whims or fears. (The one caveat to this rule may arise when the plaintiff declines treatment out of religious scruples, a situation in which the courts seem to be in disagreement about the proper approach.) Instead, the plaintiff will be required to undergo treatment if a reasonable person would do so. On the facts of this problem, for example, the procedure seems to be low risk with a good prognosis for fixing the knee injury. When the procedure has high risks of negative outcomes with uncertain chances of improvement, the balance would be struck in favor of allowing the plaintiff to refuse to undergo the operation.

7.   The answer is A. In this situation, the plaintiff's injury is not healing properly because of pre-existing problem with diabetes. Even though most victims would have healed without difficulty, the defendant must pay for injury actually incurred, even though unexpectedly severe. In other words, the thin skulled plaintiff doctrine would apply to these facts. As for the objection that future damages are speculative, the requirement is that the plaintiff present evidence of the existence and likely amount of such damages. Although somewhat speculative, such damages are recoverable if the plaintiff presents sufficient evidence. Here, the plaintiff has offered the testimony of experts regarding the need for and nature of future treatments. This evidence should be satisfy the plaintiff's burden in this regard.

8.   The answer is D. Recall that future damages are reduced to present value, past damages are not. On the other hand, the majority rule is that this rule applies only to economic losses. Most jurisdictions do not reduce future pain and suffering to present value.

9.   The answer is B. Courts are divided on whether damages for loss of enjoyment of life are a separate element of damages from pain and suffering, or on the other hand are simply a part of the

general recovery for pain, suffering and other "psychic" harms. Whatever position the courts might take on this point, however, Marta would be allowed to recover for both under these facts. The pain and suffering from the original injury is clearly compensable, but since that pain has now ended there is no basis for recovery for future pain. The future harm is the loss of enjoyment of life resulting from the inability to continue her performance on the violin, which on the facts was a major part of her life. This form of loss is well recognized, and whether it is a separate item of recovery or part of a single award for pain and suffering, Marta can recover damages for it.

10. The answer is C. The question illustrates the other side of the thin skulled plaintiff rule. Although it is no answer to a claim for damages that the plaintiff suffered unforeseeably severe injury, this principle is offset by the rule that requires the trier of fact to consider whether a preexisting condition would have produced the harm even if no accident had occurred. In this case, the preexisting cancer had shortened the victim's expected life span to six months, which the facts state is a reliable estimate. In this situation the amount of future earnings would have been limited by circumstances that had nothing to do with the defendant's tort.

11. The answer is B. Punitive damages are warranted when the defendant has an actual desire to cause harm, but they are usually also awarded when the defendant's conduct evidences a reckless disregard of the safety of others. Putting a live rattlesnake in a small enclosed space with a human being would qualify under that standard.

12. The answer is D. The Supreme Court, in developing its due process rules for punitive damages, has stated that the ratio of punitive to compensatory damages is a significant guidepost in determining whether the amount awarded is constitutionally excessive. Without stating a bright line limitation on the ratio, the Court also suggested that ratios in excess of ten to one should be looked at carefully. However, another guidepost is how reprehensible the defendant's conduct is. Recent Supreme Court decisions have involved mostly economic harms, but the facts in this problem involve the knowing creation of a serious risk of physical harm from the disease. Arguably this sort of conduct is more reprehensible than simply causing an economic injury, and might justify a somewhat higher ratio of punitive damages.

†